£13.50

GW00838884

Masters of Business?

BUSINESS SCHOOLS AND
BUSINESS GRADUATES IN
BRITAIN AND FRANCE

Tavistock Studies in Sociology
General Editor: FRANK PARKIN

RICHARD WHITLEY

ALAN THOMAS

JANE MARCEAU

Masters of Business?

BUSINESS SCHOOLS AND
BUSINESS GRADUATES IN
BRITAIN AND FRANCE

TAVISTOCK PUBLICATIONS
LONDON AND NEW YORK

First published in 1981 by
Tavistock Publications Ltd
11 New Fetter Lane, London EC4P 4EE
Published in the USA by
Tavistock Publications
in association with Methuen, Inc.
733 Third Avenue, New York, NY 10017

© *1981 Richard Whitley, Alan Thomas, Jane Marceau*

Typeset by Cotswold Typesetting Ltd
Printed in Great Britain at the
University Press, Cambridge

British Library Cataloguing in Publication Data

Whitley, Richard
Masters of business? – (Tavistock studies in
sociology)
1. Business education – Great Britain
2. Business education – France
I. Title   II. Thomas, Alan
III. Marceau, Jane
658'.007'1141   HF1141

ISBN 0–422–76500–7

Contents

vi Contents

Acknowledgements

An investigation of this kind can only be conducted with the help of many people. It is impossible to name them all, but we wish to give special thanks to Janet Cabot who made a major contribution to the British study through her unstinting efforts in the field at the London Business School. The computer analysis was made much less painful because of the work of Barry Hetherington of the Manchester Business School computing staff, and the administration of the British project benefited greatly from the attention of Mrs Jean Pendlebury and Mrs Betty Thompson. Mrs Thompson was also heavily involved in the preparation of the manuscripts, and we are grateful for her patience and hard work. We also wish to thank Mrs Barbara Kennerley of the Manchester Business School, and Elizabeth Scott, Ian Bruce, David Norburn, and Charles Handy at London.

In France, our thanks go to Dean Berry, Claude Faucheux, Henri-Claude de Bettignies, Jim Stevens, Mieke Ovaa, Jim Lyons, and Mme Hibon, all of whom have been associated with INSEAD and whose advice and assistance was of great value to the French research.

We are also grateful for the comments we have received from our colleagues and friends, and for the forbearance of our families.

Last but not least, we wish to thank all those students and alumni of

INSEAD and the London and Manchester Business Schools, without whose cooperation our researches would have been impossible.

Finally, we wish to point out that although we have all been members of staff either at INSEAD or the Manchester Business School throughout the period of the research, the views expressed are ours alone.

RDW
ABT
JM

Preface

The concern of this book is to compare and contrast the position of three apparently similar high-level specialist educational institutions, one in France and the other two in Britain. They were set up in each country as a response to similar socio-economic forces, including industrial change and company reorganization, and in particular to the influx of American capital and American management 'knowhow'. In both countries they represent an addition to the higher education system that is novel in kind and in objectives. The book seeks to elucidate the extent to which, for all apparent similarities, the three business schools nonetheless reflect differences found in their surrounding social, educational, and economic context and the implications of these differences both for the chances of entry of different groups of students and for the career chances of their graduates.

The particular institutions discussed here are the Institut Européen d'Administration des Affaires (INSEAD), situated at Fontainebleau in France, and the London Graduate School of Business Studies and Manchester Business School in Britain. INSEAD was founded in 1958 and was one of the first business schools in Europe to be created on an American model that drew much of its inspiration from the famous Harvard Business School. It is a private college financed almost entirely by business and is not linked to any university. Its students are drawn from all over Europe and beyond, but a third of each *promotion* are French and it is these students who are considered in this study. The schools at London (LBS) and Manchester (MBS) were set up in the mid-1960s after a commission under Lord Franks reported that Britain also needed high-level management education. Unlike INSEAD, they are part of their cities' universities and are partly financed by the state through the University Grants Committee. The majority of the students at these schools are British and it is they who are reported on here. All three institutions are post-graduate schools which admit only those of graduate status to their degree courses in business administration, although they also run shorter, less 'academic' courses for older managers. They are among the best known schools of their kind in Europe, with national and international reputations in the field of management education.

The research that forms the basis for this book was carried out between 1973 and 1975 at INSEAD and between 1976 and 1978 at London and Manchester Business Schools. Both studies were financed by the Social Science Research Council. The French project, conducted by Marceau, aimed to explore through a study of one of Europe's top business schools particular relationships between higher education and elite formation and maintenance in France. The research was specifically designed to complement and extend, through the special case study of an institution unusual within the French context, a series of studies on higher education and elites conducted in the 1960s by the research team led by Pierre Bourdieu. Marceau's study investigated the social origins, educational experiences, and career aspirations and paths of INSEAD students and graduates with a view to beginning to assess the extent to which the Institute provides a valuable distinguishing diploma ('cultural capital') on the managerial labour market. It probed also the less visible but equally important additional 'social capital', the network of contacts useful for a top-flight business career which passage through such a school can provide.

Set in the wider framework of the analysis of the French class structure and the role played by education in maintaining that structure made by Bourdieu and his colleagues, the study of INSEAD was intended to examine that thesis through the workings of a specific institution. More precisely, the study was to examine the degree to which the additional cultural capital represented by an INSEAD diploma was useful to young people in carrying out successful 'conversion' strategies. Such strategies, as outlined by Bourdieu and de St Martin, enable the sons of privileged sectors of a society to adjust to changes in the economic system that could be disadvantageous to them, in that such changes operate against the position of their families of origin, frequently members of the *patronat*. By changing their sector of employment and their 'condition', they maintain the position of their family of origin for themselves. In these strategies, developed in an age that believes in education, the possession of new and more 'appropriate' cultural capital, represented by a degree in business administration, is thought to be a useful ingredient in business success and hence in the maintenance of an 'expected' socio-economic position over the generations.

The study of the schools at London and Manchester and their alumni was conducted by Whitley and Thomas, and while relying less on the details of the framework suggested by the work of Bourdieu, was also intended to ascertain whether the post-graduate programmes provided by the schools functioned largely in the same way as had been found for France. This study, building on the experience and findings of the earlier one, was able to collect more complete data in certain spheres. In particular, the data collected on careers followed by business school alumni enabled a more sophisticated analysis to be made.

Taken together, the two studies provide the basis for a comparative examination, using data gathered in two countries, of the role and functioning of specific institutions, both in education and, less directly, in the business world in those two countries. The information collected allows a comparison not only of the place of those institutions and their alumni in France and Britain but also an assessment of the applicability of theories developed in one culture to the empirical situation in another. Given differences of structure in society, education, and economy one should perhaps not expect the interrelations between them as seen in the workings of specific institutions and labour markets to be identical; we hope we have contributed in a modest way to showing how and where to expect differences to occur in the countries that are the reference here. It is the contrast and comparison, the differences as well as the similarities that intrigue the observer, and we hope these are brought out in this book.

1 Introduction

Since the Second World War there has been a considerable growth in provisions for management education in Europe, yet relatively little attention has been paid to the sociological significance of these developments. In this book we examine the role played by a new type of institution which has been associated in a particularly striking way with the emergence of European management education – the high level business school. Such schools are of special interest because one of their chief aims is the production of young, qualified Masters of Business Administration (MBAs) who might be expected one day to take control of major enterprises in the modern corporate economies of the West.

The creation of business schools has a number of important implications. Business management in both Britain and France has not been recognized in the past as a technically based profession like medicine, engineering, or law. Although 'business' is usually carried on in hierarchically organized structures, access to these structures has not in principle been associated with specific educational qualifications, nor has it been linked to definite kinds of career paths. Thus, in Britain, entry to senior management posts has rarely depended much upon the possession of higher education qualifications, and has only done so in

France in certain kinds of companies. The emergence of business schools might therefore seem to indicate that significant changes have taken place in business such that a new type of business leader is in demand, trained in the new 'science of management' at the highest levels of the education system. This in turn might suggest that access to controlling positions will in future depend much more on the possession of formal management education qualifications. As a result, in so far as the education system is open to all who can demonstrate their ability, the privileges of birth in relation to business careers, so important in the past, may be weakening. It seems more likely, however, that the education system is largely used by already privileged groups to ensure that their children maintain positions in the socio-economic structure that they perceive as equivalent to their own. In an age of 'credentialism', it is frequently necessary to become better formally qualified in order to continue in the parents' occupation or to move to new fields in response to changing economic circumstances. We are concerned, therefore, both with the extent to which the business schools serve, as broader analyses of the role of the education system suggest, to enable those from privileged origins to maintain their social position, with reference to the specific sector of 'business', and with the extent to which they provide new forms of cultural capital that are publicly presented as of value for entry to top positions in business. In other words, we examine the degree to which institutionalized provision of a 'particularly appropriate' high-level educational credential is translated in practice into specific career chances in business. Much has been written about 'credentialism' in general; in contrast little attention has been paid to examining in detail the particular ways in which a 'new' credential is absorbed in the existing labour market of the social and economic processes acting to give it a 'real market value'.

In principle, the different issues involved can be separated. The schools, for example, could constitute channels of upward mobility for disadvantaged groups, even if the qualifications they dispense did not give access to the top jobs in business. On the other hand, the MBA could constitute a new *sine qua non* for entry to the top business stratum regardless of the social backgrounds of those who hold it. If both conditions were fulfilled this would indicate a major change in both the criteria of access to, and the composition of, the group of business controllers as a socio-economic entity.

An examination of these possibilities requires consideration of the social origins of the newly qualified Masters of Business Administration, and assessment of the significance of their qualification. The latter involves an analysis of the careers of business-school graduates and the roles that business enterprises have offered to the MBAs. But before embarking on this analysis it is useful to set the business schools in the broader context of the relations between education and the reproduction of social and economic inequality.

Education, occupation, and social inequality

In recent years there has been widespread sociological debate about the role of the education system in the reproduction of the social order (e.g. Bowles and Gintis 1976; Bourdieu and Passeron 1970; Boudon 1973). The education system has often been seen as playing a critical role in this process because it can at one and the same time select, orientate and certify young people for positions in the production system as well as help to legitimate the ensuing social and economic relations. In this way the education system has been held to contribute to the differential placing of candidates for given roles in the occupational structure and to the justification of unequal rewards for work. At a time during which the direct inheritance of privileged positions in the economic system has been increasingly subject to criticism, the possession of educational qualifications has become widely accepted as a legitimate basis for differential rewards. Because educational verdicts, for all their apparent neutrality, rarely work to the disadvantage of those from privileged homes, the education system, it is argued, contributes powerfully to the reproduction of the established order (Bowles 1972).

This contribution depends largely on the success of dominant groups in modern Western societies in imposing a technocratic ethos on the occupational system. This ethos emphasizes 'competence' as the basic criterion for occupational selection and promotion, a criterion increasingly symbolized by the possession of particular education certificates by those who enter the labour market and the chances of entering any particular occupation, whether in the public service or in private businesses, have come to depend more and more on the possession of educational certificates (Ashton and Field 1976; Dore 1976). Such qualifications have tended to be adopted by employers as a major means of rationalizing their recruitment and promotion decisions and of ensuring the minimization of employment 'mistakes'. The educational system, this view suggests, has thus come to constitute a major means both of legitimating occupational inequalities and of reinforcing the dominant market principle in which high rewards are justifiably related to 'scarce' talents.

In practice, however, although the education system is chiefly responsible for the production of 'qualified' manpower, the relations between these qualifications and positions in the occupational structure are not determined, on the whole, by the education system itself. On the contrary, it is the economic system that determines the availability of particular types of roles and that specifies both the criteria of access and the rewards of success. It has become increasingly clear, in fact, that there is no necessary relation between the availability of 'qualified' persons and their chances of access to specific positions in the occupational structure (Collins 1971). Moreover, it is by no means certain that where such relations do exist the required qualification is always 'functionally' appropriate. As Hussain (1976: 418) has pointed out:

> 'Strictly speaking, there is no such thing as a purely technical division of labour . . . social relations affect the division of labour by establishing a hierarchy of work – a classification and ordering of different kinds of work, by defining the criteria of selection and access to occupation . . . thus . . the factors used to select individuals . . . have a dual role and function, namely: to determine the technical competence for the work in question and to place the occupation in relation to others.'

Thus 'certification' in many spheres is not complete. It is particularly far from complete in private business where other qualities, such as ownership of economic capital, may be fundamental in determining the attribution of personnel to command roles in spite of their 'technical incompetence'. In other spheres, too, until recently, 'competence' for a post was often perceived to be unrelated to the specific subject of the 'certificate' but related to general competencies thought to be developed by the study of given subjects. Thus, 'suitability' for the path to a potentially senior post in the Treasury, or for entry to the preparation studies for the French medical profession was often judged on performance in Latin and Ancient Greek and varied – notably in the case of the Treasury – according to the institution at which such knowledge had been acquired. There have, however, in recent years been formal changes in some organizations such that the criteria of suitability for certain kinds of jobs have become more apparently 'technical'. In France, for example, entrance to medical studies is now dependent on high-level competence in mathematics – a far higher level indeed than students are ever likely to need for most careers in medicine – and for some time now the economic arm of the British Civil Service has been recruiting more trained economists, even if the *de facto* requirement of passage through Oxbridge seems to linger on.

The recruitment of initially technically trained personnel for specialist, and subsequently generalist, positions in the public service has had its business counterpart in the presentation of managers as 'professionals'. In this sense, the foundation of business schools and the 'technical' training of managers may be seen as part of a more general tendency. In this book, therefore, we will explore how far this process has occurred in business and the limitations and constraints under which the process takes place. We will further explore the extent to which the 'value' of an MBA degree depends on the uncertified capacities and characteristics of its holders, and the extent to which it serves to legitimate the continued access by those from privileged backgrounds to important positions in business.

The reproduction of business elites: business schools and the MBAs

One of the most striking aspects of the business schools is their claim to be preparing the business leaders of tomorrow. Although the schools may now be more cautious in making such claims, there can be little doubt that many of those who were involved in the founding of these institutions saw them as training grounds for the corporate controllers of the future. The business schools may thus be considered as potentially key institutions in the reproduction of the business elite. The utility of the concept of 'elite' has been the subject of much sociological debate and confusion (Bottomore 1966; Giddens 1974), but it does seem to serve to delineate a crucial social category, and for this reason we have given some attention to the question of the role of business schools in supplying new recruits to senior positions in business.

In this context we have adopted an identification of the business elite that is in keeping with the spirit of the concept used in earlier studies (e.g. Giddens and Stanworth 1978; Thomas 1978; Whitley 1973, 1974). This would include directors of the largest industrial companies in the private sector and of large banks and prominent insurance and finance houses, and top positions in the nationalized industries. Whilst being aware of the drawbacks that such 'positional' views entail (Pahl and Winkler 1974) the current state of our understanding of elites leaves us little alternative to this approach. It is clear, however, that even if the equation of the formally most powerful positions with the actual exercise of power is a matter for dispute, 'elite' positions in this sense remain amongst the best paid and most prestigious in society (Westergaard and Resler 1975 : 77–8, 162; Fidler 1977). The involvement of the business schools in the production and reproduction of this group must therefore be of considerable interest. We thus consider holders of top positions as the existing 'masters of business', and examine the extent to which the criteria of their selection may be replaced by formal education qualifications, so providing access to such positions for the new Masters of Business Administration from the European business schools. The significance of such a change relates to a great extent both to the characteristics of the student population attracted to and by the business schools and to changes in business policies.

Whatever the relation of the MBA to access to top positions in business, the wider role of the business schools in the social and economic structure can be more clearly understood through an analysis of the characteristics of their students. These attributes are the outcome of a complex process involving the interaction of factors such as the social position of students' families, their occupational milieux, the students' educational histories, their work aspirations, their employment experiences, the selection policies of the schools and of employers. We will examine many of these elements later in the book and indicate how in fact the business schools build on the inequalities that permeate British and French society, even though in both countries they have attempted to institute acceptance policies that give weight to factors beyond formal educational achievements. We can understand why the schools attract the sort of students they do by seeing individuals as operating in a market in which they must sell their competencies and credentials to employers in return for 'appropriate' rewards. The market, however, is constantly fluctuating. Because formal credentials must largely be obtained through successful participation in the education system at a relatively early age, correct decisions about the most valuable form of investments must usually be taken long before entry to the labour market. Like speculation on the Stock Exchange, these long-term investment strategies are subject to errors of prediction, to fluctuating markets, to boom and slump conditions, and to the vagaries of inflation and devaluation. Whilst certain 'blue chip' investments in cultural capital (in this case educational qualifications) can be made, such as attendance at the *grandes écoles* in France, or at public school and Oxbridge in Britain, some are riskier than others and modifications and additions to a person's portfolio are sometimes needed as conditions change. 'Conversion strategies', to use Bourdieu's term, may be needed and one such new investment is the acquisition of new educational credentials, presented, at least by the business schools, as particularly appropriate to new business conditions (Bourdieu, Boltanski, and de St Martin 1973).

New conditions for careers in business are created by a number of factors. On the one hand, the conditions of access to coveted positions in the occupational system may be modified as the productive system responds to economic and technical pressures, so that those who have equipped themselves for access to these positions may find themselves unexpectedly deficient in capital. The business world, particularly in Britain, has been an especial source of occupational uncertainty because of the general lack of visibility of career paths (Dunkerley 1975; Twigger 1978). In recent years this invisibility has been exacerbated by widespread changes in business organization associated with industrial concentration and the accelerated expansion of the larger firms that dominate the economy and the consequent diminution in the number of small and medium-sized businesses at the national level in both Britain and France.

These changes have altered managerial structures, and may have created new career paths and new types of managerial role that demand novel attributes from those who are to fill them. The business schools might well be seen as an institutional response to such changes, and we therefore examine both these and the more immediate circumstances of the funding of the three schools in the following chapters.

Even without such changes, individuals may experience career difficulties. Some persons will fail to acquire the type of cultural capital that they perceive as necessary to secure their social position by virtue of the verdicts of the educational system, verdicts that are selective and thus will fail to satisfy all those who enter into competition for its certificates. In either case, those who because of their high social origins aspire to enter high-level occupations are likely to be attracted to those institutions that provide the new forms of capital that may be perceived as ensuring preferential treatment in the struggle for advancement.

In relation to business, the business schools can be seen as just such useful institutions. They might thus be expected to attract those who are relatively well-endowed economically, educationally, and socially and who, for this reason, are particularly anxious to maximize their chances of acquiring 'suitable' social positions. The more successful are these strategies of individual reproduction, the more likely it is that the privileged position of advantaged groups will be maintained, for although both the nature of occupational roles and the criteria for access to them may change, there is no guarantee that the new forms of capital required will be any more equitably distributed than were the old. It seems likely, therefore, particularly in view of the social biases that are inherent in the workings of the public and the state secondary levels of the education systems and university systems, that they will act as agencies to aid the reproduction of advantaged groups.

The data on the MBAs reported here attempt to relate individuals' perceptions of their life chances to social 'reproductive' processes. We thus examine the social and educational backgrounds of MBAs, their career experiences prior to attending the schools, their educational and career motives, and the influences that have come to bear on their life choices. These features of the MBAs are placed in the context of the educational and occupational background of the MBAs' families over two generations, so that the wider family network of social and economic contacts and aspirations may be brought into the analysis. We also study the activities and effects of the business schools' own involvements in the selection of future MBAs. Taken together with the information we present on the MBAs careers this gives a comprehensive picture both of the business graduates, and of the role played by the business schools.

Business schools are institutions placed at the interface of two of the most important sectors of modern Western capitalist societies, the economic system and the education system. Exploring the reasons that led to their creation, and discussing the possible careers of their alumni, offer a privileged vantage point from which to shed light on a number of social mechanisms. Using the schools and the backgrounds and careers of their graduates as a focal point, this book aims to contribute through a specific study to the examination of an important and more general sociological issue: the relationship between education and occupational inequality. If, as is generally agreed, a person's social status depends overwhelmingly on his, or her, position in the occupational structure and labour market, then the mechanisms determining recruitment patterns to important posts in private business are of considerable interest. Access to, and promotion within, different managerial lines can be assessed in different types of enterprises as well as within different parts of the organizational tree in specific kinds of company. These mechanisms will also be affected by the structure of the business firms, and by structural modifications over time, which have an impact on managerial career patterns and the type of person who may be recruited to the business elite. By setting the analysis against the background of economic and socio-political changes that have occurred in Europe since 1945, and within the specific context of the development of a new type of educational institution, the 'business school', we hope to contribute to a wider and better understanding of the mechanisms both of social change and social immobility.

2 Economic change, managerial careers, and business schools

.

Among the major changes in most West European countries during the present century have been substantial alterations to patterns of industrial structure. The decline of traditional industries, e.g. steel and textiles, and the rise of new ones – often based on new sources of power such as electrical engineering (Hannah 1976; Parodi 1971) – have been accompanied by an increase in industrial concentration and the appearance of giant multi-national companies operating in a number of areas. These new firms are often organized in ways different from those of single industry enterprises (Chandler 1962), and require new managerial skills and attitudes resulting in the emergence of a distinct stratum of 'professional' general managers who operate across industries and countries (Chandler 1976). New career patterns necessitating considerable job mobility have become institutionalized in these giant companies and managerial careers in general have become more structured as the managerial labour force has grown (Leggatt 1972) and tasks become more specialized. Planning of managerial careers, as of corporate strategies and market development, has become more systematic and many large firms have 'management development' groups who concentrate on organizing managerial manpower.

Post-graduate business schools, established to provide management specialists and to train general managers for these new forms of organization, may be seen as an educational and social response to these changes. The function of business schools may be seen as an attempt to legitimate the authority of general managers by certifying their graduates as competent in this area, while also providing additional 'cultural capital' for those who are newly disadvantaged by the changes in industrial and occupational structures. They thus function to develop and institutionalize the new international corporate system.

Changes in industry structure, firm behaviour, and the development of long-range planning

The domination of major sectors of national economies by a few giant companies has occurred at different rates in different countries but has currently reached an advanced stage in most North American and EEC countries (Franko 1976 : 18; Hannah 1976; Jacquemin and de Jong 1977; Morvan 1972 : 148–50; Prais 1976). While large firms dominating particular industries were not unknown in Britain and the USA before and just after the First World War (Payne 1967), they did not usually operate in more than one industry, and their aggregate impact on the economy was not as marked as it has become since 1945. According to Hannah (1976 : 216) the largest 100 manufacturing firms produced only 15 per cent of the total manufacturing net output in the UK in 1909, yet by 1930 this proportion had risen to 26 per cent, and in 1970 was considered to be 45 per cent. Although other EEC countries may not exhibit such a high degree of industrial concentration, most nonetheless are hosts to some very large firms which employ a substantial proportion of the labour force.

As well as having a much greater aggregate effect on national economies today, giant firms are more likely to operate in a number of industries and countries and to follow an active strategy of further diversification of product ranges and of acquisition of other companies than did the large firms of the inter-war years. Although multiplant firms were known before 1914, the growth in number of plants owned by the largest 100 firms since 1958 has been very rapid. In that year the average number of plants per large firm in Britain was twenty-seven, in 1972 it was seventy-two (Prais 1976 : 62). This increase is largely due to the high rate of takeovers and mergers that dominated the 1960s and that increased the diversity of firms' product ranges. Similarly, Morvan (1972 : 146–64) has shown how there are considerable divergences between firm concentration ratios and establishment concentration ratios in some French industries, so that if the larger firms were broken down into their component factories concentration would fall dramatically. While the dominance of giant multiplant firms may not be as marked in France and West Germany (George and Ward 1975) as in the UK their role has certainly grown in importance in the last fifteen to twenty years.

Moreover, the importance of multinational manufacturing facilities has increased dramatically since the 1940s. Although British firms had established some overseas manufacturing subsidiaries before 1914, more than three-quarters of the 2,530 subsidiaries owned by large British firms in 1971 had been set up since 1955 (Franko 1976:94). Similarly, although some continental firms had foreign subsidiaries in the 1880s, 78 per cent of the 1,481 subsidiaries of French and German companies located outside the home country in 1971 had been established since 1955. Indeed, for French firms, two-thirds were founded or acquired since 1965 (Franko 1978:87–94). While major multinational firms did not develop in the larger continental countries as early as in Britain, and the number of foreign subsidiaries is still not as large, the wave of multinational expansion that has recently occurred in nearly all Western European societies has probably had more impact on continental economies, concentrated as it was within a shorter time.

Since about the middle fifties, then, most Western European countries have experienced the rise of multiplant, multi-industry, and multinational giant firms, which collectively control major industries such as chemicals, metals, electronics, vehicles, food, and oil (Jacquemin and de Jong 1977:98) on a qualitatively different scale to anything that had gone before. Industrial concentration has become much greater since the War and the largest firms have become much bigger; not only this, the firms operate in different ways and are differently organized.

The major change in large firm behaviour is, of course, a consequence of increased concentration; where markets are dominated by a small number of very large firms, they are much more susceptible to long-term planning and control than when they consist of a large number of relatively small firms, such as those that characterized the English textile industry in the early nineteenth century (Pollard 1965:89–96). Market sharing agreements and similar devices to reduce market uncertainties are not novel phenomena and are unlikely to die out with the rise of multinational giants (Richardson 1972), but these are essentially short-term attempts to maintain stability and equilibrium rather than coherent strategies to manage the development of markets in conjunction with product innovation and development. The rise of massive multi-industry firms enables the risks associated with product change to be spread over greater financial resources and to be planned so that product life cycles in different markets do not coincide, but rather cancel each other out. This allows the profits obtained in one market to be used to offset the losses entailed in new product development and launch in another market (Jacquemin and de Jong 1977 : 87–8). In addition, these giant corporations have the resources to attempt to control consumption patterns through advertising and promotional schemes (Andreff 1976 : 140–42; British Monopolies Commission 1969 : 350–80). As well as sometimes leading to increased market share and market size, the growth of such expenditure also increases barriers to entry into these industries and so renders the market more predictable (Bain 1956; Prais 1976 : 78–85; Utton 1970 : 29–30).

Besides planning market development on an international scale in a number of industries, giant firms are also able to plan the development and introduction of new products through the establishment of research and development laboratories employing large numbers of scientists and technologists. As Andreff (1976 : 108–32) among others (cf. Franko 1976 : 18–20) points out, the large multinationals spend a considerable proportion of their turnover on research and development and collectively are responsible for a substantial percentage of the total expenditure in this field (Utton 1970 : 106). In general terms, there does not seem to be a clear positive relation between firm size, industry concentration ratios, and research expenditures in large European firms (George 1971 : 54–5; Jacquemin and de Jong 1977 : 152–57; Brabowski 1968). There is, however, quite a strong relationship between very large size and stability of growth and profit rates (George 1971 : 66–7), which suggests that the giant companies are more able to manage their environment and to reduce uncertainty than are medium and small firms. This, in turn, implies that some of the 'invisible hand' functions of markets, such as allocating resources and coordinating price movements between products and product ranges, are being undertaken within large companies rather than between them. (Chandler 1977).

Long-range planning on an international scale requires the coordination of new product development in research and development laboratories with market development in particular industries and, in multi-industry firms, across industries. The formation of giant firms enables this sort of planning and coordination to take place and, indeed, oligopolist competition on a global basis encourages it. As a result, managerial discretion, in terms of the degree of relative autonomy from short-term product and capital market constraints and pressures, tends to increase in giant multinationals (Williamson 1970), with coordination and integration of diverse activities in a variety of industries and countries becoming an obvious and overt major managerial problem. The more such firms appropriate what were formerly market functions, the more complex the internal management function becomes and the more differentiated, specialized, and organized managerial tasks and roles become (Williamson 1971). Traditional modes of organizing managerial hierarchies and tasks become a constraint on organizational development, and new forms are sought which, in some cases, require new skills and establish new patterns of managerial careers (Franko 1976 : 187–212).

The developing autonomy of giant firms from short-run market forces and the growing complexity and importance of managerial structures in these firms suggest that not only is the traditional microeconomic theory of the firm inadequate for an understanding of firms' behaviour, but that studies of business elites and changing organization forms will need to be incorporated into any potentially adequate theory of the firm. Once it is admitted that markets do not uniquely determine firms' production functions, price movements, and resource allocation patterns, so that firms cannot simply be seen as the intersection of cost and revenue curves (Baumol 1959; Marris 1964, 1971b; Penrose 1959), the 'black box' of firms' decision processes and their implementation needs to be explored to understand patterns of economic change (Marris 1972; Williamson 1971). If, in fact, giant firms in oligopolistic industries do have some discretion over investment plans and are able to influence market developments, then consideration of who exercises this discretion, in what way and with what results, becomes integral to any economic theory of the firm.

Equally, the long-standing concern of social scientists with the social origins and educational experiences of business 'elites' (Domhoff 1967, 1975; Mills 1956; Monjardet 1972; Newcomer 1955; Stanworth and Giddens 1974; Whitley 1973, 1974) assumes economic overtones in so far as these characteristics can be linked to particular preferences, beliefs, and attitudes that can be shown to affect strategic decisions. In addition, the traditional focus in the sociology of organizations on bureaucratic structures and hierarchies (Burns and Stalker 1961; Perrow 1972; Pugh and Hickson 1976) becomes relevant to economic analysis as the managerial structures of large firms assume greater importance in the operation of diverse activities and constrain the development of new ones. These structures also impinge upon the development of business elites, it should be noted, in so far as they lead to distinct managerial careers that differ from previous channels of access to top positions. These career patterns may affect the sort of person who proceeds up hierarchies and their preferences, and hence the type of decision arrived at. Studies of the 'corporate economy' (Hannah 1976; Marris and Wood 1971) involve all these aspects, and the traditional barriers between sociologists and economists working on firms and elites are no longer tenable, if they ever were.

However, despite the widespread acknowledgement of these changes (e.g. Child 1972) very few studies of the interrelations between business elites, organization structures, and business policies have been carried out. The 'ownership and control' controversy has led to some analysis of firm ownership differences and growth and profit rates with somewhat inconclusive results (Holl 1975; Jacquemin and de Jong 1977; Radice 1971; Nichols 1969) but these have usually relied on rather simple assumptions about managers' motivations, ignoring organizational complexities or market changes (Marris 1971a; Williamson 1964; 1971). Similarly, most sociologists studying business elites have resolutely ignored economic variables, although some recent work attempts to incorporate market factors and business decisions in an analysis of managerial characteristics (Nyman and Silberston 1978).

One major attempt to link managerial control structures to business decisions has been carried out by a group of Harvard Business School students following the ideas of Chandler (1962) in his classic study of how product diversification strategies were followed by the development of a divisionalized organization structure in Du Pont, General Motors, Standard Oil of New Jersey, and Sears, Roebuck. This approach can be labelled the 'strategy and structure' school after Chandler's dictum that 'structure follows strategy' (1962 : 14). Subsequent work by Channon (1973, 1977), Dyas and Thanheiser (1976) among others, extended this model to European countries and more recently Bouchet (1976) has linked the development of particular diversification strategies by firms to the career paths of the top management teams in an interesting attempt to study managerial careers, policies, and market performance. Although this school is rather inclined to celebrate the survivors of competitive capitalism and does not always show the relationship of the mechanisms that link market changes to company policies, this work does provide much useful information on how giant firms have changed their policies and their managerial hierarchies with considerable consequences for managerial careers, business elites, and the development of new managerial skills and roles. These consequences may be related to developments in the provision of management education and, in particular, the functions of prestigious post-graduate business schools.

Diversification and divisionalization in large firms

The 'strategy and structure' school in Europe focuses on how, between 1950 and 1970, the top 100 firms in a country have diversified away from their basic product range in one industry to other products, and on the consequences of this diversification for the reorganization of the internal structure of firms away from a strictly functional form to a multidivisional one.[1] In the latter structure, each division is responsible for all the functions for a range of products, and is thus regarded as a profit centre. According to Chandler (1962), managerial problems arising from product change and diversification necessitate a move to the multidivisional form because of the increased difficulty of coordination and planning encountered by relatively diversified firms. In this sense, managerial structures can constrain corporate policies and/or make certain ones ineffective. Certain structures fit certain strategies better than others and giant, multi-industry firms will be unable to plan effectively and to maximize corporate efficiency if top management is still engaged on operating problems and coordinating separate functions for all product lines instead of concentrating on overall strategy and resource allocation between product ranges (Williamson 1971, 1975 : 132–54).

The managerial authority structure is also important to the formulation of strategies insofar as it affects the careers of future top managers and so enables particular people with particular experiences, beliefs, and attitudes to acquire elite positions. Whether or not the 'top management teams' of contemporary giant firms are mostly sons of executives and have been to fee-paying secondary school (Giddens and Stanworth 1978; Whitley 1974), their careers in these large and increasingly bureaucratized firms will affect their views as to desired strategies to pursue and evaluation of outcomes. The particular manner in which they rose to the top is likely to affect their preferences and strategic policy decisions, for example in relation to diversification and acquisition policy (cf. Bouchet 1976). Thus, the consequences of moving to a divisional form of organization not only facilitate the adoption of particular strategies of diversification and investment, but also concern the sort of person who will move fastest up to the altered hierarchy. The qualities and skills required to succeed in a traditional, functionally based, highly centralized structure will not necessarily be helpful in a relatively decentralized, divisionalized one where some coordination roles are decentralized to the operating divisions. The business schools' emphasis on producing 'general' managers in addition to teaching specialist techniques is, in part, an attempt to fill this perceived need.

Dyas and Thanheiser (1976 : 8–15), following Scott, have suggested that there are three basic 'stages' in the development of the large corporation, which relate to particular types of managerial structure. In relatively small, single plant firms, managerial tasks are largely confined to coordinating processes and arranging the sale of the product; manufacturing and sales are then the two traditional managerial functions. With increased volume of production and multiplant operation, growing firms establish a central administrative office distinct from operational management, and managerial work is organized into different functional departments such as marketing, manufacturing, finance, etc. (Chandler 1962 : 12–14; Penrose 1959). This type of organization, based on major managerial functions, can cope with quite considerable increases in size as long as the diversity of processes, products, and geographical spread does not become too great. Expansion backwards into raw material production and processing and forwards into distribution and receiving can usually be managed simply by expanding the functional structure and ensuring systematic coordination of the component parts. This coordination function is highly centralized at the top management level by the functional directors with the help of various specialist groups such as management services and market research.

The next 'stage' of corporate growth often involves the increasing complexity of production processes and systematic search for new product lines in some industries, leading to the establishment of research and development laboratories and the elaboration of advisory functions such as personnel and industrial relations, production planning and control, inventory management, etc. The distinction between operating managers, who are responsible for production and sales units, and advisory units, which assist these managers has, of course, been reified as the distinction between 'line' and 'staff' positions, as in the Pennsylvania railroad (Chandler 1962 : 38–9). This rather rigid distinction failed, though, to survive the growing complexity of activities carried out by large scale industrial enterprises and some formerly 'staff' groups, such as finance and personnel, became major 'line' departments with their own career structures (Legge 1978). This proliferation of functions to cope with an increasingly broad range of activities, which themselves were becoming highly complex and differentiated, in turn intensified difficulties of coordination, especially since this was usually highly centralized at the top of the hierarchy (Williamson 1970, 1971).

The increasing strain upon the centralized, functionally organized system of administration was further aggravated by moves into new products and industries that occurred in the USA between the wars in some industries, and in Britain and Europe after 1945. According to Chandler and other members of this school of thought (Channon 1973; Dyas and Thanheiser 1976) these changes led to giant firms in the food, chemicals, oil, metal, and machinery industries adopting a multidivisional form of organization. This structure decentralizes much of the coordination function to product division managers who are responsible for the total production and marketing of a given range of related products, such as chemicals, pharmaceuticals, or textiles. These divisions become 'profit centres', relatively autonomous from head office and with few mutual interdependencies. Once annual budgets and targets are set they are largely left on their own, subject to satisfactory financial performance.

The role of top management is now much more focused on strategic issues such as long-term planning, acquisition and divestiture of companies, investment cycles, and managing the general environment. As Williamson (1970, 1971, 1975) among others has pointed out, the central office of such a divisionalized firm operates like a mini capital market, allocating resources between industries on a consciously planned and continuously monitored performance basis. In orthodox economic terms, this may lead to greater efficiency in the allocation of resources (Marris 1972, but cf. George 1971 : 39–41). As distinct from the holding company structure in which the central office functions largely as a bank, the multidivisional structure involves elaborate systems of financial control and monitoring of divisional performance and the integration of divisional activities into an overall strategic plan. Whereas in the functionally organized firm, coordination was necessary between operating units with a high degree of interdependence, the multidivisional firm delegates that type of coordination to divisions and concentrates on strategic integration at the centre. This calls for a comparatively extensive head-office staff and more sophisticated managerial techniques which, in turn, implies substantial changes in accepted practices and patterns of work. They also suggest changes in the evaluation of managerial skills and hence in career paths and strategies.

This view of economic and organizational change and, in particular, the relative influences of specific market and technological factors, is not totally accepted by historians and economists, especially when applied to European economies (Alford 1976; Chandler 1976; Franko 1976; Hannah 1976). The particular sequence of events in many cases does not always support Chandler's dictum (1962:14) that structure, that is the administrative system, follows strategy, the determination of the long-term goals and objectives of an enterprise, and there have been several attempts at refining the basic classification scheme, such as those by Channon in 1973 and 1976, to allow for the European predilection for the holding company structure. Alford (1976) has drawn attention to the need to incorporate considerations of market power in understanding how strategies may in fact follow structure and, more generally, how markets can strongly influence strategies which in any case may be more *ad hoc* and reactive than the term suggests. Similarly, as Chandler himself (1976) points out, many European large companies remained unbureaucratized well into the 1950s and the development of a distinct managerial stratum with specialist skills and techniques has been a relatively recent phenomenon, despite the so-called 'management movement' claiming professional status in the 1920s and 1930s (Child 1969; Hannah 1976:87–92; Whitehead 1947). Indeed, Chandler's emphasis on the 'managerial revolution' thesis of the separation of ownership from control of giant corporations (Nichols 1969) is perhaps misplaced with respect to the USA (Burch 1972; Zeitlin 1974) and is certainly dubious in the European context (Franko 1976; Morin 1974). However, recent work (Channon 1973; Dyas and Thanheiser 1976) does show that over half of the largest European firms have now moved to the diversified, divisionalized form and the implications of this change for managerial careers, elite recruitment, and operation need to be discussed.

Managerial careers in functional and divisionalized firms

The development of functional hierarchies in large centralized firms meant that managerial careers based on steady advancement up a particular specialized ladder could develop, although there was of course no guarantee of such mobility, nor was there necessarily a strong likelihood in many firms of eventual succession to a top management post (cf. Clements 1958). Particularly where family control remained the dominant influence, as in most European countries, an integrated managerial career ladder to the top was unlikely to develop. However, the emergence of large firms relying upon an enlarged managerial labour force in the inter-war years did result in some sort of career progression developing and in functional expertise becoming recognized as a managerial skill (Hannah 1976 : 79–99) even if the managerial bureaucracy found in some US companies was relatively rare in Europe (Chandler 1976). Aside, then, from family entry to top positions after a period in the lower ranks – as at Pilkingtons (Barker 1977) – in Britain, at least, managerial careers in large firms were firmly located in functional hierarchies (Granick 1972 : 301), although according to Granick, top managers were more likely to have had some experience of another function than middle managers. In France, because firms were rather smaller and had more family control and because of the importance of educational qualifications (Granick 1972; Morin 1974; Monjardet 1972; Parodi 1971), functionally based careers were not as important as in Britain and the notion of 'professional' management as distinct from technical professionalism seems to be more recent (Granick 1972), The tendency of many French firms only to recruit to top posts graduates of the *grandes écoles*, especially Polytechnique (Bourdieu, Boltanski, and de St Martin 1973; Monjardet 1972), means that managerial careers integrating middle and top management positions were most unlikely to develop in a similar way to those in some large British firms. Relative to the French system, British upper managerial strata were fairly 'open' to new recruits from middle management because entry to these strata was not so strongly differentiated by the verdicts of the educational system (Granick 1972).

The emphasis on functional expertise in many large British firms had the consequence of making the transition from managing a functional specialism to general policy-making and strategic evaluation at or near board level more difficult than in France where, in a sense, the 'high flying' graduates of the top *grandes écoles* had always been working as 'general' managers (Granick 1972 : 362–69; Chandler 1962 : 41). The move to diversification and divisionalization in Britain has occurred at the same time as the expansion of 'general management' courses designed to assist the transition from functional specialist to managerial generalist (Gunz 1980) at least partly because of the concomitant need to develop managers of divisional 'profit centres' and expertise in managing specialists. As Dyas and Thanheiser (1976 : 20–3) point out, the move to multi-divisional structures implies new skills among middle managers as well as at the top management level. Whereas in functionally organized firms performance measures were often based on technical or cost criteria relevant to the operations of the various departments, in multidivisional ones rewards should be based much more on the overall economic performance of organizational subunits, and hence on general managerial skills. If, in fact, giant diversified firms are to operate as mini capital markets (Chandler and Daems 1974) then their constituent profit centres should operate, and be treated, as semi-autonomous decision units. General management in the sense of coordinating departmental activities hence becomes more decentralized and diffused in these firms. As a consequence, functional competence must be supplemented by 'general management' capabilities at lower levels of the organization than in functionally organized companies, and career paths based more on performance assessed by market criteria can be expected to develop.

It is important to note, however, that not all industries follow this path of diversification and divisionalization equally rapidly. As Chandler points out (1962 : 42), firms in industries where markets and technologies did not change very quickly and where growth came mostly from expansion of existing product lines, did not need to alter radically their mode of operation. It was only when existing markets were in danger of becoming saturated that, for example, the tobacco companies engaged in an aggressive campaign of acquisition and diversification (Alford 1976b; Channon 1973). Also, while the logic of divisionalization may demand the decentralization of general management functions and reward systems based on profitability rather than on functional expertise, the available evidence suggests that these implications have only taken place to a limited extent in Britain, France, and Germany (Channon 1973; Dyas and Thanheiser 1976). This is due in part to the reluctance of many top managers to delegate general operational responsibilities and restrict their focus to more strategic issues but also to the equally strong cultural resistance to basing managerial salaries upon general economic performance.

However, there are some intrinsic difficulties in moving rapidly to a fully fledged divisional structure, not the least of which concern problems of measuring managerial performance based on profit centres. Precisely because the giant firm tries to plan future strategies and optimize the coordinated efforts of its constituent units, it cannot fully operate as a simple resource-allocating system based on market performance as the holding company structure tried to do. The sub units cannot thus be regarded as fully autonomous, and devices such as transfer pricing between subsidiaries are often used to maximize the overall return to the firm at the cost of reducing unit profits. In fact, the setting of transfer prices between divisions is often a highly political activity, because it affects profits and hence future investment and managers' careers. While various technical procedures have been developed to overcome these problems (Granick 1972 : 325–54) there is still the inherent conflict between overall firm goals and strategy and sub-unit optimization. In addition, for the full benefits of the multidivisional structure to be realized, a much enlarged head-office staff is required, together with a more sophisticated financial reporting and planning system than that existing in many British and French companies after the war. This requirement, of a considerable increase in technical expertise at top management level to enable central control to be more systematic, may have deterred some firms from moving to a fully fledged divisional form.

Giant multinationals, business elites, and business schools

The development of fairly novel forms of organization in diversified giant companies, the emergence of new managerial specialisms and partial institutionalization and decentralization of the general management role, coupled with the contemporaneous establishment of prestigious educational organizations intended, in part, to produce high-level managerial generalists with an understanding of specialist competences, all imply changes in the structure and operations of business elites. The increasingly specialist nature of many managerial tasks in large, complex firms – and their concomitant increasingly systematic organization – threatens the legitimacy of authority based upon the ideal of 'all round' experience, as in Britain, and of technical expertise in engineering certified by prestigious educational institutions, as in France (Granick 1972).

In addition, the multidivisional structure necessitates some decentralization of operational control, even if it is not as great as some analysts of the 'strategy and structure' school suggest, and this in turn implies the development of new ways of behaving and of new means of exercising control through novel, systematic, procedures rather than through direct personal authority.

These interrelated developments, the growth of multidivisional multi-industry, multinational giant firms and the emergence of distinctly managerial skills and techniques, have two major sets of consequences for national business elites. First, in association with general trends of economic decline of certain industries and concomitant rise of others, they imply a restructuring of relations within national business elites and between them. At the same time, existing distinctions between economic sectors, such as financial services and manufacturing industries in Britain, become weaker as giant firms accumulate enormous cash resources, act as semi-banks, and operate directly in financial markets (Chandler 1976; Chandler and Daems 1974; Pollard 1969 : 231–34; Williamson 1970). Similarly, the large national banks have become 'universal' ones, rather than simply retail or wholesale ones, and have also begun to operate as multinational enterprises competing for corporate clients. These changes have their impact on inter-elite connections, as has been shown by analyses of overlapping directorships between financial and manufacturing firms in Britain (Stanworth and Giddens 1975; Whitley 1974), and increasing bank control and directorships of major firms in France (Birnbaum *et al.* 1978 : 36–7; Morin 1974). So the development of giant firms hastens the process of creating new alliances and dissolving old ones between national managerial elites in different sectors.

The second set of consequences for national elites concerns the growing importance of multinational managers as distinct from national ones. When national economies were dominated by largely single industry firms, overseas operations were usually a matter of vertical integration – backwards to safeguard the supply of raw materials and/or forwards to increase sales and overcome tariff barriers – and did not necessitate major changes in modes of operation and control (Franko 1976 : 24–58). Business elites were largely based on firms operating in one industry and in one country – although this was not so true of those based in small national markets such as Belgium, Holland, Sweden, and Switzerland. International alliances to share markets or to agree prices were relatively short-term and restricted to specific products and markets (Franko 1976 : 84–98), even when cemented by kinship connections.

Put schematically, the development of coordinated multinational, multi-industry firms transformed this situation of largely *ad hoc* international collaboration between single industry elites to one in which divisional managers operate in the context of a global strategy, and resources are allocated according to world-wide criteria of profitability between industries and countries. Correspondingly, the development of distinctly managerial skills, conceived to be transferable across industries, markets, and countries, enables members of elite groups who were formerly restricted to particular industries in particular countries to become mobile across such boundaries. Groups dominating national economies through their positions in particular firms and industries – and often legitimating their incumbency of these positions in terms of 'experience' and long association with the specific conditions of an industry – decline in importance as economic control is transferred to a new stratum of 'generalist' managers in the multinational giants. These top managers delegate operational control of subsidiaries in specific industries and countries to divisional managers and deal with the problem of coordinating multi-industry activities, international financial management, and planning investment strategies on a global basis. At this level of international operations, specific knowledge of particular industries or countries is less important than general management skills. The bases of national, single industry, elite groups are correspondingly devalued.

The 'professionalization' of management

The idea of management being a 'professional' activity requiring the acquisition of particular skills is not new (Anthony 1977; Child 1969; Nichols 1969) but it has received a considerable impetus with the decline of traditional means of legitimating managerial authority and development of specialist techniques for controlling and planning large diversified corporations (Harbison and Myers 1959). The recent establishment of post-graduate business schools in Britain and France has institutionalized the ideal of 'general management' as a distinct set of skills whose possessors have legitimate authority over technical specialists. These schools also offer a means for members of dominating groups in declining industries to acquire these new skills and so legitimately assume authority positions in growing sectors of the international economy. By reifying the notion of general, professional management, the business school degree or diploma enables potentially downwardly mobile groups in Britain and France to acquire the requisite cultural capital for privileged entry into the managerial hierarchies of the newly dominant giant firms and so become potential members of the new stratum of the international corporate elite. It also serves to legitimate this privileged entry by certifying the business graduate's managerial competence and, in general, the competence and efficiency of this new stratum. Schools that emphasize the international aspects of management – such as INSEAD – will obviously be particularly useful for these purposes.

The 'professionalization' of management and the development of new ways of integrating and controlling sub-units of large firms such as the use of sophisticated financial control techniques, are also likely to affect the behaviour of middle and senior managers in multinational firms. The more firms operate as mini capital markets and seek to maximize the total profit of the whole enterprise (Williamson 1970), the more the performance of individual units will be assessed on various measures of profitability and financial contribution to the whole rather than in terms of particular industry-based criteria or output growth (Dyas and Thanheiser 1976 : 25). As a result, managers should become more profit-conscious rather than less, as some 'managerialist' writers have suggested, because their managerial career will be based more overtly on their profit performance (Nichols 1969 : 108–48). This increased awareness of profit and financial criteria of managerial success among middle managers as divisionalization develops in large firms is linked to a greater emphasis on making what can be sold at a profit rather than selling what is made. Marketing as a distinct activity, dealing with product planning and development and the development of overall pricing strategies for selling a range of products, becomes more important in conditions of increased inter-national competition. Similarly, when managers are made responsible for the overall profitability of an operation rather than simply for a single functional part of it, they are forced to coordinate market strategies with production planning. Especially in consumer goods firms, marketing and general commercial skills become of considerable importance so that marketing departments often dominate product development strategies. This shift away from production-dominated structures entails the decline of the relative importance of engineering skills particularly in France (Granick 1972) in favour of commercial ones (*Table Ronde* 1978). Consequently, some of the commercial *grandes écoles*, such as HEC, are beginning to assume an importance for careers in business hitherto reserved for the engineering schools (Bourdieu, Boltanski, and de St Martin 1973).

Post-graduate business schools thus offer an opportunity for those who have already obtained the more traditional qualifications to acquire more commercially oriented ones, and so to transfer fields and/or become general managers. As well as functioning as a conversion device for potentially declining elites, therefore, these schools may also function as transfer organizations for those caught out with the 'wrong' educational background and type of skills. Legitimating chances in economic structures and systems of authority in the new types of enterprise by institutionalizing the professional general manager role, the business schools also enable those who are 'relatively deprived' by these changes to recover some of the lost ground.

Changes in managerial careers and the roles of business graduates

Changes in business strategies and administrative structures have meant that as well as functional specialists being required to develop general management skills – or at least demonstrate the capacity to become a general manager – new types of specialist expertise are now required to coordinate and control these giant enterprises and to plan their future development. The 'professional' manager with distinct skills, not based simply on functional experience, that Chandler saw beginning to dominate major US companies in the 1970s began to develop in some European countries in the 1950s and 1960s (Chandler 1973; Hannah 1976: 77. In order to cope with more market-centred corporate strategies, major European companies looked to accepted American practices and began to hire a few products of US business schools, particularly of Harvard (Business Graduates Association 1973; Granick 1972: 374–78). The move to multidivisional forms of organization was inspired in many cases by US management consultancy firms, especially McKinsey, and the desire to imitate the major US multinationals in structure and approach appeared to be particularly strong in the 1960s (Chandler 1976; Dyas and Thanheiser 1976; Franko 1976 : 198–212; Granick 1972 : 377–79; Hannah 1976 : 173–76).

Whereas previously, functional success in Britain, or graduation from the best *grandes écoles* in France, had often sufficed to acquire senior management posts in large firms, in the 1950s and 1960s it seemed that new skills were being demanded which traditional methods of recruitment did not appear to develop. In addition to sending a select group of their managers on 'management development' courses, as well as on other courses to learn new specialist techniques, some, but by no means all, firms began to recruit the graduates of the newly established business schools.

In France in particular, this move towards expanding management education became almost an explosion (Granick 1972 : 377) after 1968; several post-graduate schools were set up in addition to an expansion of the commercial schools, and a 'business university' was established in Paris. Indeed 'management' has now received the accolade of being worthy of acceptance as a subject of the 'aggrégation' examination. Although the consequences for managerial careers of this sudden interest in management education are not yet wholly apparent, there is some evidence to indicate that the higher commercial and business schools at least started to become as important for a career in business as the great engineering schools are for a career in the Civil Service (Beaudeux and Rouge 1978; Bourdieu, Boltanski, and de St Martin 1973; Bourdieu and St Martin 1978).

The existence of a privileged entry gate to managerial positions for a small group of suitably endowed young men and women is not, of course, new. In Britain, management trainee schemes have been operating in many firms since the 1950s, at least, usually for Oxbridge arts graduates and public-school educated men without any higher education (Acton Society Trust (AST) 1956, 1962). As the Acton Society Trust study of management succession pointed out, this was the most advantageous position to have as one's first job for fast promotion into middle and top management, even more so than beginning as a managerial or senior specialist (AST 1956:26–8; Melrose-Woodman 1978). However, these traineeship schemes were mostly predicated on the assumption that management was an art that could be picked up on the job rather than a set of skills that could, in part, be learnt at a suitable prestigious institution (AST 1962). Furthermore, aside from the technical part of the enterprise and the accounting skills required for elementary costing and book-keeping, the amount of technical managerial knowledge required of senior managers was often minimal, so that the lack of such expertise was not especially noticeable. The need for systematic coordination and planning, and the development of techniques and practices for accomplishing them, which became obvious with changes in market and price structures in the 1960s, however, rendered this approach to management development and succession visibly obsolete in some industries (Political and Economic Planning 1965:46–65).

Although management trainee schemes for university graduates continue to flourish in many firms – sometimes with many attendant difficulties (Acton Society Trust 1956:45; British Institute of Management 1968; Sorrell 1966) – they do not always contribute to the demand for new managerial skills and, in particular, graduates cannot be given managerial responsibilities for some time after joining the firm (Acton Society Trust 1956:45). In contrast, business school graduates have by their initial training acquired extensive skills in financial management and planning – as distinct from accounting (Berridge 1978) – and market management and development.[2] They have also been trained to look at the enterprise as a whole and to develop corporate strategies for future development. It is precisely this emphasis on long-term planning and control at many major business schools in Europe that makes business graduates appropriate for the new multidivisional form of organization, at least in the view of the business schools. Extensive training in financial control procedures, in forecasting and policy development techniques, render the graduate of the new, prestigious business schools peculiarly appropriate for high-level staff jobs in diversified, divisionalized, multinational companies. This need not mean, however, that all large companies see MBAs in this light or consider the business schools' main function to be to provide graduates for these sorts of jobs.

It can be seen from such public documents as course brochures, that major business schools do themselves place considerable emphasis on the preparation of students for general managerial responsibilities, in addition to the inculcation of particular skills and expertise. In effect, they claim to instil the capacity for taking decisions and exercising authority during the MBA programme, so that business graduates may be given preferential opportunities over other managers to demonstrate their potential and thus to develop a 'track record' at a fairly early age. Since it is difficult to assess someone's individual performance in general management positions because of the diffuse, largely non-technical nature of these positions and the lack of strong boundaries to the activity (Offe 1976), it is especially difficult to assess different people's potential performance in such posts. This is one, but not of course the only, reason for the mystification of much managerial work as an 'art' learnt by 'experience' of 'leadership', etc. (Margerison 1978) and concomitant reliance on tacit norms of social acceptability (Nichols 1969 : 126–30), as we shall see below.

One of the major methods of instilling general managerial capabilities that has been adopted by many European business schools is the use of case studies in class discussions developed by Harvard Business School (Gordon and Howell 1959 : 32). Another approach, developed particularly at Manchester, is the use of group projects to ensure that graduates are experienced in working in managerial teams on complex business problems where each member has a specialist contribution to make. These projects are often 'live' in the sense that they involve working in firms on current problems and so socialize students into senior managerial cultures as well as developing the necessary social skills for group working. They also develop coordination skills, which may be useful when the graduates are called upon to manage a group of specialists. In so far as these and other methods of learning are successful in developing self confidence and a belief in one's capacity for making decisions and managing groups (as most alumni in our study said they did when asked how business schools had been important for their careers), business schools may succeed in producing graduates who are able to convince their superiors of their potential and so are given broad managerial responsibilities in their late twenties and early thirties. This is especially probable for those business graduates who already share some of the background and educational atrributes of senior managers. The 'right' background and attributes are likely to remain important factors in giving MBAs early opportunities to demonstrate their capabilities, as they are for other managers. Nonetheless, attendance at a prestigious business school may, to some extent, compensate for a relatively non-prestigious education and/or parental background. Indeed, the sheer fact of going to such an institution is likely to imply considerable qualities – not least of commitment and perseverance – on the part of sons of manual and clerical workers given the middle-class dominance of universities and higher education generally (Bourdieu and Passeron 1970; Halsey 1972, 1974). The combination of these qualities and the cultural capital of the degree obtained from an elite business school may result in some of these relatively disadvantaged business graduates moving fairly quickly into senior management posts in large manufacturing firms.

3 Management education and the British business schools

To understand the present role and position of the British business schools it is important to know something of their history. Despite the publicity that accompanied the opening of the schools in the mid-1960s, the creation of these two small, if novel, university institutions as a result of a report by Lord Franks was a relatively minor development at a time of major expansion in the education system at university level. Understandably, it was the Robbins Report, rather than the Franks Report, that caught the attention of politicians, educationalists, and the public at large. For by comparison with Robbins's proposals for the immediate founding of six new universities and an expansion of university places in the order of thousands, those of the Franks Committee, for the establishment of two business schools, were modest indeed.

The changes foreshadowed by Franks's proposals were modest, however, only in terms of scale and in relation to the development of the education system as a whole. Seen in the context of the history of British management education they were of considerable significance. To many of those who had witnessed the varying fortunes of management education in Britain since the War, the birth of the university business schools seemed, indeed, to be a momentous event which marked a key stage in the progress of a 'management education revolution' (Wheatcroft 1970). The schools appeared to symbolize a new partnership between business and the educational world, founded upon fundamental changes in the attitudes of the state, the universities, and above all, business, and seemed to demonstrate by their very existence that management education had at last come into its own (Mosson 1965 : 159; Turner 1969 : 93).

Traditional attitudes to management education

If the mushrooming of provisions for management education in the 1960s seemed to some to be a revolutionary development, this was only partly because management courses had by then come to exist in profusion where few had existed before. What seemed equally, if not more, significant was the change in the traditional attitudes and practices of British business that this growth seemed to reflect, for the prevailing view had for long been that formal education had little or no role to play in the development of a manager. British managers, like British gentlemen, were born rather than made, and management itself had been seen principally as an art learnt by long years of practical experience in the workplace rather than in the groves of academe. As Florence (1961 : 324–25) has said:

'To have discussed education for management a hundred years ago would have been thought grotesque. Management as such hardly existed. There were entrepreneurs, proprietors, partners – businessmen generally; but management was merely an incident, almost a side-line, in the work of those industrialists. To be educated for that side-line was preposterous. You were either born to a great business as the son and heir of a family concern, or you achieved greatness by successful competition against rivals, or you had it thrust upon you by promotion from the ranks of clerks or foremen. You never trained for business as for the law or the church or medicine.'

Such conceptions of the proper mode of advancement in business persisted well into the twentieth century, although they were not to go unchallenged. The reactions of businessmen to the questioning of their traditional attitudes and practices showed, however, that they were highly resistant to change.

In the 1920s and 1930s, a new conception of management began to be developed by a small group of 'management intellectuals' who came to be known collectively as the British 'management movement' (Child

1969). Although not always united in their views, a common strand in their thinking was that it was no longer adequate to define management purely as an art. Rather they sought to establish a new definition of management as an activity based on scientific principles and which, if an art at all, was an art informed by science. Basic to this notion was the belief that there existed a distinct body of knowledge which could and should be used as the basis of management practice. Such a claim was made possible in their eyes by the emergence of a number of works on industrial organization and administration by writers such as Taylor, Follett, Mayo, and others. The existence of a generalized body of knowledge, to which they themselves contributed, implied that education for management need no longer be confined to direct experience on the job, but might instead be provided, as was the case for other professions, within the education system.

The precise role that education for management might play in managerial recruitment was, however, a matter of debate. Lee (1921), for example, argued that managers were a distinct professional class whose right to control was based on their scientific expertise, and that only those possessing this should be recruited to, and promoted within, managerial ranks. The acquisition of such expertise could, Lee believed, be achieved to a substantial degree through formal education, most appropriately within the universities. James Bowie (1949) even suggested that management should become a 'closed shop' to which only those who had been formally trained would be admitted. Others, such as Urwick (1954, 1957) saw a more limited though still substantial role for management education. Although scathingly critical of those who insisted that management was purely an art, and repeatedly advocating the need for formal management education, Urwick nevertheless accepted the idea that certain personality attributes were essential in a competent manager. In that sense, the new management-as-science view represented not so much a radical alternative as a significant modification of the ideas of management-as-art. Nevertheless, the most important implication of the new thinking was, from our point of view, that the attribution of managerial competence, or at least a fundamental component of it, could in future be made by educational institutions. It was no longer grotesque, in the eyes of the management movement, to discuss management education.

These ideas received very little support from business, the universities, and the state. If businessmen had heard of the new thinking on management at all they greeted it with at best indifference and at worst outright dismissal. The members of the management movement found themselves preaching to a largely unreceptive audience, and were sometimes driven to bitter criticism of employers for their extreme conservatism in the face of new ideas, their lack of interest in business research, and their unbending resistance to management education (Child 1969 : 103). The metamorphosis of the ugly duckling of the management craft into the majestic swan of the management profession seemed as far away at the outbreak of the Second World War as it had at that of the First.

The dominant business view of management-as-art appears, however, to have shifted in the 1940s and 1950s in such a way as to enable both the art and science conceptions of management to be incorporated within a single framework. The matter was addressed explicitly in these terms by Sir Frederic Hooper in his book *Management Survey*, first published in 1948 and reissued in 1960 with minor changes. Although it is difficult to know the extent to which his views were representative of those of the major industrialists of the day, such evidence as there is suggests that they were widely held (Child 1969 : 140).

Hooper began by summarizing the alternative views of management as art or science. It was the former view, said Hooper, that has 'held good in Britain until recent times, and, indeed, still holds good in many quarters'. He went on:

'The art of management turns mainly on personality; that is upon the possession of, and the relation between, certain qualities. These qualities can be armed by study. . . . But if the necessary qualities are not already there in the first place, or at least latent close below the surface, no amount of training, however scientific, will put them there. Nor can the art of management, as such, be made the subject of examination; least of all written examination. . . . There is only one valid test for management as an art – the production of successful results on a sufficient scale over an adequate period of time.

By contrast, the science of management is very little dependent upon personality. . . . It can be taught and studied in a classroom, and the degree of mastery acquired can be tested validly and to a useful extent by written examination.' (Hooper 1960 : 14–15)

In Hooper's opinion, management was neither art nor science but a blend of art *and* science. Thus the fundamental qualities necessary in a manager were those which a man had 'built at birth into the fibre of his being', which were 'the true index to what he may become', and which could be 'developed, built upon, brought into balance, and equipped'.

Acquired qualities, by comparison, could prove to be but superficial and temporary.

These fundamental qualities were those essential to leadership. The list included the ability to evoke loyalty and devotion and to exact discipline, an objective mind, earthiness, and 'above all that indefinable thing called judgement'. Evidence of quality included 'the present showing, in bearing and speech, of the man at his selection-interview', and 'acceptability to others'. The latter was particularly important:

> 'The quality of acceptability ranks high where management is concerned, whether in business or elsewhere. Appraisal accordingly covers general personal appearance; absence of unpleasing mannerisms; the existence of pleasing ones; the absence of disturbing or flamboyant traits of character. It takes account of how the candidate gets on with others, and whether he has poise and is at ease in company.' (Hooper 1960 : 171–72)

Hooper then considered the role of education, for although inborn qualities were 'undoubtedly primary' they could be enhanced by the right educational background. Top management, in particular, required qualities of mind that neither a specialist managerial or technical training could convey, nor even practical experience of business. Indeed the specialization of management, which was 'becoming split up into a number of channels', made the training of the whole man even more important. Such a training was most effective in the early, formative years of general education, and a liberal university training seemed highly appropriate. Industry had in general extended a 'cold hand' to the arts graduate, but would now have to turn more often to such men (no mention of women is made in this discussion) as the universities would increasingly cream off the most intelligent minds leaving fewer potential managers to enter business direct from school.[1] Apart from this, the aspiring manager, be he 'ranker, technician, graduate or proprietor's son', needed three kinds of training: general training in the science of management, practical training related to the particular type of business he is entering, and training to develop the 'whole man' so that he can 'practice the art of management as distinct from the science'. General training would be acquired in technical or commercial colleges or similar institutions, whilst practical training would be carried out within the firm. At a more specialized level, functional training could be obtained by working for the examinations of the professional institutions associated with management. Finally, the 'larger view' necessary for top management could be developed by attendance at the Administrative Staff College, Henley (a private institution founded in 1947 – see below), to which those who had reached the peak of their careers as junior executives would be sent. Here men would be given 'a final finish, an impulse, and a cutting edge. . . .'

The role of formal education and training for potential managers was thus to differ according to the level of authority of the manager who was to receive it. At the lower levels it was to consist of the 'science' of management. At the higher levels, however, it was the 'art' of management that was predominant. If management was both science and art, the weighting in favour of art increased progressively as the topmost levels were approached. The willingness to 'disenchant' managerial skills was limited to those which could be exercised at the lower levels. It followed that since the 'art' of management would neither be taught nor examined in any formal sense, it was impossible to 'qualify' as a top manager. One could be 'broadened' but for that purpose it was the private college, such as Henley, rather than the state education system, that would administer the appropriate rites.

Hooper's view thus constituted a synthesis of the ideas of management-as-art and management-as-science. His emphasis on management-as-art, to which science was supplementary, seems to have represented the typical orientation of British business in the 1940s and 1950s. A study of management in large manufacturing companies conducted in the mid-50s by the Acton Society Trust indicated objective consequences of selection policies that closely match what would be expected from the application of notions similar to Hooper's. Thus the most advantageous 'promotion factor' among the managers studied was an Oxbridge arts degree (the requisite liberal education), followed by attendance at a major public school (the right qualities of personality and leadership) (Acton Society Trust 1956 : 28–9).

The activities and publications of the management movement provided the basis for a change in the prevailing system of managerial recruitment and promotion, but even after a quarter of a century of persuasion there was little sign of movement. Most businessmen found the view that formal education could play a part in the making of a manager wholly unacceptable (Turner 1969 : 92–3). Employers were generally opposed to the idea of management education, were suspicious of university graduates, and tended to believe that the proper mode of access to managerial positions was either by inheritance or through the grisly process of working one's way up from the bottom (Wheatcroft 1970 : 87).

The advent of the Second World War did, however, have important consequences for management education. The exigencies of wartime operations brought the state and industry into close contact, and what the state found was not always to its liking. Bevin, for example, found such an absence of provisions for personnel management in factories that he instituted direct Government appointment of personnel officers at all but the smallest, and the compulsory introduction of welfare amenities (Child 1969:111). The state thus became more aware of the inadequacies of existing management practices, an awareness heightened when a number of study groups visited the United States to look at American management methods in connection with the Marshall Aid scheme and returned with glowing accounts of US management and US management education (Anglo-American Council on Productivity 1951; Hutton 1953). These two factors, a consciousness of the outdated managerial methods prevalent in British industry and the contrasting modernity of American practice, encouraged the state to take action at a time when it was in an increasingly interventionist mood (Williams 1971:115–19; Thomson 1965; 206–07).

One consequence of the state's awakened interest was the founding of the British Institute of Management (BIM) in 1947. Set up as the result of the report of the Baillieu Committee, created by the Board of Trade, the BIM was intended to act as a centre for the dissemination of information on modern management methods and was encouraged to turn itself into a professional body (Board of Trade 1946; Robertson 1965:76, 82; Wheatcroft 1970:91–2). Initially it was treated with a good deal of reserve by most firms, perhaps partly because the BIM's membership was split from the first between those who believed management could be taught and those who held that managers were born and not made (Nichols 1969:127). The BIM did, however, fare better than its predecessor, the Institute of Industrial Administration, which had been founded nearly thirty years earlier by members of the management movement. An expression of the movement's belief in managerial professionalism, it collapsed in 1924. Although it was revived some years later, in 1939 it had only 517 members and was eventually merged with the BIM (Child 1969:113; Dunkerley 1975:43).

Of greater importance for management education was the establishment of a working party whose recommendations resulted in the first relatively large-scale provision within the education system.

The National Scheme of Management Studies

In 1945 the Ministry of Education established a committee 'to advise on the educational facilities required for management in industry and commerce' (Wheatcroft 1970:89). Chaired by Lieutenant-Colonel Lyndall Urwick, a long-standing and prominent member of the management movement and a strong believer in management education, the committee recommended a National Scheme of Management Studies to be run in the technical and commercial colleges. First launched in 1949, this scheme constituted the major contribution to management education by the state education system until the emergence of the university business schools in the 1960s.

Under the scheme, a two-stage course was to be taken by those who had already had an appropriate general education. The first stage involved the study of 'background' and 'tool' subjects and led to qualification for membership of one of the 'professional' institutions which had sprung up in the 1930s to cater for specialist branches of management (e.g. Institute of Labour Management, Works Managers' Association). The second stage led to either a qualification in a specialized field or one in general management. The course as a whole was to be taken by part-time study over a period of five years or more. The final examination in a specialized field could not be taken before the age of twenty-five, and in general management not before twenty-eight, thus ensuring that positions of responsibility should not come too readily into youthful hands. A revised scheme was introduced in 1961. Entry requirements were raised to a degree-level qualification, and the course was now to last three years, leading to the award of a Diploma in Management Studies, which replaced the original Diploma of the British Institute of Management. The first year again emphasized 'background' subjects whilst the second and third years were to be devoted to the study of management principles and practices, personnel management, industrial relations, and 'higher business control'.

But this effort in state management education was not well received by employers. Both the quality of the teachers and the calibre of the students were soon questioned and the scheme rapidly fell into disrepute. Despite revisions, business criticism continued and eventually even the BIM, under whose auspices the scheme had originally begun, felt obliged to withdraw its support. Not surprisingly, enrolments for the revised course diminished. After a flying start with an intake of nearly 1,600 students in its first year, the numbers had slumped by 1963 to 564. Even the initial intake had been far from massive, for it was estimated that 11,000 managers each year were in need of initial management training (Political and Economic Planning 1965:237). Moreover, very few of the students who did attend were sent on the courses by their firms. On the whole then, the courses were quietly ignored by the bulk of British industry.

The unpopularity of the National Scheme in employers' eyes reflected in part their general lack of belief in the need for, or possibility of, vocational education for management. A second important factor, however, was that the courses were administered through the unprestigious technical and commercial colleges (Robertson 1970). Businessmen tended to look with disdain on these institutions which they thought unsuited, by virtue of their traditional tasks and intake, to the job of educating managers. As Mosson (1965 : 172, 191) noted:

'The demand for technical instruction which arose in the nineteenth century was essentially an effort to elevate the working classes and in a society with a predominantly middle-class management the institutions which grew up to satisfy that demand continue to be, to some extent, socially suspect. . . . The technical colleges . . . have long been associated with the improvement of the working classes and to a middle-class management bear the indelible stigma of providing a satisfactory training for supervisors and foremen.'

The colleges were caught in a vicious circle. Because of their low prestige they were unable to attract the promising young managers from major companies to their courses whose presence might have served to raise prestige. Employers seemed equally unwilling to give much recognition to the 'qualification', so discouraging those who might have attended as 'independents'. There were criticisms of the lack of business experience on the part of the teachers, but few firms would second their senior managers to the colleges to teach. And whilst there was a feeling that part-time study was an inferior substitute for full-time education, the alternative of granting young managers full-time release proved likewise unattractive. Business did not do much, therefore, to help remove the causes of its discontent.

Developments that took place under the National Scheme showed the absence of any widespread change in business thinking about management education. Employers' reactions were much as could have been predicted from the experience of the management movement before the War. When it is remembered that it was not a business organization but the Ministry of Education that originated the committee devising the scheme, and that this committee was chaired by a 'management intellectual' whose views were far from representative of those of business, it is easy to understand how this pioneering step came to meet with such a dismal response. Clearly, to make provisions for management 'qualifications' was one thing, but to secure their recognition quite another.

Developments in the universities

Until the founding of the business schools, universities made little contribution to management education (Mosson 1965, 1975). The Manchester College of Science and Technology offered the first post-graduate management course of its kind in Britain in 1926, at a time when some of the famous American schools were already twenty to thirty years old; but in general, the calls of the management movement for high-level management courses fell on deaf ears. Without the backing of the state, and in the face of the insouciance of the universities and the equal, if not greater, indifference of business, they were condemned to a lengthy period of fruitless exhortation. It was only after the Second World War that the universities showed any signs of serious involvement with their concerns.[2]

The universities offered courses both at post-graduate level (now widely accepted as the lowest level at which vocational studies in management can begin (Rose 1970 : 12, 113, 115)) and short courses for experienced managers. By the early 1960s the number of institutions giving such courses was, however, extremely small. In 1960, just three years before Franks published his proposals for the business schools, only five universities were running full-time post-graduate courses in business administration (McGivering 1960 : 74). They catered for but a few hundred students each year and, as in the case of the technical college diploma courses, very few of these were sent by firms. Rather more popular were the post-experience courses, particularly those that were intended to 'broaden' senior managers (Mosson 1965 : 178, 186–87). Their attractiveness stemmed in part from the fact that they were short, lasting weeks rather than months, so that firms could release their managers without creating a serious 'manpower gap' and without much expense. They also fitted more adequately with employers' conceptions of management education by virtue of their non-academic orientation and the absence of academic entry requirements. In addition, these courses rarely, if ever, involved the examination and certification of their participants. Unlike the post-graduate courses, they were not concerned with the assessment of managerial competence. Instead, they seem often to have been used as a reward for those who had already been judged competent and worthy of promotion by business itself, and in this they performed much the kind of role envisaged by Hooper.

In general, however, industry showed as little interest in the universities' provisions as it did in those of the technical colleges. The post-graduate courses in particular were thought of as being excessively academic and insufficiently related to the pragmatic concerns of business. Businessmen were not, of course, always encouraged by the attitudes of the universities themselves (Allen 1961; McGivering 1960:135; Mosson 1965:195, 214; Nichols 1969:85; Turner 1969:92–3; Wheatcroft 1970:3). Universities traditionally presented themselves as aloof from the sordid world of practical affairs, so that the addition of management subjects to universities' curricula would represent a humbling of their status and a diversion from their historic role as guardians of the nation's intellect; 'training' was not a fitting task for a university. Although it is difficult to know how widespread such views were, the universities cannot be said to have gone out of their way to welcome the new discipline of management. They thus did little to modify industry's views, and indeed reinforced the latter's lack of interest with their own.

The private sector

The largely negative orientation of business to management education in the state system contrasted sharply with its attitudes to provisions in the private sector. After the Second World War, and especially since the late 1950s, there was a considerable growth of private facilities for 'management development' and training (Robertson 1965), both in the form of private colleges and in-company schemes. By 1965 there were more than sixty residential colleges catering for managers, most of which had been founded during the previous ten years, and there had been a steady increase in the use of internal management training schemes and in the number of training officers, advisers, and consultants needed to organize and staff them. It was here, in the private sector, that business put its money and its manpower, for here at least the customer was always likely to be right.

The prototype of the private management centre was the Administrative Staff College at Henley. Founded soon after the War, it was financed entirely by industry and had been established as an independent institution, without ties to the state or the education system, in part because of apprehension about academic interference with business affairs (Wheatcroft 1970:91). Oriented to courses for top management, its criteria for admission reflected the preferences of business, favouring practical experience above academic achievement. Entry to the College was widely sought after; to be sent on the general management course was often regarded as a sign that top management status either had already, or would soon after, be conferred (Mosson 1965 : 191).

Where business went outside its own organizations in search of management education, it was to institutions such as these that it usually turned. Unlike the technical colleges, there was no question of their social correctness, and in contrast to the spartan facilities that the colleges offered, they frequently provided the amenities and ethos of a country-club. The courses placed a strong emphasis on the practical. Course content stressed the development of social skills and the broadening of outlook thought essential for those about to enter the higher ranks of management. At these institutions, practical men met with other practical men to discuss practical matters in an atmosphere far removed from that of the lecture theatre, seminar room, and examination hall. This orientation was reflected in the teaching methods adopted, the 'syndicate method', in which participants exchanged experience principally with their peers, being frequently used. Certification on the basis of examined performance was also thought unnecessary. Symbolically, those who completed the Henley course were awarded not a diploma but a green tie (Turner 1969 : 97). Since the 'arts' of top management were believed not to be susceptible to examination, this is, perhaps, not surprising. The preference for the private colleges was, to some extent, incidental in that where the state system operated in a similar fashion to these colleges it also found favour. In the universities, for example, the most popular courses were those for relatively senior managers. They too were concerned largely with 'broadening' and the development of social skills, were of relatively short duration, and were not formally assessed. And, like the private colleges, participants were selected on the basis of the judgements of business.

Support for the private colleges was supplemented by the growth of schemes for management education and 'development' within companies, made possible by the quantity of resources available to large firms and the size of their managerial labour force. These developments seem also to have taken place largely after the War, and are reflected in the growth of personnel management during this period. Such internal provisions were probably much encouraged by the passing of the Industrial Training Act of 1964, which imposed a training levy on companies and which included within its terms of reference the training of managers.

It is difficult to know what role these in-company schemes play in managerial promotion, but clearly, by their very nature, they offer many advantages. They are under the direct control of firms. Those who are to be exposed to such schemes can be chosen by the company. They do not leave the organization for any substantial length of time. Training in abstract principles can be integrated with attention to company-specific problems. And those who attend are not equipped with symbols of excellence that they could exploit in the labour market. Whatever their significance, in terms of sheer numbers it is these in-company schemes that constitute the chief expansion in management education (Rose 1970; Weston 1972; Leggatt 1972) and their existence underlines the fact of industry's relative functional autonomy in this respect. Business, it has been pointed out, does not need the educational system to inculcate the new skills of management. It is capable, or so it might claim, of doing the job itself (*Industrial Management* 1971 : 1). As was noted at the time, British management education was not on the whole concerned to produce managers; rather it aimed to 'develop' those who were already afforded managerial status (Mosson 1965 : 198).

The founding of the business schools

The early 1960s seemed an inauspicious time at which to launch new institutions of high-level management education, for in those days, as Lord Franks himself was to note, 'there was widespread doubt in industry, and in the universities, in the Government and in the Civil Service, about the need for, and the feasibility of, management education' (Franks, in Wheatcroft 1970 : v). But there was also an increasing concern about the quality of British management, which eventually resulted in the expansion of both private sector facilities and those in the state system. Within business, large companies were facing new problems of organization and control in an increasingly competitive environment, and this stimulated attempts to discover and develop new forms of managerial talent (Robertson 1965 : 73; Turner 1969 : 65, 72). At national level there was a growing mood of frustration and anxiety over the persistently poor performance of the economy. It became fashionable to compare countries' growth rates, and whereas before 1950 Britain's had seemed to compare reasonably well with her competitors, there were now signs that the British economy was falling behind (Williams 1971 : 126–27). The deep-seated nature of these problems was becoming more and more evident, and it was factors such as these – the growing importance of large firms, the unsatisfactory record of industry, the failure to compete successfully in export markets, and the awareness of the fundamental unsoundness of the economy – that encouraged the search for new and more effective solutions. Not least amongst those proposed was the rejuvenation of British management through education and training (Mosson 1965 : 199).

Such a solution to the country's economic problems seemed all the more plausible in view of the development of an influential school of economic thought that posited a close connection between investments in education and training and national productivity (Tyler 1977 : 24). According to this theory, the road to economic salvation lay in the direction of increased expenditure on education and a heightened attention to 'human resources' or 'human capital'. This idea was grasped so fervently by Western governments that it became thought of as a new 'secular religion' (Illich 1970) and British governments, of either party, were no exception. Their faith in the role of education in economic development was expressed, for example, in both the Crowther (1959) and Robbins (1963) reports, which emphasized the relation of the one to the other (King 1969 : 114). In such an atmosphere the state developed a considerable enthusiasm for both education in general and management education in particular (Chester 1965 : 3). The message that the productivity teams had brought back from America soon after the War, linking business success to managerial quality, and that in turn to management education, took on a new relevance. More than ever it was the example of the United States that was used both as the model for British development and the measure of her current failings (cf. Thomson 1965 : 271–72).

As Turner pointed out, 'business schools are about as British as drum majorettes' (Turner 1969 : 92). That senior businessmen and civil servants came to talk quite unapologetically about the need for 'business schools' is something of an indication of the potency that transatlantic concepts had at this time. Yet if the inspiration for the schools was drawn from America, the manner in which they were created was impeccably British.

Urwick had called for the immediate establishment of a residential, American-style business school in connection with an existing university as early as 1950, but no action was taken (Urwick 1950). Gradually, however, a number of industrialists became convinced of the need to improve the availability of facilities for high-level management education. A feeling developed in the late 1950s that existing provisions were inadequate and that more courses should be offered at under-graduate, post-graduate, and post-experience level. Since the technical colleges were not well thought of, attention focused initially on the universities.

The first initiative came from a group of young but senior managers, some of whom had been to the renowned Harvard Business School, who attended a series of luncheon meetings with politicians at the House of Commons (Robertson 1965:80; Wheatcroft 1970:94). In 1960 they created the Foundation for Management Education (FME), which raised funds to finance a set of teaching experiments at three universities. In 1963 they extended their patronage to a further nine. These developments sparked off something of a controversy over the legitimacy of university involvement in management education, and the whole subject became a matter for public debate (Allen 1961; Robbins Report 1963:134; Smith 1961).

One result of this wooing of the universities was the establishment of a second group of industrialists who were far from impressed by the thrust of the FME's work. They too met as a dining group but in the more palatial surroundings of the Savoy Hotel. This 'Savoy Group' was convinced of the need to create a 'British Harvard' but was pessimistic about the possibility of grafting such an institution on to any existing university. In their eyes, what was needed was a completely new kind of college which would be tailor-made to fit industry's requirements. Many of those who found their ideal for this new entity in the American-style business school supported this view with arguments which were not far removed from those of the 'human capital' theorists. America had business schools and was successful; Britain had no business schools and was not (Lupton 1972).

When proposals for a new 'business' university at Warwick emerged, the 'Savoy Group' advocated that a business school be founded in association with the university. With the assent of Lord Rootes, a prominent industrialist and Chancellor-Elect for the new university, its future Vice-Chancellor was summarily despatched to the United States to study American business schools (Wheatcroft 1970:95). These events were, however, overtaken by new moves on the part of the state.

In 1961, Selwyn Lloyd had proposed that a National Economic Development Council (NEDC) should be created as a forum for discussion between the Government, industry, and the unions on economic planning. The NEDC's second report, *Conditions Favourable to Faster Growth*, issued in April 1963, indicated that there was a 'need for at least one very high-level new school or institute, somewhat on the lines of the Harvard Business School, or the School of Industrial Management at the Massachusetts Institute of Technology' (NEDC 1963). This seemed to cast the die strongly in favour of business schools, but the report gave little indication of how or where such schools might be established. In the traditional British spirit of compromise and fair play, the FME, the Savoy Group, the British Institute of Management, the Federation of British Industries, and the NEDC itself commissioned Lord Franks to produce a concrete set of proposals which would finally resolve the disagreements about the form that future provisions for high-level management education should take.

THE FRANKS REPORT

Franks's task was undoubtedly made easier by the recommendations of the Robbins Committee which published its report in October 1963, just one month before his own. Caught up in the fervour for educational expansion, it suggested that 'two major post-graduate schools should be built up in addition to other developments already probable in universities and other institutions' (Robbins 1963). Its awareness of these 'other developments' was no doubt due to the fact that the FME, the FBI, and the BIM had submitted evidence to the Robbins Committee. Franks produced his report in November 1963 under the auspices of the BIM, his principle recommendation being that two business schools should be established in association with the universities of London and Manchester.

The Franks Report showed clearly that the road to the British business school had been far from smooth. There was, he noted, a considerable difference of opinion on the part of academics and businessmen over what the proper role of a business school should be. (Franks 1963: paras 17–19, 28, 29, 34). Businessmen were much concerned that the schools should be geared to the practical needs of industry and feared that, as university institutions, they might well become dominated by academic interests. Many wanted the emphasis to be on short, sharp, non-theoretical training courses suited to thirty- to forty-year-old experienced managers. As Professor Ball of the London Business School wrote, 'there seems little doubt that those who thought of the establishment of the business schools had predominantly in mind the needs of existing middle management (Ball 1967: 5; cf. Robertson 1970: 15; Turner 1969: 94–5). The academics, in their turn, feared that they might be reduced to the mundane task of 'retreading' middle managers, and wished to emphasize the importance of developing a new breed of young professionals equipped with the latest ideas and techniques of modern management. United through both businessmen and academics might have been in their desire for a business school, they were clearly divided over what its principal function should be.

With considerable sensitivity to these deeply held views, Franks proposed a compromise that he hoped would satisfy both parties. He acknowledged that there was a place for both post-experience and post-graduate courses and advocated that the schools should develop both. The existence of the latter, he noted, would help to attract and retain a high quality staff and thereby benefit those attending post-experience courses. He also thought that initially a number of those on the post-graduate courses would not hold degrees, and that 'no-one should be excluded on this ground provided he has the capacity and the knowledge to profit' (Franks 1963 : 10). It does not seem to have been envisaged at this time that the post-graduate courses would lead to the award of degrees, and that possession of a degree-level qualification would thus be a mandatory entrance requirement. Franks seemed to expect that they would be open to all young managers irrespective of their formal qualifications.

To further ensure that the new schools would reflect the interests of both camps, Franks suggested that they should be financed half by industry and half by the state, and that responsibility for policy should be similarly shared between business and the universities. 'Then and then only', he wrote, 'will the positive commitments of university and business be sufficient, both being irrevocably involved in the success or failure of the school' (Franks 1963 : 7).

Since the state was so clearly in favour of the sort of developments that Franks envisaged, his recommendations were speedily put into effect. On industry's side, the sponsors of the Franks enquiry met the month after the Report was published and agreed to accept his proposals. A second committee was set up under Lord Normanbrook to examine the detailed costing of the plans, and immediately following the publication of its report in May 1964, the Conservative Government agreed to a pound-for-pound funding of the schools. Franks's sponsors then launched an Appeal to industry to raise the requisite sum and within six months had exceeded their target of £3m by more than half. More than 300 organizations contributed to the Appeal, and in the light of past experience the level of support for the new, high-level, university business schools seemed almost startling. Business was no longer simply talking about the need for more management education. It backed its words with hard cash.

THE APPEAL TO INDUSTRY

Closer inspection of the sources of support for the Appeal shows, however, that there were considerable variations in both its quantity and quality. The Appeal report (Nelson 1964) indicated that over 350 subscriptions had been received and that, making allowance for subsidiaries which had made donations through their parent companies, this represented a contribution from more than 700 firms, ranging from £400,000 to a derisory £2 given by Remington Rand Limited. The bulk of the donations, although in four figures, were not particularly large; nearly two-thirds of them were for a sum of less than £10,000 and only a fifth were for £25,000 or more.

The group of sixty-four 'large' contributors included some interesting names. The largest single donation came from the British Iron and Steel Federation, whose gift was nearly three times the size of the next largest (from Ford). Sir Robert Shone, Director General of the National Economic Development Office of the NEDC and a sponsor of the Franks Report, had been a member of the Iron and Steel Board since 1953, an important channel of government influence over the industry. There were large donations from eight public sector organizations which in total exceeded that of the BISF. Five of these, including the British Railways Board, the National Coal Board, and the GPO, gave an identical sum of £70,000 each, the result perhaps of a Government round-robin. Overall the public sector's contribution, including £35,000 from the Bank of England, made up 10 per cent of the Appeal's total.

'Large' donations from the private sector were represented by those of forty-seven industrial and commercial companies. About forty of these were among the 100 largest firms of the day, which suggests that there were a significant number of large firms which did not support Franks's proposals or at least did not back them with a substantial donation. Whilst companies such as Ford, ICI, Shell, Unilever, GKN, AEI, Courtaulds, Dunlop, English Electric, and Imperial Tobacco gave sums of £100–£150,000, there were others who seem to have treated the Appeal much as they would have any 'worthy cause'. EMI, for example, gave a mere £500. By contrast, the large banks were unanimous in their support, even though the business schools tended on the whole to be presented as institutions that would chiefly serve the needs of industry rather than the City. Each of the Big Five gave at least £25,000.

The response to the Appeal was thus uneven and reflected the divisions of opinion (Mosson 1965 : 176) within the business world which Franks had noted, but which he and his colleagues had managed only partially to dispel. The sizeable donations from the nationalized industries, however, were perhaps a measure of the backing from the 'highest authority' of which Lord Nelson spoke in his report on the

Appeal (Nelson 1964 : 5). Whatever the variations in the amount of enthusiasm for business schools, the total committed to the Appeal fund by late December 1964 was more than enough to enable them to begin. The following year saw the opening of the two 'British Harvards', the London and Manchester Business Schools.

The business schools: control

The implementation of Franks's compromise solution to the 'business school problem' produced two hybrid institutions, each of which stood rather awkwardly with one foot in the academic world and one in the world of business. Jointly controlled, jointly funded, and offering both post-experience and post-graduate courses, they soon developed something of a split personality, with all the attendant discomforts such a condition brings. Intended as a bridge between the universities and industry, there was a constant danger that the two sides would move apart and send the whole structure crashing into the abyss.

From the beginning both the schools were determined to establish their own identities and saw themselves in competition to become Britain's top business school. The operations, policies, and organiz-ational arrangements at each thus developed in somewhat different ways. As business schools they were aware of the need for 'product differentiation', and this, together with their different socio-geographical milieux and the difference in emphasis in the attitudes of their leading staff, ensured that each would take on its own unique character.

At Manchester the formal status of the school in relation to its 'host' university differed from that of London. The Manchester Business School (MBS) has been at one and the same time both an 'autonomous' institution and the Faculty of Business Administration of Manchester University. As such it has been subject both to the control of the University, through the Faculty Board, and to that of the business community through the school's Council, each body being linked by the presence on each of senior members of the school's academic staff and the Vice-Chancellor of the University. Whilst the Faculty Board is an exclusively academic body, the Council has included a strong representation of senior businessmen, most of whom have been drawn from the large firms which made substantial donations to the Appeal fund.

At London, however, the school was instituted as a sponsored body within the University of London under the auspices of the London School of Economics and Imperial College. Its top policy-making body has been the Governing Body, which, as at Manchester, has included a large number of high-ranking businessmen among its members. The initial difference in emphasis can be illustrated by the fact that, whereas at Manchester the Vice-Chancellor of the University chaired the meetings of the Council for the first five years of the school's existence, at London it was the chairman of Tube Investments, Lord Plowden, who performed this task.

The effects of these differences upon the activities of the schools are difficult to judge. In theory, London has had a greater degree of autonomy from the University than Manchester, though it has by no means been free from University-imposed constraints. It has more freedom over staff appointments, for MBS professors are also professors of the University and representatives of other University departments participate in the selection of the Business School faculty (cf. Ball 1967 : 3). Even so, both schools have repeatedly bewailed the limitations that academic regulations place on their ability to attract the right kind of business-orientated staff at the right price.

Whilst the controlling bodies of the schools constitute the main formal channel for business influence over their activities, the ability of the business nominees to guide the schools in the directions that most industrialists seemed to prefer has been rather limited. Once the schools got under way, they began to develop in an unforeseen, and to many in business, unwelcome fashion, yet the controlling bodies were either unwilling or unable to curb these inclinations. In practice, business has made its influence felt by other means, through its willingness to continue the flow of funds and to patronize the schools' courses, and through the medium of such 'representative' organizations as the BIM. The foci of these unwelcome developments were the business schools' courses intended for young post-graduates at the start of their managerial careers. It seemed that the British Harvards that were now in production were not quite what their initiators had had in mind.

The business schools: curriculum

The Franks Report did not go into great detail about what the business schools should do nor about how they should do it. Their aims were stated by Franks in a very general way as to 'increase competence in managers or those who will be managers' (Franks 1963 : 3), and by Lord Normanbrook as 'to improve the efficiency of British industry and commerce by ensuring a larger supply of managers or potential managers who are familiar with the new techniques and tools of management' (Normanbrook 1964 : 6). Franks envisaged twenty-week courses for experienced managers and a one-year course for a younger but imprecisely defined group (cf. Ball 1967 : 5). The curricula would draw on the best American practice, at that time enshrined in the reports of the Ford and Carnegie Foundations (cf. Earle 1965 : 3), but would need to adapt to British conditions and eventually become firmly based on British conventions. What the British industrialist wanted, noted Turner (1969 : 432–33) was the flavour of the American way of doing things; any more fulsome embrace was regarded with considerable distaste. Such an ambivalent attitude to the American model of management education was not, however, adopted by the academics who were now in the process of fashioning the schools' curricula.

On the whole, both the London and Manchester schools identified strongly with what they thought of as their American counterparts, though again there were differences of emphasis. London was particularly keen to acknowledge its debt to the United States. The full title of the School, for example, the London Graduate School of Business Studies, was a borrowing from Harvard practice, and its literature spoke of 'Programmes' (Senior Executive Programme, London Executive Programme, Master's Programme, etc.), an 'Alumni Association', and 'electives'. Manchester stuck to the more parsimonious 'Manchester Business School', and was more inclined to talk of 'courses', a 'Manchester Business School Association', and 'course options'. Even so, in 1968 it drew particular attention to the number of its staff who were training in the major American schools, such opportunities being particularly welcome 'in view of the fully established and highly advanced state of graduate business education in the United States today' (Manchester Business School 1968 : 3–4). Such differences were no doubt due in part to the contrasting backgrounds of London's Principal and Manchester's Director, the former an abrasive Canadian and ex-Managing Director of Hoover, the latter a former Oxford don with family-business connections.

At Manchester the new School inherited a diploma course, previously run by the University's Faculty of Economic and Social Studies, which it used as a basis for development. The post-graduate courses at the London School were especially open to American influence because they were created *de novo*. The first course offered by LBS was, in fact, the Executive Development Programme for experienced managers, its first post-graduate course starting a year later in 1966. When this course began, it did not follow the one-year pattern adopted by Manchester and advocated by Franks. Instead, it was to last two years and lead to the award of an MSc. degree.

Two reasons were given for this move. First, the academics thought that it would be difficult to bring students from varying academic backgrounds up to a high level of competence within a single year of study. This fitted in very much with their view of the role of the post-graduate courses as long-term investments and, of course, was not unconnected to their personal academic interests. A longer period of study implied the need for more staff and would give greater opportunity for a wider range of teaching inputs. But second, there was the argument of comparability with American practice, for 'no major American graduate school', it was pointed out, 'now offers a one-year programme, leading to the MBA' (Ball 1967 : 6). Since 'the aim was to establish on British soil a school of the high quality and established success of the great American Business Schools' (London Business School 1970 : 5), it appeared necessary to follow their example and institute a two-year degree course. If the businessmen on the schools' controlling bodies were opposed to such a proposal, they did not have much success in blocking it, for London duly began its two-year course and Manchester soon followed suit. MBS did, however, retain its Diploma course as a common first year for the new MBA.[3] The academics, it seemed, had clearly won the day (Turner 1969 : 95) although there were signs to show that this might prove to be a Pyrrhic victory.

The Manchester MBA course has not changed greatly since its inception in 1968. It starts with 'background' subjects before moving on to more specialized and more business-oriented topics. The first term of the first year deals with areas such as accounting, finance, law, economics, psychology, sociology, organizational behaviour, and quantitative methods, and aims to bring everyone up to a basic level of knowledge of business functions and management disciplines. The teaching at this stage is mainly in the traditional forms of lecture and tutorial. The next two terms deal with problems of decision making, resource allocation and policy making, in which students are presented with a variety of management problems that they are expected to tackle either alone, or more frequently, in groups. In the break before the second year, most students take jobs in business and are expected to use this experience as the basis for a 10,000-word dissertation, which must be completed as part of the degree requirements. The main activity of the second year is project work, in which groups of students work on open-ended problems faced, and sometimes provided, by operating companies. Topics for the projects have included operations management, industrial relations, entrepreneurship, and international business. Students must also take a small number of optional courses which are often associated with the main business functional areas. Among the most popular have been those connected with marketing and business finance; this reflects the possibilities for rapid advancement which students believe these functional areas offer.

The London course has undergone a much more marked change. In its early years, the curriculum was heavily biased in favour of quantitative and economic studies, with relatively little time devoted to the behavioural areas with which Manchester was to become particularly associated. Considerable stress was laid on academic excellence, intellectual rigour, and 'fierce drilling' in the basic analytical disciplines, a preoccupation with mathematics arising from the Principal's belief that it was a subject that was as much a necessary part of a manager's education as Latin had once been of a gentleman's (Aris 1965). The first year, as at Manchester, was largely concerned with broad 'foundation' topics, followed after a two-month summer vacation project by courses in the business functions and the 'high-level' areas concerned with business policy, structure, and strategy. Students were also required to take two 'elective' courses. The teaching methods were eclectic and included group projects, management games, and case studies, the latter being largely drawn from the United States.

In 1970 a revised curriculum was introduced. Although this retained the quantitative emphasis in the first year, much more prominence was given to electives in the second. Seven of these courses had now to be taken, two of them in the form of a project. Further changes were made in 1974, when the second year was made 'fully elective', students choosing five main courses in their first term and seven electives in the remaining two. The quantitative element in the first year was now reduced and more attention was given to more directly 'managerial' topics, such as marketing, finance, business policy, and 'management problems', the change being facilitated by the resignation of the school's first Principal early in 1972.

Both the London and Manchester Schools provided the sort of curriculum that they believed was appropriate for the young professional manager who would one day move into a position of high responsibility. Courses such as these on corporate strategy, business policy, mergers, and policy formulation made clear the schools' perceptions of the role of the post-graduate courses. The growing trend in the teaching methods towards more student participation and group work similarly reflected the schools' beliefs about the need to produce not just technicians but socially skilled men capable of bearing the responsibilities of leadership. There was, indeed, an element of the traditional public school ethos, the rigorous and punishing regime that would make men out of boys. In this, as in other ways, they expressed the strange contrasts created by their Anglo-American origins.

Although we are mainly concerned with the post-graduate courses and their students, the schools have by no means been exclusively geared to these provisions. Both institutions responded to Franks's suggestion that post-graduate and post-experience courses should be offered by running short courses for middle and senior managers. At Manchester, a major aspect of the school's activities has been its ten-week Management Course, and it has also run a three-week course for senior executives, these post-experience provisions having had a roughly equal share of the school's resources with those for post-graduates. Similarly, the Executive and Senior Executive Programmes have figured prominently in the activities of the London School. The schools have also provided a wide range of other short courses. Thus they have not been narrowly concerned with post-graduate education, but have divided their attention and resources between this and the post-experience areas in keeping with the spirit of the Franks Report.

Reactions to the business schools

The modifications that were introduced, most noticeably to the London curriculum, were not made simply for academic reasons, for within a few years of the opening of the schools it became abundantly clear that the business world was decidedly unhappy with the post-graduate courses. The divisions of opinion that seemed so recently to have been dispelled re-emerged with renewed force.

In 1967, Professor Ball of the London Business School admitted that 'more weight has been placed on the development of graduate education than the Franks Report envisaged' (Ball 1967 : 5). He also noted that letters in the correspondence columns of some newspapers expressed alarm that the breadth of coverage of the business schools' post-graduate courses seemed destined to turn the students into instant managing directors. 'Business schools in business – but still a long way to go', declared *British Industry Week* in September 1967, adding the comment that the business schools had come in for a surprising amount of adverse criticism in their short life, a consequence, thought the writer, of academics letting their hair down. 'Companies facing snags over "blue chip" graduates', said the *Daily Telegraph* in October 1968, reviewing the problems faced by employers over what to do with the new breed of graduate. 'Hardly a week goes by', reflected Robertson (1970), 'without some major attack being launched in the press against business schools', whilst Sir John Partridge, President of the CBI and

Chairman of the Council of Industry for Management Education, wrote that 'there is now a very wide gulf between what the British business schools want to do and what industry thinks they ought to do' (Partridge 1970). All this amounted to what Mosson (1972:74) aptly described as 'business-school bashing'. Ironically, at this time the progenitors of the business schools, the American institutions, were themselves under attack (Ball, in Lawrence 1972:19; Hekimian 1969; Livingston 1971; McClelland 1971).

As if to confirm that these criticisms were not simply the invention of the British press, the BIM and the Council of Industry for Management Education issued their own critical report, somewhat austerely titled *Business School Programmes: the Requirements of British Manufacturing Industry* (otherwise known as the Owen Report 1971).

THE OWEN REPORT

This report summarized 'the current views and requirements of manufacturing industry on the subject of post-graduate and post-experience education at business schools', the latter including business schools,[4] university management centres, and departments of business studies (but not the independent institutions). Although the report was based on information gleaned from only fifty-three large and medium-sized manufacturing firms, excluding finance and service companies, the authors believed the views presented would command 'substantial support' among such firms. The report began by noting that there had already been a 'forceful exchange of views' between the academic and industrial worlds. However, management education was 'a young and tender plant' and it was too early to pass a definite judgement upon it. Early in 1970 the Advisory Panel on Management Education, set up by the BIM and CBI in 1969, 'had become concerned at the growing unease and the doubts in industry about some developments in the rapid expansion of under-graduate and post-graduate courses in business studies'. Thus a study was instituted in 1970 and the results submitted to the Advisory Panel in May 1971.

The investigators had talked to managers and directors in the line and in the personnel function, and although they found 'ignorance and prejudice' as well as 'considered opinion', they were surprised by 'the strength and basic uniformity of view on major issues', and felt that the report presented 'a true consensus of opinion amongst those surveyed'. Predictably, the findings were that the employers did not like what the business schools were doing, and that they particularly did not like the 'academic' post-graduate courses.

'Whereas most of the people we met were, in varying degrees, perplexed, worried or angry about post-graduate education, the question of post-experience education found them much more relaxed. . . . Industry, however, feels that it can control the selection of people to go on post-experience courses reasonably well so that it can ensure that the people selected are the right basic management material and are going on the courses for a clearly defined purpose; and it sees the post-experience courses at the business schools as only one relatively small part of a total range of management development tools in which commercial institutions, consultants, internal training, career planning and many other initiatives are both proper and effective.' (British Institute of Management 1971 : 12)

Significantly, employers wanted higher standards of entry to post-graduate courses and more attention to be given to 'the qualities which will be needed by the business graduate if he is to succeed in management'. Industry required people 'of high calibre and of real management potential'. Selection criteria were 'too academic', the critical attributes in business eyes being 'able to achieve results through people and being able to make effective pragmatic judgements'. Furthermore:

'it is not too much to say that there can be no long term future for the business graduate who cannot establish his acceptability in the short term and the significance and credibility to industry of the post-graduate course would be immeasurably enhanced *if entry to the course was confined to people of proved managerial effectiveness.*' (British Institute of Management 1971 : 8, emphasis added.)

The Report went on to say that too many business graduates were lacking in skill, knowledge, calibre, and potential. They sometimes had 'less to offer than the good graduate recruited direct from the university'.

There was also some indication of what industry did *not* want:

'It does not require business graduates to be trained in the skill of directing strategy in a large organisation, since this skill is unlikely to be needed for some years. Nor does it require business graduates who are arrogant, who regard themselves as an elite, who have no regard for the views of the experienced managers with whom they work, or who are preoccupied with theoretical solutions to practical problems. This was described by one Deputy Chairman as the 'I am trained to be a Managing Director' syndrome and he added that it was the result of attitude rather than of syllabus. It is industry's

belief that this attitude tends to be fostered in the business schools.'
(British Institute of Management 1971 : 11)

Finally, the majority view in industry was for a one-year, rather than a two-year, post-graduate course. The latter tended to be thought of as 'two years wastefully lost practical experience for the business graduate and an improper use of national resources for the country'.

It is possible, of course, that these reactions were representative only of the companies consulted by the investigators, and not all of these might be considered as dominant firms. There were undoubtedly some major companies that reacted favourably to the business schools. A survey by the Business Graduates Association showed that those who employed MBAs (30 per cent of the responding firms) were quite pleased with them, although less than half (42 per cent) of the companies which replied were planning to recruit business graduates in the near future (Business Graduates Association 1971). However, two further indications of industry's attitudes support the view that, on the whole, business did not see, and had never seen, the business schools as institutions for the production of young, qualified managers. What business had said it wanted was practical training for existing middle managers and its use of the schools confirmed this very fact.

We have analysed data on companies contributing to the 1964 Appeal for funds and on companies sponsoring students to the MBS post-graduate course over the years 1965–74. Over 300 organizations contributed to the Appeal, but only ninety students were sponsored over a ten-year period (out of 495 British entrants) by forty-six companies. Sixteen of the ninety were sent by a single group of firms (Shell), and only nine firms sponsored more than two students. Only five of the eleven firms that contributed upwards of £100,000 to the Appeal sponsored any students, and only twenty of the sixty-three firms that gave at least £25,000 did so. Moreover, sponsorship steadily declined from 1968 (fifteen students) to 1974 (one student), and the vast majority of those were supported not for the two-year MBA course but for the one-year Diploma. In other words, sponsorship for the post-graduate course has been minimal and declining. At LBS, the picture has been much the same.

It seems that the contributors to the Appeal were hoping that everyone else would send their young graduate managers to the schools, for they have clearly sent very few of their own. On the other hand, as has been said, business did not really see the schools as qualifying institutions for management. A second appeal to industry for funds in 1970 fell short of its target by £1¼m, and there was talk at this time of converting the schools into wholly private institutions which would render them even more amenable to the 'needs' of business (Weston 1972).

The schools' responses to these harsh criticisms were fairly cool. Both schools took some pre-emptive measures in anticipation of the publication of the Owen Report, setting up new liaison committees to improve their relations with business. The London School modified its selection criteria[5] for applicants to the MSc. course so as to place more weight on managerial competence, and initiated a study of the future requirements of the government and of industry. It also made the curriculum changes already described above. Neither school was, however, prepared to retreat from its policy of running two-year post-graduate courses. At Manchester it was even possible to welcome the Report as 'an endorsement of the directions the School is taking both at the graduate and post-experience levels' (Manchester Business School 1971 : 2–3). The school subsequently organized a conference to discuss the role of the business graduate in industry, which seemed to induce a more positive attitude in business (*The Times* 1973), or at least in those companies that had attended. Eighteen of these had been amongst the sixty-four 'large' contributors to the 1964 Appeal.

The 'problem' of the post-graduate courses was, however, soon displaced in the schools' concerns by more pressing matters. Both of them depended, and still depend, upon the income they received from fees for attendance on the post-experience courses for a substantial proportion of their finance. The onset of the oil crisis in 1973 with its consequent effects upon companies' investments in both physical and 'human' capital posed a potentially serious threat to the schools' viability (Manchester Business School 1974; London Business School 1975). Under the same conditions, industry became increasingly preoccupied with its more central concern of economic survival. By April 1974, the *Daily Telegraph* was able to report that the controversy had died down somewhat, and by July 1976 it seemed that criticism of the business schools had largely abated (*The Times* 1976).

The 'revolution' in perspective

With the benefit of hindsight, industry's reactions to the reality of business schools do not appear particularly surprising. Those businessmen who had been fired with enthusiasm for a British Harvard had never really envisaged it as a post-graduate, degree-awarding institution. Discussions in the press on the topic in the early 1960s spoke not of Harvard's two-year MBA course but of its thirteen-week

Advanced Management Programme (Mosson 1965 : 186–87; Shanks 1963), and firms which had sent their high-flyers there had supported the short courses rather than the MBA (Robertson 1965 : 77). What many seem to have meant by a 'high-level' school was not so much one that would operate at a high academic level, as one that would cater for high-level managers. Nevertheless, once the decision had been taken to locate such a school in the universities it was almost inevitable that academic interests would soon find vigorous expression.

It would be wrong, of course, to imply that there has been unanimity in the business world over the status of MBA. Yet in so far as it is possible to generalize, it appears that the MBA, and indeed any formal management qualification, has continued to be regarded with ambivalence by substantial sections of British industry (Daniel 1971 : 60–61; Leggatt 1972 : 3; Sibbald 1978 : 22; Watling 1970 : 40; Wheatcroft 1970 : 2). Analyses of press recruitment advertisements for managerial posts, for example, have revealed very little demand for academic management qualifications (Baldwin 1978; Sibbald 1978 : 22), and such credentials seem especially unlikely to carry much weight in the competition for senior, general management positions. In this sphere, the traditional values of British management show few signs of change. If anything there has been a tendency to reassert the importance of personality, attitudes, leadership ability, and track-record against a background of increasing 'technicalization' of management tasks (Finniston 1978; Parker, in Mann 1970 : x–xi; Watling 1970 : 22–5).

The partnership of which Lord Franks spoke in his report on the British business schools has not been an easy one, and has been subjected to severe strains. The whole subject of the proper role and locus of management education continues to be a matter for debate (cf. Eglin 1977; Handy 1977; Department of Industry 1977), though now of a more muted kind. No doubt the need for a more systematic education and training of managers is more widely accepted now than ever before, and it is this, rather than a radical re-orientation of recruitment and promotion practices in favour of formal management qualifications, that constitutes the most significant change of recent decades. Businessmen have not, however, been noted for their revolutionary tendencies, and their use of the schools expresses more the continuity with the past than any fundamental break with tradition.

4 Management education in France and INSEAD

The conversion of French business to 'management' ideas

In France, in some contrast to Britain, high-level positions in *major* businesses have long been filled by scientifically trained graduates from the same prestigious schools as those that provided recruits for the senior echelons of the public service, although this was not 'business' education in any sense. The major economic changes occurring in France after 1945, in particular the concentration of industry, the inflow of American capital and business ideas, and increased international competition for markets, however, provided the impetus for the foundation of management schools. While commercial training had existed in formal institutions of schooling since 1881, business education in the wider, more 'administrative' sense of *gestion* only began in France in the 1950s.

In the first decade after the end of the Second World War, French Chambers of Commerce participated actively in the work of the European Productivity Commission and subsequently sent groups of their own members to the United States to study business organization and management methods. With the acceptance and implementation of new forms of business organization came a new belief in the importance of professionalized management. To certain groups of French businessmen, it seemed that the way to train these 'professional' managers was by providing educational institutions on the renowned American models such as that of Harvard, and to a lesser extent, Stanford, Wharton, MIT, and Carnegie. Indeed, the conversion of the French to beliefs in the American system appeared to be complete in the final years of the 1950s and the decade of the 1960s. As Story and Parrott (1977) have recently put it:

> 'In no European country has American management been embraced so enthusiastically as in France . . . *le management, le marketing* and *le cash flow* became part of the French vocabulary and US corporations the model of business success . . . The whole love affair with American business started in the 1950s when streams of French businessmen poured across the Atlantic to sit at the feet of sales guru Jose Trujillo . . . The French enthusiasm for US management techniques was the more surprising in that French employers had until then (the 1960s) been among the most conservative in all Europe. In a completely hierarchical system in which promotion was decided more by education and family connections than by performance, the executives or *cadres* ruled their companies like feudal overlords.'

The acceptance by French businessmen of American management methods seemed to represent a radical change in attitudes to a whole range of business practices, including senior personnel recruitment and managerial promotion. Story and Parrott go on to point to the increasingly competitive market that was a major stimulus to the change:

> 'In a protected market, these graduates from engineering schools were more concerned with turnover, production and technology rather than profitability, marketing, selling budget control and long term planning which are such important elements of the US business approach. Paternalistic and secretive, more concerned with status than with money, strong on theory but weak on practical experience, French managers were just no match for the aggressive products of the US system.'

Thus behind this enthusiasm lay certain economic elements. To these were added political considerations. The *patronat* was frightened of political tendencies in the immediate post-war years, manifested in nationalization, prolonged strikes, and a general trend towards 'socialism' (in the sense of putting public interest first as the criterion for action). This fear was admitted quite frankly by some *patronat* leaders. As the author of a recent article points out (*International Management Development* 1977 : 11):

'In the immediate post-war period the *patronat français* (CNPF) considered that something immediate and quite radical had to be done to combat the rising tide of nationalization. One of the piles in this breakwater was to ensure that the managerial class not just made proper use of modern management techniques but considered, studied and acted in consequence about the meaning and nature of the *entreprise libre* . . . It would be difficult to dissociate these patronal efforts from the success of French management not only in coping with, and gradually using to the advantage of free enterprise, the instruments created to enhance *dirigisme* but also in stemming for at least three generations the political surge of the left.'

In the 1950s, these trends culminated in a movement within business and government circles towards the reform of the existing *écoles commerciales* and the introduction of management education and American-style business schools.[1]

Business education before business schools

'Management' (a term the French claim has a French origin, *ménager*) appeared in the French dictionary only in 1972, where it is stated that *le management* concerns techniques applied to the different forms of activities of an enterprise: production, accounting, finance, personnel, sales, etc. These techniques constitute a specific set of tools, corresponding to the different functions, whose use constitutes the management (*gestion*) of the firm.

Business schools teaching this *ensemble* of techniques have only recently been established in France. Before the founding of these schools, there existed a well established network of commercial schools. Beginning with the creation of the Écoles des Hautes Études Commerciales in 1881, many other schools were brought into existence during and after the later decades of the nineteenth century by the local Chambers of Commerce and Industry established in nearly every town of any size in France. Most of these local schools took young people immediately after the *baccalauréat* or even without it. The provincial schools adapted to a local market and, probably recruiting the great mass of their students from among the sons of local businessmen, largely destined their graduates for middle-level careers in small to medium-sized businesses or helped to prepare sons of businessmen for the 'proper' running of inherited concerns. Specializing in law and accountancy, the curriculum was designed to train the students in basic technical skills rather than in decision taking, human relations, or any of the other attributes associated with modern management or *gestion*.

In recent years, under the influence of the Fondation Nationale pour l'Enseignement de la Gestion des Entreprises,[2] and following the 'modernizing' example of the major Paris schools, the provincial establishments gradually revised their teaching methods and emphases, raised their standards of entry in some cases, and began to offer specialisms so that certain schools became known as strong in particular new fields. It has, however, been much harder for them to raise their image from fabricators of accountancy specialists to providers of management generalists in the eyes of industry, as witnessed by the still low salaries proposed (Beaudeux and Rouge 1978) and limited career profiles offered. Many of the schools continue to have considerable difficulty in their reorganization and feel themselves to be in a period of crisis. In even the major schools, there is a considerable amount of student unrest, and at least one remains 'unreformed' and dominated by older conceptions of commercial education, offering a curriculum weighted towards the traditional subjects of law and accountancy, supplemented by short courses in micro-economics and psychology (source: private communication, ESSEC student, 1978).

In contrast to the 'lower level' provincial commercial schools, there also existed three major Parisian ones: the École des Hautes Études Commerciales (HEC), the École Supérieure des Sciences Économiques et Commerciales (ESSEC) (which is part of the Parisian Catholic faculty and second to HEC in the hierarchy of prestige recognized by French students and employers), and the École Supérieure de Commerce de Paris (ESCP). The foundation of HEC in 1881 constituted the reaction by the Paris Chamber of Commerce to the increasingly favourable recruitment position of graduates from the major state engineering schools in large sectors of business within the expanding industrial climate of the late nineteenth century, a period of major economic and political change, the development of financial institutions and commercial enterprises, and the rapid extension of the French colonies. From the beginning, these elite schools imitated the 'best' parts of the state system and the entry *concours* became increasingly difficult and separate from those of their provincial counterparts.

A hierarchy of prestige, social origins, and career possibilities within the employing enterprises was thus created for the commercial system as it had been for the engineering system. In subsequent years, business education came to be incorporated into the same model as the engineering and under-graduate commercial schools. However, preparation for business, while imitating the organization of the public system of engineering education, remained for many years in private hands.[3] The universities found it hard to be persuaded that management education constituted a discipline worthy of study, and they were reluctant to take on any task related to the running of business enterprises. In France, for example, there have never been professorial chairs financed by industry. Until 1955, when the French Government introduced a certificate of management, it was remarkable that no state institutions of higher education offering courses in management existed. Not until 1968 was a business university (that of Paris IX, Paris Dauphine) founded and that at a time when the role and structure of all French universities were being called into question.

Public management education began in a very small way. In 1955, five Instituts d'Administration des Entreprises (IAE) were created, gathering together 209 students, all already holding a degree and studying part-time for one year for the IAE certificate. By 1973 there were eighteen such institutes, with a total of 5,500 students. While apparently considerable, this increase is noticeably far lower than that seen in the growth of many other new university courses. In spite of the new 'management' nature of the IAE courses, industry's attitudes towards the holders of IAE diplomas have always been lukewarm, resembling British attitudes towards technical college education. The IAE suffered from the same 'low prestige' image as British technical colleges in comparison with the 'royal route' through the *grandes écoles*, especially the engineering ones, and increasingly over the period, the high-level commercial ones. Moreover, situated as the IAE are in the universities, industry feared it could not control criteria of admission to them, nor even directly influence the content of the curricula or teaching and examination methods. As the prestige of the universities fell, so the products of the IAE seemed to suffer by becoming tarred in the eyes of industry with the unfavourable image of the surrounding faculties, which were perceived as hostile to business and as encouraging attitudes to work, orderliness, and discipline that did not conform to those of potential employers. As with the undergraduate level provincial *écoles de commerce*, the low estimation by industry of the value of IAE diplomas is reflected in the low salaries accorded to the holders. The modernization of the curriculum, by using, for example, the case method of teaching, has not been enough to persuade potential employers that the IAE can transform a 'university' man into a potential high flyer in business.

The teaching of 'management' in France did not, therefore, really begin until the 1960s, with the reform of teaching methods at the Paris commercial schools. A recent writer, himself a graduate of both HEC and Columbia Business School and hence a member of the new wave of 'true managers', describes the astonishment of the director of HEC, when confronted in 1959 by a group of his ex-pupils who had recently returned from the United States and who suggested that the French school should develop training based on American methods and techniques (Xardel 1978 : 25).

When it did get going, most of the new management education remained within the semi-public or private sectors. The modification of courses and teaching methods, and the creation of INSEAD would seem to indicate changes in the attitudes of French businessmen towards business education.

Business attitudes to business education

By the 1960s French top management had become convinced of the need to rationalize management techniques, and publicly believed wholeheartedly in the value of specialized education in business skills, both to enable the production of the senior managers of the next generation and to improve the performance of those currently in office in middle, and even senior, positions. To this extent, it was drawing on a well established tradition that related educational credentials to management recruitment and promotion. In France, the upward limits on the possibilities of career development open to managers in many kinds of enterprise have long been largely determined by the diplomas held. These educational certificates have been turned into qualifications through their recognition by employers, and their labour market value has by no means been only theoretical. In this France has differed considerably from Britain.

The importance of the educational credential does not lie in its signifying technical competence alone, but relates equally to the more general intellectual and social characteristics attributed to its holder by virtue of being a product of particular sections of the education system. Thus, for example, while the necessity for technical expertise as a basis for access to certain types of command post in industry has been verbally recognized by employers, it is noticeable that the *grande école* whose graduates stand the best chances of acquiring top management positions in the largest French companies (the École Polytechnique) is one that does not supply a 'practical' training in engineering. Rather, the curriculum concentrates on developing abstract mathematical reasoning. The hierarchy of the *grandes écoles* and the attraction of their graduates in the eyes of many employers thus seem linked to the association of the 'best' schools with pupils of the highest social origins, and to the position of the schools as the distributors of a culture that attracts the most 'gifted' products of the school system, rather than for any more 'technical' reasons.

The attitudes expressed by industry towards the significance of management education *per se* as an ingredient of the successful 'manager' have, however, carried over this ambivalence towards the relative worth of technical and social skills. While the merits of a skilled engineer are relatively easily recognizable, the skills of a financial manager can only partly be recognized by the balance sheet. 'Management', especially at the more senior levels, involves the creation and maintenance of cooperation between different functions, between clients, suppliers, and factories, and between different levels of the hierarchy, as well as the application of technical skills. While many sectors of business recognize management education as useful for the inculcation of specific skills in finance or marketing, they are often reluctant to admit that the schools can create a 'true manager'. Argument continues unabated about the degree to which managers are 'born' or 'made' and about the most appropriate mix of 'personal' and 'technical' qualities. As in Britain, ambivalence on this score is reflected in uncertainty about the best way to train managers – at school or on the job – and about the criteria for recruitment and promotion.

These attitudes have been apparent in the discussions conducted in management and other journals, and in the attitudes of firms towards business schools, MBA courses, and short 'training' courses for established managers, and they ultimately affect the kinds of career possibilities offered in different sectors of the executive labour market. These arguments are presented in different ways. Some involve notions of 'lag' and 'evolution'; thus many observers regard businesses as not yet 'ready' to accept modern management techniques and, by implication, not ready for the integration of men and women trained in those techniques into important posts. Thus Veyret, writing in the business journal *L'Expansion* in 1968, was obliged to report that: 'In the majority, French business controllers do not yet feel the need for modern methods of management and thus for executives trained in these methods'. He goes on to note that most of the French holders of Harvard MBAs work in international, mainly American, companies and that the few who were working in French firms 'believe themselves to be employed in tasks below their level of competence'.

Veyret indeed pointed out that at that time, business education in Europe was the equivalent of a product without a market. Many industrialists feared the prolongation of years of study, complaining that their *cadres* started work at the age of twenty-five but still had to be taught everything. That argument still continued in 1978, as could be seen from another article in the same journal, in which business leaders are reported as advocating that young people go straight to work after their *baccalauréat* to learn the 'real' problems of business life.

Other arguments rely on assumptions about the type of person required for the job. Failing to recognize that problems can be seen as a mix of 'technical' and 'ideological' factors, they present views on what management is 'essentially' about and couch them in psychological terms. This seems to be true not only in France but throughout Europe. For example, a survey that asked more than 400 top managers in France, Germany, Austria, Belgium, and Switzerland what they thought of on hearing the word 'manager', resulted in more than half the respondents placing personal traits and leadership first. Such factors as 'leadership, ability to communicate, social attitude, ability for teamwork, persuasiveness' went with 'sense of responsibility, performance of duties, creative talent, superiority, technical knowledge and skills, decisiveness, personality, broad general knowledge, readiness to accept risks, vitality, ability to make things happen, intelligence'. These beliefs were expressed in such replies as:

> 'The director and manager must have a good general education, good breeding, ability to command, psychological talents . . .'

> 'A man in a leading position has a distinctive personality, good professional knowledge, strength, energy, common sense, leadership qualities, knowledge of human nature, organizational talents, and rational thinking.'

and

> 'Character, knowledge, corrected and improved by experience. The manager is determined by his character. Education and knowledge rank in second place.'

> 'A manager must be vigorous, healthy, obliging and just.' (Harmon 1971 : 19, 14)

These attitudes inevitably reduce the importance that industry and commerce attach to the role of business education and its potential in the production of the best managers. Most seem to believe that the most such education can achieve is the development of innate, latent talents and abilities. As Xardel sums it up: 'Let's be clear; in a school one acquires information (*connaissances*), one can develop aptitudes already existing in an embryonic state, but one can hardly create them (1978:25).

It is important not to confuse *gestion* and management. Thus managers, whether trained in business schools or not, react with their 'intuition', their 'sensitivity', their 'past experience', which in the crucial moments often dominate 'management techniques' even of the most elementary kind. The language used to describe the qualities necessary for decision making at the level of these men, among France's most successful 'managers', verges on the mystical: 'To conquer a market or lead a team of men towards victory, one must sometimes make use of the resources of emotion, of the irrational, of passion, or sometimes even of hate and the spirit of revenge (Xardel 1978:27).' Such qualities are not those taught in schools (although business schools do try through such courses as 'organizational behaviour' – see below). Many believe they cannot even really be developed there. As Daniel Jouve, who at twenty-nine years of age was Director General of the Groupe Expansion, summed it up:

'The best training for a manager is first military service, the responsibility for men, the fact of being an officer. Commanding a section of 60 to 80 men at the age of twenty is an extraordinary education! In relation to what one can learn as a student which is theoretical [in military sense] you are given power and learn practical matters . . . Commanding men young is fundamental.' (Quoted in Xardel 1978:58)

Even the business schools themselves share those conceptions to some extent. The application forms for INSEAD, for example, as at Harvard, invite candidates to relate experiences occurring during their military service that have taught them important lessons, and much emphasis is laid on the early occupancy of posts of leadership, even if only in the Boy Scout movement. The French Foundation for Management Education even went so far as to state:

'Management is an art. It can therefore not be taught, even if one can develop it. It cannot be described rationally in its entirety and in its substance, even if one apprehends certain of its aspects. It is an affair of character and of personal qualities.' (Quoted in Xardel 1978:61)

One can thus hardly produce 'businessmen', managers, or entrepreneurs in schools. One can, on the other hand, develop their
analytical capacity, their economic culture, and their aptitude for
decision making. Xardel concludes:

> 'The major characteristics thus required of the manager are thought
> to be the sense of permanent adaptation to events, the sense of
> innovation and 'character' [*Pour l'affronter (la vie des affaires) avec
> succès, il faut . . . un caractère particulièrement trempé*]. The major
> role of business education may even be conceived of as a negative
> one. For one needs human warmth and there's no boss, or man with
> a vocation to become a boss, if he does not possess a personal
> attraction [*rayonnement*] and an authority that can make for
> obedience without imposition – education's role should be to
> discourage all those who do not have this quality.' (Xardel 1978 : 74)

The development of specific styles of leadership and 'man
management' are some of the important elements of a business-school
curriculum, while at the same time they are those that business as a
whole still seems to think are essentially innate. These styles of
leadership vary over time and with the circumstances of the firm and its
environment just as the predominance of certain functions in the firm
as a whole vary. While Bourdieu and others (1973) have suggested that
with the new style of business comes a new style of leadership so that
the aged *patron* is replaced by the young, suave manager, skilled in
techniques of 'group' work, cooperation and coordination, this
development seems to depend on the circumstances faced by the firm.
In an easy age of market dominance, 'soft', persuasive management
techniques are seen as 'appropriate' or at least as acceptable. When the
economic horizon darkens, firms look more to managers of harder
reputation (cf. Xardel 1978 : 92).

In summary, then, there would seem to be considerable ambivalence
and divergence of view within business about the degree to which
'management' qualities can be rationalized into codifiable techniques
and taught to managerial novices. While many employers in France
hastened during the 1950s and 1960s to express belief in the new
'scientific' management techniques imported from North America,
few are prepared to define managerial talent solely in terms of the skills
recognized and taught as disciplines in business schools. While the
functions corresponding to the disciplines do indeed exist as major
units in many firms, the successful manager running, and especially
coordinating, those functions is perceived as possessing characteristics

that are innate or social, and that may be developed but not created by education. Management is still felt to be more of an art than a science, at least at the highest levels.

The Institut Européen d'Administration des Affaires (INSEAD)

INSEAD, the Institut Européen d'Administration des Affaires, was founded in 1958 in temporary accommodation in Fontainebleau[4] where it now occupies purpose-built premises set on the edge of the forest, about sixty kilometers south of Paris. The Institute was sponsored by a group of businessmen belonging to the Paris and International Chambers of Commerce and the European Productivity Agency, set up to administer Marshall Aid. Technical assistance on curricula, standards, teaching methods, recruitment, and organization was provided by Harvard Business School. Two men were outstanding in the founding of the Institute, General Georges Doriot, French by origin but a professor at Harvard Business School; and Jean Marcou, president of the Paris Chamber of Commerce from 1958 to 1960, a leading businessman with a multitude of interests, the founder and first president of INSEAD. Other public men, notably Olivier Giscard d'Estaing, brother of the former French President and a Harvard MBA holder, and Roger Godino, brother of another holder of an American MBA, became early and powerful directors of the Institute with wide-ranging connections in the business world, especially in the 'new' industries and groups developing in the 1950s and coming to fruition in the 1960s.

These men combined views about the necessity for closing the transatlantic 'management gap' with a strong belief about the desirability of unifying and creating a strong Europe. The creation of INSEAD was, therefore, the result of the interaction of a number of political, economic, and ideological beliefs and aspirations. A strong Europe based on competitive and efficient industries would be, it was believed, a counterweight to the influence of both power blocs and would strengthen European stability and security both at home and abroad. If the 'Common Market' Europe were to be created, implying the development of large European companies, then these companies must be given the benefit of American expertise and management skills with a European slant. Hence, they felt the need for a European Institute of Business Administration. To respond to the needs of a new situation, 'new men' had to be created.

AIMS AND POLICIES

European and international themes constantly recur in any description or discussion of the Institute's role, aims, and purposes. It was to have a unique blend of social, political, and economic objectives, and was to represent and develop private business interests:

> 'INSEAD was to be the work of private business, European or even international, better placed than anyone to determine the profile of its future high-level colleagues, to infuse them with a dynamism capable of general social and economic progress, and to solder friendship among young peoples from diverse disciplines and countries who will be called upon to participate in the creation of a Europe we hoped to see one day united and prosperous.' (Jean Marcou speaking at the Diploma Ceremony, INSEAD, June 17, 1977)

The European and international character of INSEAD is indeed written into its statutes. Article One of the statutes decrees that the Institute 'has as its aim the education of businessmen and women of all countries and the pursuit of research related to business administration and the economic integration of Europe'. Yet by the mid to late 1970s, INSEAD's position in the field of management education was as different from that of 1958 as were the hopes of European unity. While maintaining its European emphasis, it came to look well beyond Europe, as can be seen from the nationalities of students attending both the post-graduate and post-experience programmes. And, while maintaining its emphasis on *management* skills, the thrust was shifting towards the public sector. INSEAD began to develop new strings to its bow.

The economic organization of business and the social climate surrounding education, business, and business education has changed dramatically, and this is expressed in a recent brochure:

> 'Today we have a new Europe. And in that new Europe there are many more professionally trained managers. Access to management techniques is widespread, but demand still grows. A business school in Europe must respond to these demands but it must analyse today's problems and try to anticipate those of the 1980s. Today's answers will not solve tomorrow's problems. Already the arts and skills of politics and diplomacy are [as] essential to business as the techniques of science. And the developing countries in their turn are seeking to help in acquiring the management expertise they need. It

is in that spirit, and to meet that challenge, that INSEAD exists.'
(INSEAD publicity 1977)

The mission of INSEAD, according to a member of its staff, is the provision of:

'high quality business education that is international in scope, European in content and managerial in emphasis. Its objectives in pursuing this mission are:

- to contribute to the discovery, adaptation and dissemination of relevant management knowledge and thereby to improve the practices of management
- to retain a growing, independent and truly international institution where skills in living and working with other nationalities combine with effective knowledge learning

Our strategy in attaining our objectives is:

- to provide business education rather than teaching its techniques
- to offer international business education activities to a primarily post-experience market
- to design and deliver education to both individuals and organizations
- to attract and develop a faculty qualified to educate both the aspiring and the practising manager
- to concentrate, in our learning and teaching, on participative and experimental methods.'

Within this statement are suggested the rationales for INSEAD, its clientele, and its methods of teaching and learning. Behind this policy and its effective implementation lie a number of opportunities and constraints, and a number of modifications of general policy orientations largely made in response to changes in demand from client firms and potential customers. The changes reflect too different stages of the Institute's development and especially the creation from 1971 onwards of a largely permanent and full-time faculty.

TEACHING AND RESEARCH: A DIFFICULT BALANCE

In the 1970s the Institute claimed to have become a 'complete service' institution, offering courses of the three major kinds: post-graduate MBA courses, post-experience courses of a 'public kind' for executives working in firms at middle management and senior levels, and 'tailor-made' courses for companies, akin to in-house training schemes. The latter include the 'consortium' type of course and the more conventional in-house programmes. The first, and the most important for INSEAD as a quasi-university institution, was known initially as the one-year post-graduate programme (PGP) and now as the MBA programme. This existed from the beginning.

All these teaching and learning activities developed and grew but not always as originally envisaged. The relative balance of effort to be allocated to each was for long a subject of continual and sometimes heated debate among members of INSEAD's faculty and supporting companies. Each type of course requires a considerable investment of resources, and the development beyond a certain point of each necessitates a fundamental rethinking of the aims and orientation of an institution such as INSEAD. Each represents a different, and sometimes mutually conflicting, market and major investment in one sometimes means drastic changes in the others and in the staffing and purposes of the institution. There are, however, severe constraints on the development of the post-graduate programme in particular, and financial deficits run up by *that* programme have come near at times to causing the Institute to change direction fundamentally. This kind of balancing problem is common to many business schools, even those financed by state agencies, and arises in part from the rather uncertain, ambivalent, and even internally contradictory situation of such institutions poised as they are between a 'university' and a 'business' ethos. The problem is however particularly acute at INSEAD, dependent as it has remained on the generosity of private donors, especially business corporations.

FINANCE, STUDENTS, AND STAFF: THE MARKET FOR A
BUSINESS SCHOOL

INSEAD began in 1958 with sixty participants (as MBA students are called) on the post-graduate one-year programme, which for many years remained the only course offered. These students, from fourteen countries, were taught by a staff drawn on a part-time basis from among practising high-level managers in major European and American firms. It had always been the intention, however, to build a permanent full-time staff on a par with the standards of the American management schools and capable of teaching managers and potential managers at a number of different stages in their respective careers. From 1970 onwards, under the impulsion of a newly appointed Dean of the Faculty, the building up of the permanent staff began vigorously. In order to attract the kind of people he needed to make INSEAD a first-order school in international terms, the Dean needed to offer salaries and conditions of work comparable with American ones, and normally, therefore, well above those usually offered in Europe. INSEAD was making a heavy commitment to the future by investing in this way. This heavy investment, accompanied by necessary increases in administrative staff and back-up facilities, coincided in the later period with the worst recession Europe and America had seen since the Second World War. Certain financial difficulties became apparent at INSEAD as elsewhere. The crisis over financing brought to a head the contradictions involved in the ambivalent positions held by business schools, and forced into the open discussions about the vision held by both business supporters and staff about what business education was about and for. These involved bringing to the surface even deeper underlying notions of 'management' as an occupation or a profession, about who should provide education and when, and indeed whether the 'discipline' of management existed at all. These ambivalencies related to differing perceptions of the demand or market for the various courses the school offered.

There have also been student recruitment variations. The intention during the period of the Ford Foundation Grant in the early 1970s was to increase dramatically the number of students on the PGP (one-year, MBA course) to around 540. In practice, not only was it not possible to find sufficient well-qualified students to reach that number, but overall applications for the programme actually dropped over the period from an all time high of nearly 600 in 1971 to a low much nearer 500 in the following years. Many of these were of course unsuitable for the MBA programme. The reasons for this drop are multiple: potential students with jobs preferred to hold on to them in a situation of general economic uncertainty and the demand by firms for executives, particularly those with MBAs wanting high salaries and rapid promotion, was low. Finally, as a number of INSEAD staff themselves noted when reflecting on the medium-term future of the Institute in 1974, demand by European firms for graduates of MBA-type programmes was a relatively recent phenomenon. Indeed, the majority of European firms seemed to be only just discovering how best to use the MBA graduates. The Institute found it rather difficult to recruit suitable students to the PGP at the same time as it began to seem likely that that kind of education would always lead to financial deficits. For INSEAD to remain competitive, the fees charged to participants for the PGP (except for the 10 per cent sent by firms) were set to cover rather less than half the total cost, and this in spite of rapid fee increases in the 1970s to such a level that they could not easily be raised any higher. By 1974, therefore, it was already apparent that much of the revenue for INSEAD would have to come from elsewhere. The relative importance to be allotted to the different programmes offered therefore became of prime concern. The question even arose, and for a short time was debated around the Institute, of whether the PGP should not be scrapped and INSEAD turn itself into a short-course executive programme establishment, an institution of a very different kind.

The reasons why this proposal gained support are interesting as an illustration of business attitudes to management education. Although the PGP was creating deficits, short courses for executives were, on the contrary, financially extremely viable and continued to attract increasing interest from many European and American firms. Demand for executive education in the 1970s was still strongest at the middle to senior management level, where the impact of the increasing decentralization of European firms was greatest. In the absence of a large stock of managers with a broad business education (as exists in the USA), European firms have had to find other ways of strengthening middle management and could not wait for the MBA market to grow. Demand for short public programmes for company executives had therefore been growing in Europe and this growth was expected to accelerate. Many firms ran their own programmes but many contracted them out and supplemented them with public courses. Longer programmes with a general management orientation were also much in demand, for these were the courses which catered for the 'catch-up' needs of Europe. At an even more senior level, demand for general management programmes dramatically outstripped supply. The proportion of INSEAD's resources raised from post-experience courses by the mid-1970s was thus very considerable. Indeed, at the time, and as is consistent with the attitudes of employers described above, many observers were forced to the conclusion that business in Europe was far more interested in financing courses for practising middle and senior managers, courses from which the firms concerned got immediate benefit, than they were in contributing funds to the training of a new generation of young managers who might not even wish to work in the donating firms. There seemed to be an increasing feeling on the part of major European businesses that financing educational deficits was a matter for the state and not for individual private companies.

Advocates of the abandonment of the PGP and reliance on short courses did not, however, win the day. There were strong arguments for the retention of the PGP, which was the most academic of all INSEAD's courses, the one on which its major international reputation was based, considered as it was the 'masthead' of the institution, as well as the development of many of the aspects of the school's work that were the closest to those of a 'university' department.

Other questions in relation to the Institute's development were also raised and again underline the particular situation of institutions of management education. For example, many members of staff felt that the Institute should devote more time to fundamental research and to the production rather than simply the transmission of management knowledge, and this was finally agreed. The chosen strategy for the early 1970s was therefore in the end a compromise between building a long-term institutional reputation and building a deficit-free institution delivering what would, inevitably it was felt, eventually become medium-quality, middle-management education.

INSEAD thus chose to establish itself in the 1970s and beyond as a major centre of what it conceived of as management *education* as opposed to training, and a place where research and the creation of new knowledge, not necessarily directly linked to individual business problems, could be produced.

CONTROLLING BODIES

By the statutes of INSEAD, the governing power is located in the General Assembly who elect the Board. Membership of the General Assembly is by financial contribution to the Institute, by charter, and by election. Operating policies are in theory carried out by the Board, who are self-selecting and self-perpetuating, but in practice it is the Executive Committee, a sub-group of the Board composed of six or so members, that takes the major decisions.

In principle, and in line with the international aims of the Institute, membership of all the governing bodies was to be international. In practice, in the early years at least, representation was mainly of French, British, and American companies and these, especially the French, still dominated membership in the 1970s in spite of active efforts in the 1960s to recruit non-French members.

In 1973–74, a crisis of governance arose at the Institute, reflecting the ambivalent status of a school that spanned university-level education and business. As a result, a management committee was created in 1974 and eventually the faculty gained official representation on the Board.

By 1977 the Board was composed of:

'Civic leaders, the Paris Chamber of Commerce, members from

multinational corporations, from private finance and from national-ised industries, from academic life, diplomacy, the European Parliament and international public administration. They guarantee our private and independent status in the pursuit of our European mission for European management and society.' (Kitzinger 1976)

The change in the direction of the mission of INSEAD towards research and towards training managers for all parts of the public sector was thus felt to be faithfully represented in membership of its governing body.

FUNDING OF THE INSTITUTE

INSEAD long depended largely on company gifts to cover the deficit between programme revenues and total costs. In later years, increased efforts were made to raise money both from private and public sources, notably from the French Government.

INSEAD has raised funds from a number of different sources. Financial problems have arisen because many donors were corpor-ations, subject to squeezed budgets themselves from 1973 onwards. Most donations were not guaranteed against inflation, while INSEAD's costs were largely tied to inflation, especially the highest cost of all, the salary bill. In Europe, moreover, there are few tax concessions to encourage individual and corporate contributions. In recent years, two ways have been devised for companies to contribute to the Institute over a period of five years, the Affiliate and Associated Programmes. Before these started in 1972–73, 175 companies gave more than 5,000FF to INSEAD. Of these, ninety-five were French, by far the largest proportion, followed by the Americans (twenty-nine companies), with Britain, the Netherlands, Switzerland, Germany, and 'other European' contributing fifty-one companies between them.

CURRICULUM OF THE MBA PROGRAMME

What and how students learn at business school is an important element in understanding their position on the labour market after-wards, for it provides important guidance as to why firms employ MBAs. What students learn, how they learn, and the informal and social results of the learning process all contribute to what an INSEAD MBA is, and to the aura of MBAs in the eyes of employing companies. It is important, therefore, to present here the major developments of the curriculum, teaching methods, and staffing.

The early teaching at INSEAD – indeed, for almost ten years of the school's existence – was carried out virtually entirely by part-time staff from industry, supplemented by visiting professors from American business schools. This was thought to ensure the 'relevance' of teaching to students' needs as the teachers were largely using their own managerial experience. It was also a function of the rather less-than-well-established financial stability of the institution. Even more important, perhaps, it was inevitable given the almost total lack of any teachers trained in the discipline of management in France as well as in almost every European country. Around the mid 1960s, however, INSEAD began a policy of recruiting promising young teachers from among students on the MBA programme and sending them to the United States, largely to Harvard, to prepare Doctorates in Business Administration (DBA).

The staff – professors, associate and assistant professors – more than doubled in number over the period 1969–70 to 1973–74. In 1971, there were twenty-two permanent full-time staff and thirty part-time ones. By 1973–74, the end of the major staff expansion period, there were fifty-one permanent full-time staff, five visiting staff, one research fellow, and an executive-in-residence. The national and educational origins of the staff in 1973–74 varied enormously, as did the number of years they had been teaching at the Institute, but American and French teachers predominated.

In terms of what they taught, 'the standard diet of a business school is still with us', a senior member of INSEAD's staff recognized in an interview in 1977. The five staple ingredients of the diet remained finance, accounting and control, management sciences, including the use of computers, marketing, organizational behaviour (OB), strategy, and environment. The latter includes business policy and a reinforced version of what was the major speciality distinguishing INSEAD from US schools – a course called the European Environment of Business.

In common with many American business school practices, in the early years of the Institute no departments existed as such, and until the early to mid-1970s many members of staff resisted the idea of such specialisms, reiterating their belief in the unity of management education and the cross-disciplinary team work needed to teach any aspect of it. The growth of staff numbers, however, finally overcame such opposition, and by 1976 five 'areas', corresponding to the studies mentioned above, had been created.

While the 'areas' taught at the school have since largely remained unchanged, there have been a number of modifications to content and a number of shifts in emphasis. Thus, for example, finance came to include many options, of which students choose several, covering international finance, banking, consolidation accounting, the effect of inflation on financial planning, and so on. One particularly significant and recent addition to the INSEAD curriculum has been the study of industrial relations, first as an option and then as part of the core course, but it seems still to remain very much a secondary consideration in the training of tomorrow's senior managers.

The aim of the curriculum as stated by its teachers is not to provide specialist training in functional areas but to develop the general manager with a global view of the problems of an enterprise. The general emphasis, in line with the school's vocation, is on the international enterprise or the international sections of national companies. The MBA programme consists of a number of core courses and a choice from a wide range of electives. The course as a whole has remained closely structured. During the year, students attend between 1,500 and 2,000 classes of one hour and ten minutes each. The primary objective of the first part of the programme is to bring everyone to similar levels of understanding of the basic subjects of business education, much as is the case at the British schools.

The rather technical, functional courses of finance and marketing are perhaps subsidiary in some senses for potential general managers to those on Business Policy and the European and International Business Environments. These courses, much developed in recent years, provide syntheses of the functional courses and develop the participants' general management skills by training them to evaluate the potential of the firm in its environment, to develop strategies and to build within the firm the organizational structure and management processes needed to implement them.

Last, but certainly not least, there has always been a course of particular importance to the general manager and to the career aspirations of the young executive. It is the course that perhaps best represents some of the aspects of the changing corporate image in the public eye, relating as it does to the 'human' side of business organization and to methods of command and styles of leadership. This is the course, long established in all business schools, on Organizational Behaviour. The course as developed at INSEAD follows a delicate path between the development of the 'man' and the development of the 'managerial' man. It is largely staffed by clinical and social psychologists, and the emphasis is on individual interaction. The objective of the course has been described by its teachers as being to 'increase individual responsibility in dealing effectively with human and organizational problems encountered in organizations and in society'.

It develops personal skills for listening, communicating, and decision making by increasing the 'participant's understanding of himself and his organizational environment'. The issues examined include in- dividual behaviour, interpersonal relationships, leadership and group processes, inter-group conflict analysis, and the dynamics of change and development in organizational structures. 'The aim is also to increase a manager's flexibility and self-awareness of others – in short, to instil certain behavioural and attitudinal changes.' However, person- nel management as such for long received little explicit treatment.

The curriculum at INSEAD has thus been much concerned with the 'needs' of the top general manager of tomorrow.

TEACHING METHODS

The major teaching methods of the Institute are those borrowed from Harvard: the case method and group work. The year's students are divided on arrival into four sections, each of which is further divided into a number of groups of six people. The student composition of these groups is very varied: a Swiss engineer, a French lawyer, a German economist, mixed ages, mixed backgrounds, mixed skills. The groups, intended to provide the working unit for students for the entire year on the compulsory courses, are assigned to a section with its own classroom where groups meet for all plenary sessions of the core courses and where each student has a fixed place with his or her name on it. The composition of the section follows the same principle as that of the groups and the constancy of place of meeting and seating arrangements contribute to the students meeting on a regular basis and getting to know well others from a wide variety of backgrounds of all kinds.

Subject teaching within the classroom is largely done through the case method. It developed from teaching techniques in use at Harvard Law School and refined by the Harvard Business School in the 1920s, and involves the presentation to students of a problem, drawn from a real business situation and set in the details of that situation. The problem demands a decision, frequently of a policy kind, by managers with fairly general responsibilities. For most cases there is no one 'correct' solution and participants are expected to use the material to develop their understanding of the elements lying behind business decisions. The essence of the method is to develop in them managerial skills normally needed at quite high levels of the management hierarchy[6] and accords with the stated aim of the school to produce general managers rather than specialists. The teaching methods have thus sought to give the student the kind of decision-making powers he or she would need at relatively high levels of management and to do so in a way – group work – perceived as associated with the techniques of international business management of the future.

INSEAD and the British business schools

There are many differences in detail in the origins, structure, and development of INSEAD and the two British schools. Whereas INSEAD was founded as a European school with the missionary purpose of creating a new breed of European manager, the British institutions seem to have originated from more parochial concerns about the ailing condition of British management. The British schools have always been embedded in the state education system at university level, whereas INSEAD has been a private college. INSEAD only later added post-experience courses to its activities, whereas at London and Manchester courses of this kind were offered from the beginning. INSEAD has emphasized linguistic ability in its recruitment policies, whilst the British schools have not. Yet despite these differences there are striking similarities in the roles the schools have set themselves and in the pressure to which they have been subjected.

Both the British and the French schools have seen their MBA courses as preparing the high-level managers who, in the decades to come, will staff the major corporations. Their curricula and teaching methods have much in common. At the same time, all three schools have found themselves caught in a conflict between the demands of the business world and demands that originate from their status as institutions of high-level education. Business scepticism over the MBA courses was much the same in France as it was in Britain, and raised similar questions about the desirability of continuing to offer the courses as they stood, and indeed, of continuing to offer them at all. All the schools have also been forced by economic circumstances to reconsider their role, and to re-orientate themselves, most clearly in the case of INSEAD, to new markets that lie outside the private sector.[7] Although the British schools have been partially insulated from the effects of market fluctuations by virtue of their part-public funding, they, like INSEAD, have moderated their expectations about support from private business. The uncertain position of the schools has thus been as evident in France as it has been in Britain, and although the attitudes of French business to the MBA are even less clear than those of the British, it seems that there too, its acceptability as a high-level management qualification remains yet to be fully established.

5 MBAs: social origins and educational paths

Studies of the social composition of the student bodies of educational institutions in Western industrial societies tend to show increasing dominance by those from privileged origins as the level of education rises. In both Britain and France, those born into the higher social strata have been strongly over-represented in the student bodies of the institutions of higher education, so that the distribution of the most valuable kinds of certificates has tended to reflect the inequalities in the distribution of other types of capital in the population at large. Thus, to the extent that educational qualifications have become increasingly important as a means of access to different levels of the occupation structure (and this is, of course, a matter of some debate), and that high-level certificates are advantageous or essential for entry to high-level positions, it is those from the most privileged homes who have been best placed to reproduce in their own generation the advantages of their families of origin.

An examination of the origins of the students who attended the business schools enables us to assess the extent to which these institutions operate in a way similar to others in the higher education systems of each country. Our purpose at this stage is chiefly to describe the business graduates in terms of their social and educational backgrounds so as to locate them in the social structure. In the following chapter we will look at some of the factors that have influenced the formation of the student population, and that help to explain why they manifest their particular characteristics.

Sex, age, and marital status

The French students we are concerned with attended INSEAD between 1959 and 1973, and during this period over five hundred studied at the School.[1] The British students attended either the London or Manchester Business School between 1965 and 1974, and nearly a thousand British graduates passed through the two schools during these years, divided fairly evenly between the two institutions.

At both the French and British schools the overwhelming majority of students were men. During the period studied, fewer than 5 per cent of the British students were women and even fewer of the French, which is doubtless partly a consequence of the particularly strong male stereotype that has been associated with managerial occupations. In Britain, for example, managerial rhetoric has tended to treat 'managers' as virtually synonymous with 'men' in keeping with the very low numbers of women actually engaged in managerial occupations (Department of Industry 1977). Although in recent years a conscious effort has been made to attract more women to the British schools, in the past the male orientation of the managerial culture has inevitably been reflected in their ethos.

Most of the students entered the schools in their early or mid-twenties, very few being younger than twenty-one or older than thirty. In Britain, over half were between the ages of twenty-three and twenty-six, with little change in the age distribution of the intakes. The INSEAD students were, on the whole, an older group than the British, less than 10 per cent being under the age of twenty-three on entry, and over the years the proportion of older students increased. Changes in INSEAD's recruitment policies have favoured slightly older applicants, for in the mid-1960s it introduced the requirement that military obligations be fulfilled before entry, and more recently it has given preference to candidates with at least one year of work experience. In general, however, the French students, although older, were less likely to have had work experience than the British, because of the time spent in military service. Three-quarters of the British had at least one year of work experience before attending business school in comparison with only half of the French in the sample studied.

Most of the students were not married at the time they entered business school, although the proportion of the unmarried declined at INSEAD as the average age of the students rose. In the early years, almost all the French students were single. In Britain more than two-thirds of the students were unmarried, and this proportion changed little over the years.

The students at all three schools were, therefore, fairly similar in these terms, being generally young, unmarried men in their early to mid-twenties, at or near the start of their working careers.

Socio-professional origins

An analysis of the socio-professional origins of the alumni, in terms of father's occupation, shows that the majority were drawn from the privileged strata of each country (*Table* 5 (1)).

Almost 90 per cent of the British students' fathers were, or had been, engaged in non-manual occupations, usually of a professional, administrative, or managerial nature. Over half of the fathers were either owners of 'substantial' businesses (defined as large enough to warrant incorporation), company directors or senior managers, senior administrators, or independent or 'higher' professionals (lawyers, doctors, engineers) that is to say, members of the higher social strata. Many students thus had what is presumably the special advantage of at least one parent with experience in the same field as the one in which they intended to pursue a career. While our information on the type and size of firm owned or directed (in the case of company directors and senior managers) by the fathers in the higher business groups is incomplete, the indications are that the business owners' firms were probably of small to medium size, whilst the directors and senior managers, although associated with significant firms, were only rarely in top positions in the very largest companies. The number of students whose fathers were, for example, directors of 'elite' firms (Giddens 1974) was, so far as we can tell, rather low. Similarly, although 11 per cent of the fathers were senior administrators, often in the Civil Service or in local government, and a further 15 per cent were in the more prestigious and better-paid sectors of the professions (independent accountants, solicitors, doctors, qualified engineers, research scientists, tertiary level teachers, etc.), the number of fathers who could be regarded as holding elite positions was fairly small. The socio-professional origins of the British students were thus often high, but less often of the highest, elite kind.

In comparison with the population as a whole, the students were,

Table 5 (1) Socio-professional origins of the British and French alumni

Britain[1]

	Business owners	Top managers	Independent professionals	Higher professionals	Administrative	Other managers	Lower professional	Employers/proprietors	Routine non-manual	Skilled manual	Other manual	Other	Total
n	78	58	14	57	49	69	31	38	25	30	12	3	464
%	17	12	3	12	11	15	7	8	5	6	3	1	100

France[2]

	Patrons[3]	Professions liberales	Public service[4]	Cadres supérieurs (private sector)	Cadres moyens[5]	Shopkeepers/Artisans	White collar	Manual workers	Farmers	Others	Total
n	135	49	45	41	50	20	8	8	14	8	378
%	36	13	12	11	13	5	2	2	4	2	100

[1] Questionnaire data for British alumni entering LBS 1966–74 (n=255) and MBS 1965–74 (n=219). No data=9
[2] File data for French alumni entering INSEAD 1959–73, selected years (n=415). No data=37
[3] Business owners, chief executives, and board members
[4] Civil servants, military and naval officers, secondary and university teachers
[5] Includes ingénieurs. Cadres moyens are principally 'middle managers'

nevertheless, drawn in very disproportionate numbers from high-status families (*Table* 5 (2)). The proportion of alumni with fathers in managerial or professional occupations was five times as great as the proportion in the comparable group of economically active males, while there were four times the proportion of clerical and manual workers in the population as there were among the alumni. A good deal of the disparity can, of course, be accounted for by the composition of the graduate population, biased as it is to the higher groups, but this bias is further accentuated for the business graduates. Thus those with fathers in managerial or professional occupations were found amongst the business graduates almost twice as often as they were in the undergraduate population. The over-representation of the sons of managers and administrators is particularly noticeable in contrast to the under-representation of the children of professionals. The former

Table 5 (2)   Occupational distributions of males, university entrants, and British alumni (percentages)

Registrar General's occupational grouping	Males aged 45–9 1966[1]	Fathers of university entrants 1968[1]	Males aged 45–9 1971[2]	Fathers of university entrants 1974[2]	Fathers of LBS/MBS alumni 1965–74
Administrative, managerial	6	14	7	15	55
Professional, technical	8	30	9	34	22
Clerical, sales, service	22	28	21	25	14
Manual, agricultural	64	28	62	26	9
Total	100	100	100	100	100

[1] Adapted from Table B, *UCCA Statistical Supplement to the Sixth Report, 1967–68*, p. 23. Columns refer to economically active males, aged 45–9, in Great Britain (Census 1966), and accepted home candidates, United Kingdom

[2] Adapted from Table K4, *UCCA Statistical Supplement to the Twelfth Report, 1973–74*, p. 18. Columns refer to economically active males, aged 45–9, in Great Britain (Census 1971), and accepted home candidates, United Kingdom

The reclassification of the alumni data into the Registrar General's occupational groupings to enable comparison with the Census figures cited in the UCCA reports, provided a close, but not a perfect, fit. In particular, a number of cases classified as 'clerical, etc.' according to the Registrar General, have in the case of the alumni been classified as 'manual'. If anything, the disparity between manual workers among the alumni and the other groups has been under- rather than over-estimated.

group of students consisted largely of those whose fathers were business owners or managers, and their very frequent appearance suggests a high degree of inheritance of occupational aspirations. Similarly, the relative under-representation of children of professionals is consistent with the preference for graduates from this background for professional rather than business careers (Kelsall, Poole, and Kuhn 1974; Universities Central Council on Admissions 1968).

The social origins of the French students shows that, like the British, they came from a very small section of the working population. What might be called the 'significant minority' of the students, nearly 40 per cent, came from families headed by a father who owned or controlled one or more business enterprises. Many of these were, or had been, substantial businesses, frequently in the textile industry. Other sectors of business were also well represented by managers' children: 11 per cent of the students were the sons of senior and top managers and a further 13 per cent came from families headed by middle managers. A number of students came from privileged families in other socio-economic spheres of activity. Thus 13 per cent of the fathers exercized the professions of either medicine or law or were in independent occupations servicing business and the public, such as insurance brokers, stockbrokers, and engineering consultants. These were joined by a similar number whose fathers were engaged in the public service, whether as high-level civil servants working in the central administration, or as teachers in secondary and higher education, or as officers in the armed forces.

By comparison, the proportions drawn from manual working-class homes were very small, smaller even than those at the British schools. Working-class students numbered only 2 per cent of the 378 INSEAD alumni with known social origins; in Britain the figure was 9 per cent, the bulk of these being children of skilled manual workers. Even with the addition of the sons of routine white-collar workers, the numbers rise only to 4 per cent for France and 15 per cent for Britain.[2] The 'working-class MBA' from either INSEAD, London, or Manchester is thus a very rare product indeed.

As in Britain, the representation of the highest social groups was far greater than their proportion in the population (*Table* 5 (3)). Although the *patrons*, *cadres supérieurs*, and members of the liberal professions made up only 15 per cent of the French working population over the period, they constituted nearly three-quarters of the INSEAD alumni. Manual workers, on the other hand, comprised half of the working population but only two in a hundred of the business school's students.

The student composition of the major *grandes écoles* reflects a similar

Table 5 (3)   Occupational distributions of male population and INSEAD alumni (percentages)

	Males 1962	Males 1968	INSEAD alumni 1959–73
Patrons	10	10	36
Liberal professions, *cadres supérieurs*	5	6	36
Cadres moyens	7	9	13
White-collar workers	8	9	7
Manual workers	50	50	2
Farmers	15	12	4
Others	5	5	2
Total	100	100	100

Data on the occupational distribution of economically active males adapted from Salais (1969)

social selectivity to that in British universities, and as in Britain, the tendency is for these imbalances to be accentuated still further at the business schools (*Table* 5 (4)). It is indeed remarkable to find that the proportion of students drawn from the top socio-professional groups at INSEAD was twice that found at the ultra-prestigious Ecole Polytechnique and at most of the other top *grandes écoles*. The strong representation of the sons of *patrons* at INSEAD in comparison with the *grandes écoles* is illustrated by the fact that the proportion of *patron* sons at the former was higher than that of *patrons* and *cadres supérieurs* together in most of the latter.

In both France and Britain, the schools have thus attracted a generally high-status clientele with a general bias in favour of those from business backgrounds. In France, however, the sons of *patrons* made up a much more significant proportion of the student body than did the sons of business owners in Britain, 36 per cent at INSEAD but only 17 per cent at the British schools. The difference may be accounted for by the differing prominence of medium-sized family businesses in the industrial and commercial structures of France and Britain (Cornwell 1974), the differing facilities for financing studies at the French and British schools, and the different emphasis by big business in each country on educational qualifications as a means of advancement.

Although the majority of firms in both countries fall into the category of small to medium-sized, privately owned concerns, the

Table 5 (4) Social origins of students in *grandes écoles*, late 1960s (percentages)

Socio-professional category	INSEAD	Polytech- nique	Mines (Paris)	Centrale	ENA	HEC	Ulm lettres	Ulm sciences	ESCP	ESSEC
Patrons* and cadres supérieurs private and public										
public	59.5	24	28	30	19	38	25	16	13	6
Liberal professions	13	10	8	5	17.5	8	10	14	28	25.5
Senior Civil Servants		3	1	1.5	9	7	3	5	12	12
(group total)	72.5	37	37	36.5	45.5	53	38	35	53	43.5
Ingénieurs	13.5	20	13.5	13	6	11	5.5	14.5	12	16
Teachers		15	8	11	11	5	25	21	5	4
Middle executives		11	20	15	13	13	12	11	10	19
(group total)		46	41.5	39	30	29	42.5	46.5	27	39
Artisans/Shopkeepers	5	5	6	8	8	13	4	6	8	9
White-collar workers	2	5	4	6	7	2	8	6	6	4
Manual workers	2	4	5	4	4	1	5	2.5	2	2
Farmers and farm workers	4	2	6	5	6	2	3	3	2	3
Other	—	1	1	—	—	—	—	—	—	—

* Industriels

Sources: For INSEAD, Marceau (1975). The other figures are from a study by the Centre de Sociologie Européenne (1967) and the ESCP and ESSEC data are from Ministère de l'Education Nationale, Service de Statistique (1971)

School Names: ENA: École Nationale d'Administration; HEC: École des Hautes Études Commerciales; Ulm: École Normale Supérieure (Rue d'Ulm); ESCP: École Supérieure de Commerce de Paris; ESSEC: École Supérieure des Sciences Économiques et Commerciales (Catholic Faculty, Paris) degree of industrial concentration and the extent of the domination of very large firms is much greater in Britain than in France. There are far fewer very large firms in France than in Britain or Germany (Rowley 1974) and the significance of the medium-sized family business is much greater in the French industrial structure than in the British. The French economy seems to be at an earlier stage in the process of transition to a 'corporate economy' (Hannah 1976) than is Britain, so that the threat to independent businesses has perhaps been more acute in France in recent years. The pressure on the less powerful sector of the bourgeoisie to take advantage of new ways of securing the social reproduction of its scions has probably been greater in France, and has affected a greater number of families whose offspring now have to compete on the wider labour market. Apart from this, the existence of only limited sources of public finance for studies at INSEAD has inevitably placed the relatively wealthy, business-owning families at an advantage, whereas in Britain the majority of students have been eligible for various forms of state grant-aid. Finally, the heavier reliance in French business on educational qualifications for access to top positions in large firms (Granick 1972; Hall *et al.* 1969; Monjardet 1972), has probably been particularly important in drawing the attention of business families whose sons are less well endowed with high-level educational diplomas to institutions such as INSEAD. In Britain, it seems plausible to suggest that the relevance of attendance at a business school will have been much less obvious to business-owning families, and that this will tend to have weakened their representation at the schools.

Economic and social capital endowments: four groupings

The students in both countries have in general been drawn predominantly from those groups best endowed with various forms of capital, and in particular from those families directly involved in business. The impact of the student's initial endowments of capital, given him by his membership of a family located within a structure in which capital is inequitably distributed, can be seen more clearly when they are grouped together according to the volume and type of their endowment. Thus, for the British we can consider the owners, directors, and senior managers of substantial firms as sharing to some degree a common economic position, and as having a similar experience and understanding of the business world (in other words of relevant social capital – social knowledge). The independent professionals, higher professionals, and administrators also share a similar economic position, both in relation to each other and to the top business group, but are less directly acquainted with business and may indeed hold the business world in low regard. We can see these two groups (business and professional) as differing principally in the amount of business knowledge at their disposal and in their attitudes towards business and professional careers.

The remaining occupations are differentiated in terms of control of economic capital, and can be internally divided according to their links with business. The managerial group may be considered as having more detailed knowledge of large-scale business than the rest. On the other hand, more junior managers are less well endowed economically than the owners, directors, and senior managers of substantial firms. We therefore treat them as a distinct group, combining a relatively modest economic position with a significant degree of experience and knowledge of business. The final group comprises those whom we regard as having the least capital economically, socially, and culturally. This group includes the small employers and proprietors, lower professionals (such as school teachers, social workers, and technicians), 'routine' clerical workers, and manual workers.

The French category groupings reflect the same principles of organization, but vary slightly to allow for the differing socio-economic significance of belonging to any given group and to show the particular importance in that country, and in the INSEAD population, of the *patronat*. In relation of entry to INSEAD, the sons of the *patronat* constitute the most significant group. Numerically they outweigh by far any other section – while more than a third came from *patronat* families, the next biggest group accounts for fewer than one in seven. Examination of almost every variable of interest here – education, age at entry, previous professional experience, aspirations for future career – show the significant differences associated with belonging to the *patronat*. Those differences seem to be associated with particular configurations of ownership and control not only of economic capital but also of social capital, particularly of social knowledge relevant to business and to business careers. A particular set of values and class *habitus* are, in France, associated with *patronat* families, especially those from the older industries, such as textiles, situated in the more conservative provinces in the North and East. It is from families such as these that a considerable number of INSEAD students are drawn.

Similar reasoning suggests the importance of separating, again on the same basis as the British, those holding high-level positions outside business. In the first instance, while the economic capital possessed may be important (doctors and lawyers in France being amongst the wealthiest groups in the population), the *habitus* of the group, in terms of attitude values and expectations is likely to differ in the kind of social knowledge available to its children. Contacts and information directly relevant to business are likely to be fewer and less up-to-date. Some kinds of independent service enterprise, the 'non-hierarchical' service business, may in some senses be considered to be close to the traditional liberal professions and have therefore been included in the category. For similar reasons, the group also includes the children of senior civil servants, the armed forces, and secondary and university teachers. The professions these groups pursue are largely closed to people not 'certified' as competent by the education system and they may be expected to place considerable faith in the education system as a means to the professional advancement of their children.

The third grouping combines those groups which, although associated with business, differ in important ways from the *patronat*. Managerial families headed by *cadres supérieurs* in private or nationalized business to some extent share the life style, values, attitudes, and social knowledge typical of the *patronat*, but they differ significantly from *patrons* in their separation from the ownership of the companies they serve. *Cadres moyens* (middle and junior managers) share the business environment of their professional lives with senior and top managers, but they differ in important respects from the latter. Their economic resources, gained only from relatively low salaries, are likely to be minimal; they are not owners of capital, and their social knowledge, contacts, and cultural capital are likely to be much reduced. For present purposes, both these groups have been considered together since they are similar in their occupational milieux (business) but differ markedly from the *patronat* in economic terms.[3]

Finally, the remaining groups have been combined into one. Members of these groups are low in all three forms of capital, although to varying degrees. They include small shopkeepers and artisans, white-collar and manual workers, and farmers. While small shopkeepers are in the business world as owners of economic capital, they do not control significant amounts, and their life styles and *habitus* separate them from their more grandiose business cousins. Farmers too, are frequently owners of economic capital, often in considerable quantities, but they are largely separated from the business world. Salaried clerical and manual workers are distinct from the other categories not only in terms of their general lack of economic capital, but also because they have little in the way of social and cultural capital, particularly of the kind likely to be of use in business.

Table 5 (5) shows the populations of the schools when the students have been grouped together on the basis of the categories described.

Table 5 (5)   British and French alumni within socio-professional groupings

British alumni			French alumni		
	n	%		n	%
Business owners, top managers	136	29	*Patrons*	135	36
Higher professional, administrative	120	26	Liberal professions, cadres supérieurs (public)	94	25
Other managers	69	15	*Cadres moyens,* * *cadres supérieurs* (private)	91	25
Lower professional, small proprietors, clerical, manual	139	30	Small proprietors, clerical, manual	50	14
Total	464	100		370	100

*Following INSEE practice, in this study *cadres moyens* include some people whose profession was noted as *ingénieurs.* Some of these should perhaps be included in higher management. As it is not usually clear, we have adopted the practice of coding down.

Educational background

In both countries the students had followed educational paths typically valued by families of the classes from which they came. This schooling both reflects and confirms their position as members of privileged groups. It is striking, however, that in secondary education in Britain, and in higher education in France, the institutions attended by the sons, like the occupational positions of the fathers, were not, on the whole, quite of the 'very best'. Comparisons with the education of the total population in each country nonetheless show that the students had made 'maximum' use of the educational provisions available, both private and public. Where families could assist their offspring in the acquisition of suitable cultural capital by buying prestigious education, usually at the secondary level, or could encourage them to pursue particularly 'fruitful' lines of study (especially in France), then they usually did so. The importance of family decision making with regard to choice of educational routes, for example, emerged from nearly every interview carried out with the French students. Yet while families may enormously increase the chances of access to the best types of education, they cannot wholly guarantee results.

The importance of the increase in chances of access is, however, reflected in the educational backgrounds of those finally admitted as graduates to the business schools. This may be seen in the proportion in Britain who had attended public schools and in the proportion in France who had attended the best secondary schools, especially for the crucial, frequently private classes taken in preparation for the entry examinations to the *grandes écoles*. In both countries, the links between schooling at secondary level and entry to prestigious institutions are well known and are confirmed here. In Britain, the chances of entering Oxford and Cambridge are greater for the graduates of public schools; in France, the chances of entering the better *grandes écoles* are greatly increased by preparation in certain *lycées* and private schools situated in or near Paris.

SECONDARY EDUCATION

Britain

In Britain over half the students had attended a public school. The degree of concentration in this sector is illustrated by the fact that fewer than 5 per cent of the school-age population gains entry to these 200 institutions (Halsey 1972 : 165). More than half of the students at the London Business School had been to a public school, and in one year the proportion approached 75 per cent. At Manchester, the numbers were lower but still substantial.

Of those who did attend a public school, 40 per cent had been to one of the 'Clarendon Nine' or to a 'well known' school such as Marlborough, Uppingham, or Stowe. Those who had been to the 'best' schools represented one in five of all the students, which, although a minority, still far outweighs the proportion that would reflect those schools' numerical contribution to the education system. In contrast, about one-third were educated in the state system, which caters for the vast majority of the population. Of these, nearly all had attended maintained grammar schools. Secondary modern and comprehensive schools appear very infrequently indeed (2 per cent) among the alumni's educational histories. In general, the British alumni had received the best, if not always the very best, that the private and state secondary education systems could offer. They had thus received an advantageous start in the struggle for cultural capital in the education system, and in the majority of cases acquired an attribute that appears in the past to have been particularly valuable for the successful pursuit of a British business career (Fidler 1977; Hall and Amado-Fischgrund

Table 5 (6)   Type of school attended by the British alumni (percentages)

	Owners, top managers	Profes- sional, adminis- trative	Other managers	Clerical, manual, etc.	Total
'Clarendon' public school[1]	16 ⎫	16 ⎫	3 ⎫	4 ⎫	10 ⎫
'Well known' public school[2]	21 ⎬ 69	9 ⎬ 63	1 ⎬ 40	4 ⎬ 33	10 ⎬ 52
Other public school[3]	32 ⎭	38 ⎭	36 ⎭	25 ⎭	32 ⎭
Other independent	3	4	3	2	3
Direct grant grammar	5	8	13	9	8
Local authority grammar	23	22	41	49	33
Secondary modern, comprehensive	0	1	1	4	2
Other, abroad	1	2	1	3	2
Total	100	100	100	100	100
(Base)	(135)	(119)	(69)	(138)	(461)

[1] i.e., Charterhouse, Eton, Harrow, Merchant Taylor's, Rugby, St Paul's, Shrewsbury, Westminster, Winchester

[2] As selected by David Boyd in his *Elites and their Education* (1973; 41–2) partly in terms of Oxbridge scholarships. The schools are: Bradfield, Cheltenham, Clifton, Fettes, Haileybury, Lancing, Loretto, Malvern, Marlborough, Oundle, Radley, Repton, Rossall, Sedbergh, Sherbourne, Stowe, Uppingham. It should be noted that this list excludes Gordonstoun and Wellington

[3] Schools other than those in [1] and [2] having membership of the Headmaster's Conference

1969; Leggatt 1978; McGivering 1960; Thomas 1978; Whitley 1973, 1974). That access to these advantages was highly dependent upon the father's socio-professional position can be seen from *Table* 5 (6), where the proportions attending public school fall from 69 per cent for business owners and top managers to 63 per cent for the professional and administrative group, 40 per cent for the middle managers, and 33 per cent for the least endowed group. The proportions attending one of the Clarendon schools were identical for the owner/top manager and professional/administrative groups (16 per cent), four times the proportion for the middle managers and others. But for the 'well known' schools, a fifth of the owners' and top managers' sons had attended, ten times the proportion of middle managers' and others' sons and twice that of the professional/administrative group. Thus the owners'/top managers' sons were not only the most likely to have attended public school, but were also most likely to have attended a 'well known' or Clarendon school.

The likelihood of students having been boarders, rather than day pupils, follows a similar pattern. One-third had had residential places at their schools, but the proportion was almost half for the top business and professional groups. Overall, nearly half had been fee-payers at school, but two-thirds of the top groups had benefited in this way from the economic position of their parents. In a significant number of cases, therefore, the students' parents had used their economic capital to purchase a particularly valuable type of secondary education, frequently of the classic public boarding-school variety.

If the proportion of the business school students who had attended public or other independent schools is compared with the numbers of the graduate population who attended such schools, it is found that the former is two to three times the size of the latter.[4] The greater representation of those from high origins at business school, as against university, is thus repeated in terms of school background. As we shall show later, the socio-professional origins and secondary schooling of the business graduates come, in this way, closely to resemble those of the existing big business elite.

France

In France, with no real equivalent of the British public schools, the secondary education received by students at INSEAD nevertheless remained closely linked to the social position of the family, as well as its geographical location.

Table 5 (7) shows that the owners and controllers of business, the *patronat*, had made between two and three times as much use of the private school system as had the other professions grouped together. For their secondary education, from the age of eleven years onwards, almost a third of *patronat* children had attended only private schools, as against only one in seven children from the other group of the sample, in spite of the inclusion in the latter of some children of high social origins. A further fifth of the *patronat* children had acquired at least part of their education in private schools. Moreover, the 'best' *lycées* are largely to be found in Paris and its immediate suburbs, and attendance at these is also linked to the social origins of the students. While around one in four of the children of the three more privileged groups had attended the Parisian *lycées* only one in six of the 'rest' of the INSEAD

Table 5 (7)   Type of secondary school attended by French alumni
(percentages)

	Patrons	Liberal professions	Cadres moyens	Clerical, manual	Total
Lycée only	38	61	60	74	54
Private school	36	17	16	12	23
Mixed (*lycée* and private)	21	16	16	12	17
Abroad	5	6	8	2	6
Total	100	100	100	100	100
(Base)	(126)	(84)	(82)	(43)	(335)

population had done so, the latter being more frequently 'relegated' to
the state schools, frequently in the provinces.

A similar picture appears in relation to attendance at the special
classes préparatoires, which prepare a student over a period of between
one and three years for the entrance examinations to the *grandes écoles*.
The predominance of business-owner and top managerial attendance
at private schools for these crucial classes reappears and they more
clearly dominated the Paris *lycées*. The names of individual schools
attended (at some time during secondary education) show how much
the best ones were used, both private and public. Schools such as the
lycées Janson de Sailly and Louis le Grand in Paris, or the private
institutions of the Paris College Stanislas, or the École Sainte
Geneviève at Versailles were attended by 41 per cent of the *patronat*
children, and by almost a third of the offspring of the liberal
professions and public servants. In contrast less than a quarter of the
cadres moyens sent their children there, and less than a sixth of the rest.

HIGHER EDUCATION

Britain

The pattern of prestigious but not ultra-prestigious secondary education is repeated, although less clearly, at the post-secondary level. One
might expect that such self-consciously 'high quality' institutions as
business schools would attract those who had already attended the
foremost institutions at the preceding level in the educational hierarchy, and to some extent this is true.

Table 5 (8) Higher education of the British alumni (percentages)

	Owners, top managers	Profes- sional, adminis- trative	Other managers	Clerical manual	Total
Oxford	14 } 38	22 } 50	9 } 31	17 } 31	16 } 38
Cambridge	24	28	22	14	22
Other university	55	40	57	56	52
Polytechnic	2	2	7	6	4
Professional qualification only	4	8	4	7	6
Total	100	100	100	100	100
(Base)	(135)	(119)	(68)	(137)	(459)

Of the British alumni, 38 per cent attended Oxford or Cambridge for their first degree, a slight majority having been to Cambridge (*Table* 5 (8)). This can be compared with the contribution of these two universities to the national graduate population over the equivalent period, which ranges from approximately 14 per cent in 1967 to 9 per cent in 1974. The business and professional groups are again distinguished from the middle managers and others with 44 per cent of the former group having been to Oxford and Cambridge but only 31 per cent of the latter.

The professional group was most likely to have been educated at Oxbridge, which perhaps reflects the long-standing connection between these institutions and careers in the professions and public service and their relative unimportance for careers in business. Nearly all the other alumni had attended other British universities, although 4 per cent were drawn from polytechnics; most of these were from the lower two occupational groupings. About 6 per cent had neither attended a university nor any other institution to read for a degree, but had obtained equivalent professional qualifications, usually in accounting.

A wide range of first degree subjects had been taken by the alumni, but the areas of science, engineering, and technology predominated, accounting for just over half of the degrees. Although this partly reflects the large number of male graduates who qualify in these areas, it also stems from the very high proportion of graduates who enter industry with such degrees. In 1975, for example, nearly 81 per cent of all graduates who entered manufacturing industry had degrees in engineering, science, or technology (Department of Industry 1977 : 5). More importantly, qualified engineers and scientists have generally been recruited in Britain as technical experts rather than as potential top managers, unlike the situation in France and elsewhere in Europe (Department of Industry 1977 : 4). The ambitious scientist, and in particular the engineer, in British industry is likely to become rapidly aware of his limited career prospects, particularly if he has entered the field of production management, and many in the past have reacted by trying to escape into marketing or general management. Business school degrees are particularly attractive to this group because they constitute a much needed symbol of managerial, rather than technical, potential. As a recent Government report noted:

> 'In Britain it may therefore only be after an engineer has acquired his practically oriented professional qualifications (which generally require some experience in a position of responsibility) that his employers recognise his potential value. In contrast, a graduate on the continent emerges from higher education with a qualification seen as having equipped him to be a generalist decision maker as well as a highly trained technologist.' (Department of Industry 1975: 33)

As we shall see in the next chapter, one of the largest groups entering business school with previous work experience consisted of engineers and scientists who had worked in production management.

Given the 'high quality' image of the schools, it is perhaps surprising to find that only about half the students had 'good' first degrees. Of the degree holders, only 9 per cent had first-class degrees and 44 per cent upper or undivided seconds, so that almost half of the alumni had a lower second or below. Indeed, if we include those who only held professional qualifications, then a majority had a lower second or below or no degree at all. Although the schools have not recruited disproportionately few candidates with 'good' degrees, the wide range of academic attainments does reflect their market position in respect of academic high-flyers, and confirms that as business-oriented institutions, academic ability is by no means the only nor necessarily the most important recruitment criterion.

France

Nearly all (98 per cent) of the French students at INSEAD were graduates of an institution of higher education, mostly in France but sometimes abroad, particularly in Switzerland. A large number also had second and even third degrees, usually from universities in the USA. In France, once the *baccalauréat* has been taken, the decision must be taken about whether to enter the special classes preparing for entry to the *grandes écoles* and in which subject areas. Because of the 'railway line' nature of French secondary education, much depends on previous success in mathematics, which will already have determined the *baccalauréat* specialism taken. The academically brightest students do not enter the universities, except in certain subjects, but instead sit the competitive examinations giving access to the Parisian *grandes écoles* and their less prestigious provincial counterparts. Unlike the universities, which must accept everyone holding a *baccalauréat*, the *grandes écoles* are highly selective and their graduates are effectively guaranteed a 'better' career in business and the public service. These schools open the door to career ladders with rapid promotion possibilities and attractive salaries. The basic divide in French post-secondary education is thus between the *grandes écoles* and the universities. The *grandes écoles* are comprised chiefly of engineering and commercial schools. The best students at mathematics usually enter classes preparing for the engineering schools and the rather less good for the commercial ones. Students who are mediocre or bad at mathematics may go to the universities and fill the faculties of law and letters, although if they are good academic all-rounders they may well prepare for the Instituts d'Etudes Politiques, especially the high-prestige 'Sciences Po' in Paris.

At INSEAD, these basic institutional divisions reappear amongst the educational qualifications of the students, for while in the national population, greater numbers of students attend the universities than the *grandes écoles*, at INSEAD the relationship is reversed. Throughout the history of the Institute it has recruited over-whelmingly from selective schools, both engineering and commercial, more than four-fifths of the students having attended such top-level institutions. Only a minority, however, had been educated at the very best, top quality *grandes écoles*.

In engineering, if we take the location of the schools in Paris or the provinces as a rough indicator of the prestige of the schools concerned, we find that over a third of INSEAD's French engineering graduates held diplomas from the less prestigious establishments located in the provinces. A further 15 per cent had been educated in engineering schools abroad. Thus, over half of these students were from the not-so-prestigious schools, a figure that is increased considerably if those Parisian schools of lesser renown are included. Rather more (56 per cent) of the commercial graduates had been through the top schools,

(HEC, ESSEC and ESCP) all of which are located in Paris. A further quarter had been to schools in the provinces and 17 per cent to 'Sciences Po'. The few remaining students had done their degrees in the faculties, 30 per cent of them in Paris and 42 per cent in the provinces, covering the three subjects of science, law, and economics, and 27 per cent had studied at other faculties or abroad.

The type of higher education received (engineering, commercial, etc.) did not vary much with the students' social origins, but the prestige of the schools attended within each academic field did. Members of the top status groups had frequently not received the sort of education they might have expected or hoped for. Only a quarter of those who had attended an engineering school had been to the most prestigious engineering *écoles* in Paris, and over half had either been to a provincial school or had gone abroad to avoid 'relegation' to a provincial institution. Indeed, a higher percentage of those from the lowest group had attended the top Parisian *écoles* than of any other group, although they also had a higher percentage educated at provincial schools, only rarely being able to 'escape' abroad. Although the tendency for those from high origins to have been to the less prestigious schools is not found so markedly in the case of the commercial schools and the faculties, a quarter of these students had also attended provincial institutions.

Some students had also done second and subsequent diplomas. Fifteen had second degrees in engineering and scientific studies (mostly scientific), eighteen in commerce and political science and 125 held second degrees from the faculties of law and economics. Of these, forty went abroad to do the degree, largely to the USA, and a further forty-three had started a higher degree but had not finished it at entry to the Institute. A further fifty-six students already possessed three university degrees and 14 per cent fourth ones. By comparison, 6 per cent of the British had a higher degree and 13 per cent a professional qualification in addition to their first degree. Clearly, INSEAD's French students had utilized the higher education system to a maximum, even before embarking on a course in business administration.

The awareness on the part the the students, particularly those from high social origins, of their relatively second-best education played an important part in motivating them to attend INSEAD, and was more obviously apparent than it was amongst the British. In both counties, however, as we shall see, high aspirations coupled with an insufficiency of the 'right' kinds of capital played an important role in bringing the students to the business schools.

Table 5 (9) Higher education institutions attended by the French alumni (percentages)

	Patrons	Liberal professions	Cadres moyens	Clerical/ manual	Total	
Engineering schools						
Polytechnique, Paris	7	12	7	11	9	} top grandes écoles 38%
Ecole Centrale, Mines, etc.	22	15	24	25	21	
Other grandes écoles, Paris	16	22	22	7	17	} all grandes écoles 83%
Grandes écoles, provinces	29	40	37	57	38	
Abroad	26	10	10	0	15	
Total	100	100	100	100	100	
(Base)	(69)	(40)	(41)	(28)	(178)	
Commercial schools						
HEC, ESSEC, ESCP, Paris	59	55	55	47	56 }	
Sup de Co, provinces	24	21	32	40	28	
Sciences Po	16	24	12	15	17	
Total	100	100	100	100	100	
(Base)	(49)	(38)	(40)	(15)	(142)	
University Faculties						
Paris	36	36	14	25	30	
Provinces	36	36	71	25	42	
Abroad	27	27	14	50	27	
Total	100	100	100	100	100	
(Base)	(11)	(11)	(7)	(4)	(33)	

The wider family background

Although the analysis of the students' social origins in terms of the father's occupation enables us to situate them broadly in the socio-economic structure, the resulting picture is much enriched if members of their wider families are taken into account (Zeitlin and Ratcliff 1975). Details of the occupations and education of the grandfathers, for example, when taken with those of the fathers, enable us to observe the processes of acquisition, accumulation, and maintenance of advantages that take place over the generations, and to illustrate the continuities of privilege in which the acquisition of the MBA is but the most recent stage. Similarly, some consideration of the network of kin available, at least potentially, to the students, and the types of capital at their disposal, helps us to situate the students more firmly and to give some assessment of the value of this social capital to their future business careers.

With these ends in view, students in both the interviews and the questionnaire survey were asked to provide information about the occupations and education of their grandfathers, mothers, siblings, aunts, uncles, cousins and their spouses, and where married, of their own spouse and parents-in-law. Because of the very demanding nature of such a request for information, the data on the wider families are sometimes incomplete, and the considerable amount of information that resulted only permitted a very general analysis. In the case of the British, for example, reasonably complete information was obtained from 80 per cent of the respondents for over 6,000 relations, each student giving details for an average of nineteen relatives and in one case as many as sixty-eight. The quality of the information given must also be taken to be variable, from vague recollections of occupation or education, to detailed descriptions of a type or even name of a school or university or educational qualification. Within the constraints of the study, such drawbacks were, however, found to be inevitable.

GRANDFATHERS

The occupations of the grandfathers are shown in *Table* 5 (10). Of the British, about a third had been members of the upper classes. However, nearly two-thirds of both the maternal and paternal grand-fathers had been employed in the least advantageous types of occupation, twice the proportion found for the students' fathers. Almost 30 per cent of the fathers could thus be considered to have experienced intergenerational upward mobility, moving to a position as business

Table 5 (10)   Socio-professional origins of the alumni: fathers and grandfathers (percentages)

French alumni

	Maternal grandfather	Paternal grandfather	Father
Patrons	21	25	25
Liberal professions	13	11	12
Public service	15	9	10
Cadres supérieurs (private)	11	6	16
Cadres moyens	11	9	16
Shopkeepers, artisans	10	11	8
White collar	5	3	1
Manual workers	5	6	1
Farmers	8	15	5
Other	2	5	6
Total	100	100	100
(Base)	(141)	(167)	(173)

Bracketed sub-totals (French):
- Maternal grandfather: Liberal professions + Public service = 28; Cadres supérieurs + Cadres moyens = 22; Shopkeepers + White collar + Manual workers + Farmers + Other = 30
- Paternal grandfather: Liberal professions + Public service = 20; Cadres supérieurs + Cadres moyens = 15; Shopkeepers + White collar + Manual workers + Farmers + Other = 40
- Father: Liberal professions + Public service = 22; Cadres supérieurs + Cadres moyens = 32; Shopkeepers + White collar + Manual workers + Farmers + Other = 21

British alumni

	Maternal grandfather	Paternal grandfather	Father
Business owners	4	10	17
Top managers	3	5	12
Independent professions	6	3	3
Higher professional	10	8	12
Administrative	12	8	11
Other managerial	4	2	15
Lower professional	4	5	7
Employers, proprietors	18	17	8
Routine non-manual	7	6	5
Skilled manual	22	24	6
Other manual	10	11	3
Other	0	0	1
Total	100	100	100
(Base)	(389)	(383)	(464)

Bracketed sub-totals (British):
- Maternal grandfather: Business owners + Top managers = 7; Independent professions + Higher professional + Administrative = 28; Lower professional + Employers + Routine non-manual + Skilled manual + Other manual + Other = 61
- Paternal grandfather: Business owners + Top managers = 15; Independent professions + Higher professional + Administrative = 19; Lower professional + Employers + Routine non-manual + Skilled manual + Other manual + Other = 63
- Father: Business owners + Top managers = 29; Independent professions + Higher professional + Administrative = 26; Lower professional + Employers + Routine non-manual + Skilled manual + Other manual + Other = 30

Table 5 (11)   Mobility of fathers of British alumni between socio-
professional groupings (percentages)

	Fathers				
Paternal grandfathers	*Owners*	*Professionals*	*Managers*	*Lowest*	*Total (Base)*
Owners, top managers	66	14	5	16	100 (58)
Professional, administrative	32	45	11	11	100 (71)
Managers, lowest group*	20	24	15	40	100 (254)

* As only 9 paternal grandfathers were classified as 'other managers', this group has been combined with those in the lowest grouping

owner, top manager, professional, or administrator. Nevertheless, there had been considerable socio-professional continuity over the generations (*Table* 5 (11)), the sons of the grandfathers in the top two groupings being very largely successful in reproducing their fathers' positions in the course of their own lives. Eighty per cent of the sons of business owners and top managers themselves entered this category or became professionals or administrators, as did 77 per cent of the sons of the latter groups. On the other hand, nearly half of the sons of the grandfathers in the lowest occupations managed to attain positions in the top two categories.

Looked at from another direction only about half (47 per cent) of the students' fathers who were in the top socio-professional groups had come from families in which *their* father had had the same status. In this sense, although a majority of the alumni were drawn from privileged families, this privileged position extended to the grand-fathers' generation in only a minority of cases. Thus in only a quarter of the cases had both the student's father *and* his father's father been located in one of the top two socio-professional groupings, which might suggest that, on the whole, the business schools do not attract the scions of the well established *haute bourgeoisie*.

The French grandfathers were more concentrated in high-level occupations than were the British. Nearly half of both the maternal and paternal grandfathers were clearly located in the upper classes. One in four of the paternal grandfathers had been *patrons*, as had one in five of the maternal ones, and similar proportions had been occupied in the liberal professions or the public service. There were also a few who had been *rentiers* or landowners. The numbers in the lower-level occupations were, concomitantly, rather fewer than for the British, manual workers in particular being very poorly represented. Only about 5 per cent of the French grandfathers had been manual workers, in comparison with over 30 per cent of the British.

In the case of the French, it is important to remember that students from the upper groupings were under-represented in the sample of respondents to the questionnaire when compared with the information available on the total sample obtained from the file analysis. The questionnaire data indicated that mobility from the bottom two to the top two socio-professional groupings had occurred less frequently than for the British (16 per cent), and assuming a similar rate for fathers in the total sample about a fifth of the fathers appear to have been intergenerationally mobile.

Like the British, the sons of the grandfathers in the top groupings had largely maintained the positions of their families (*Table* 5 (12)).

Table 5 (12)   Mobility of fathers of French alumni between socio-professional groupings (percentages)

	Fathers				
Paternal grandfathers	*Patrons*	*Liberal professions*	*Cadres moyens*	*Lowest*	*Total (Base)*
Patrons	51	19	28	2	100 (43)
Liberal professions	18	46	24	12	100 (33)
Cadres moyens	17	8	71	4	100 (24)
Lowest group	12	18	23	46	100 (65)

Seventy per cent of the sons of *patrons* themselves became *patrons* or entered the liberal professions, as did almost as many of the sons of the grandfathers who had been in the liberal professions. Thus two-thirds of the students' fathers who were in the top two groupings were sons of fathers who had been in the same types of occupation. Correcting for the under-representation of high-status fathers amongst the respondents, it is probable that 40 per cent of the alumni had been born into families in which both father and grandfather had followed high-level occupations, a much higher figure than for the British. Given the comparative rigidity of the French stratification system this is not, perhaps, surprising (Marceau 1977).

OCCUPATIONS OF THE WIDER FAMILY

There is evidence to suggest that having a number of well placed relatives in business can be of considerable importance to a business career, in very direct ways in obtaining jobs and also through privileged access to information about job opportunities (Granovetter 1974). The task of determining the extent of such social capital is by no means easy, and it is even harder to show that such privileged contacts are, or are likely to be, brought into play. We can, however, give some indication of the positions of the alumni by reference to the occupations of their relatives in the older generation. This provides a very general picture of the social capital which is at least potentially available to the graduates.

We have already shown that about half of the British graduates' fathers worked as business managers or ran their own businesses, leaving aside the 'small' employers and proprietors. If we now include other relatives in the older generation (i.e. other than siblings and cousins but including the grandparents), the percentage of alumni with at least one relation in management increases to 70 per cent. Both the owner/top manager and other manager groups do, of course, possess this minimal increment of capital by virtue of their fathers' occupations, but as well, nearly two-thirds of the professionals' sons have at least one relation in management who is not their father. By contrast, over two-thirds of those from lower origins did not have even one managerial relative.

A very similar picture emerges if occupations in the 'higher' professions are examined. Apart from the alumni whose fathers were professionals or administrators, over half of the sons of the owners and top managers had at least one older relation in this field, as did 38 per cent of the middle-managers' sons. In the case of the least endowed group, however, only one in five could count even one higher professional among his relatives. This group thus had few resources in the wider family that could compensate for the lack of capital held by the father.[5] Thus, although a quarter of all the alumni came from families where the father was a higher professional or an administrator, twice as many had at least one relation in the older generation who pursued this type of occupation.

Amongst the French alumni, the representation of the higher levels of business activity was noticeably high amongst wider kin, including both close male blood relatives and affines (sisters' husbands). While 8 per cent of brothers were *patrons*, a much higher proportion, nearly a third, were *cadres supérieurs* as were 42 per cent of sisters' husbands and between one in four and one in five of the uncles and male cousins. To these one should probably add some of the *cadres moyens* who were young at the time of the study and could be expected to rise in the course of their careers. Noticeably smaller proportions than in the earlier generations are shopkeepers or artisans or are in the liberal professions, the civil service, or the armed forces, and there seems to have occurred a movement of concentration towards business occupations over the generations considered.

As a result of such movements, the French families now seem to be concentrated in a relatively small number of occupations. On average, the working males in each extended family were engaged in only two to three occupational fields between them and several families had all their males in the same one (senior managers, liberal professions, etc.). By becoming concentrated in business they have cut themselves off from many close links through family members with other sectors of the economy, and in this as in other ways, the families concerned can probably be considered as occupying 'sub-elite' rather than elite positions.

EDUCATION OF THE WIDER FAMILY

An important component of an individual's initial quota of capital, in addition to that given to him by the socio-economic positions of his parents, is the degree of education that his parents have received. We do not know much about the education of the British grandparents, for the students were simply asked whether each of their grandfathers had attended a university. One in ten of the paternal grandfathers had done so and about one in eight of the maternal grandfathers. Such proportions, although not substantial in themselves, are very high in comparison with the general situation for that generation (Westergaard and Resler 1975 : 322).

Attendance at university by the paternal grandfather was closely related both to the type of occupational position he ultimately attained and to the type of education his own son received. The vast majority of the paternal grandfathers (and indeed the maternal ones) who had been to university ended their careers in one of the top two socio-professional groupings, mostly in professional or administrative occupations. However, having been to university was little correlated with the number of grandfathers who became business owners or top managers, whereas those who had been to university were seven times more often to be found in professional or administrative occupations as those who had not. This highlights the traditional independence of British business careers from high-level educational qualifications.

The paternal grandfathers who had been to university were much more successful in securing the best forms of education for their own sons. Eighty-five per cent of their sons went to a public or grammar school, and 70 per cent continued their education at university. Yet only 59 per cent of the sons of the less educated grandfathers attended public or grammar schools and only 18 per cent went on to university.

Overall, more than a quarter of the students' fathers had received their secondary education at a public school, and a further third had been to a grammar school. Two-thirds of the fathers had therefore had what, in their day in particular, was an especially scarce advantage (Westergaard and Resler 1975 : 320).

Nearly 90 per cent of the fathers who had been to a public school had sent their sons to one, as had more than half the fathers who had been educated at a grammar school. Although the minority who had attended an elementary school had generally secured a better education for their sons than their own, this usually took the form of grammar school. These fathers had much less often been able to raise their sons into the public-school sector.

The proportion of fathers who had attended university was also high in comparison with the adult population as a whole (Westergaard and Resler 1975 : 322). Just over a quarter of the fathers had been to university, a further 10 per cent having continued their education at a non-university institution. Taking the relations of the alumni in the older generation as a whole we find that nearly 60 per cent had at least one relation with an education of this kind. However, it was those whose fathers were in the higher occupations who were most likely to have access to a fairly well-educated relative, for almost twice as many of those with fathers in the bottom two groupings had no relation with a high-level education as did those with fathers in the top two groupings. Thus, those from lower origins were both least likely to have had an older relation in a managerial or professional occupation and least likely to have even one relative with previous experience of advanced education.

In the case of the French, a very high proportion of the grandfathers, fathers, and other male relatives had themselves received higher education whether in a university or a *grande école*. Almost three-quarters of the fathers for whom we have information had had higher education, as had 63 per cent and 71 per cent of the paternal and maternal grandfathers and 80 per cent of the uncles. These proportions are very high when compared with the education of the older generations as a whole.

The male kin had not only usually received higher education but also had often attended the best institutions. Among the fathers, for example, a quarter had been trained as engineers, and most of these had been to one of the top Parisian schools. Rather fewer of the older generations had been to commercial schools in comparison with the alumni, and overall, it was the universities that had been attended most frequently. Between a third and a half of the male kin had been educated in university faculties and a large proportion had received a degree, though not necessarily their first degree, from a faculty abroad. They were on the whole even more likely to have been abroad than to have gone to a faculty in Paris, and the provincial universities had trained hardly any of the INSEAD graduates' relations.

On the whole, the French alumni were drawn from well educated families, and in at least half the cases, had both a father and grandfather who had received a higher education. Such a background helps to distinguish them even more strongly from the bulk of their contemporaries.

Summary

The backgrounds of the graduates of both INSEAD and the British business schools show them, on the whole, to be highly unrepresentative of the members of British and French society. In each country, the majority of the alumni have been drawn from families that are well endowed socially, educationally, and economically, and have been well placed to take advantage of the educational privileges that each country's educational system has made available. The fact that, for example, over half of the British alumni had received their secondary education at one of the two hundred or so public schools is a sharp reminder of the continuing significance of these institutions.

Despite the high origins of the graduates, the evidence we have on the occupations of the fathers and the occupations of other members of their families suggests that only a vew few of the MBAs could be regarded as scions of elites. The graduates were, on the whole, drawn from well placed families, but not from those with wide-ranging kinship connections within elite strata. Indeed very few of the fathers could be considered as members of an elite. In the case of Britain, we suspect that this reflects the continued marginality of high-level qualifications for rapid progress in a business career, those 'in the know' perhaps knowing better than to spend two years at a business school.

In this chapter we have simply reported our observations of the results of the process which brings young graduates to business school. As yet we have not considered how these results occur. To do this it is necessary to examine both the effects of the schools' selection procedures and the circumstances that have motivated the students to attend, and in doing this we will give the MBAs a chance to speak for themselves.

6 Entry to business school: selection, motivations, and ambitions

The social origins of the business school students show them to have been drawn, on the whole, from the more privileged sectors of British and French society. The processes by which this composition of the schools' student populations has developed are important for they shed light on the means of maintaining privilege in an overtly open system in which everyone has a 'fair' chance.

Attendance at business school is, of course, voluntary and the characteristics of the student bodies are determined by both the activities of the schools and the ambitions and motivations of the potential students. Most directly, the schools' selection policies and practices effectively delineate the attendants and determine who will, and will not, have the opportunity to obtain an MBA. More indirectly, the nature of these decisions serve more or less effectively to communicate to those who might apply an image of the sort of person who is thought suitable.[1] Together with the picture the schools present of themselves through their publicity material, disseminated through the most 'profitable' channels, the pool of applicants is given boundaries even before the explicit process of selection begins. On the other hand, the decisions of those who are in principle eligible to attend must also be taken into account, involving as they do evaluations of the opportunity-cost of attendance. These calculations are influenced both by the individual's socially determined aspirations and by his or her assessment of the career possibilities available and their likelihood of 'paying off'. In turn, these possibilities are determined by the operations of career systems that are subject to macro-level influences, such as changes within business organizations in the degree of favour afforded to particular types of experience and/or educational quali- fication in the struggle for advancement. The interaction of factors of this kind serve to determine the objective characteristics of the business schools' student bodies. It is therefore important to examine the ways in which the schools have affected the constitution of their student bodies through selection policies and practices, the ways in which they have been drawn to the attention of different social groups, and the motives of those who have succeeded in gaining admittance.

Selection policies of the British Schools

The ambiguous position of the business schools in relation to the academic and business worlds is well expressed in their selection policies for the post-graduate courses. Although there has been some variation over the years, these policies have usually tried to define the entrance requirements in such a way as to meet both the universities' demands for academic excellence and those of business for more pragmatic qualities summed up in the phrase 'management potential'.

At both schools a basic requirement has been the possession of a first degree (preferably of 'good' honours standard) or an equivalent professional qualification, and in practice the vast majority of the entrants have been graduates. Academic criteria have, however, been supplemented by the use of those related to business. Most students are expected to have had some years of work experience, though not necessarily in business, and applicants must take an admissions test (the 'Princeton Test') to demonstrate their business aptitude. This test originates from the United States where it is widely used as a screening device for those who wish to pursue business studies.

These indicators of academic and business ability have not been rigidly interpreted by the schools. A good showing in terms of degree result, for example, may be taken to outweigh a poor one on the admissions test and vice versa. Maintaining a balance between these has not always proved easy, as was demonstrated when the London school shifted the emphasis of its selection criteria more towards business in the early 1970s. Partly in response to the Own Report's criticism that business schools paid too much attention to academic qualifications and not enough to managerial ability, LBS looked more for the latter amongst applicants and less for high degree grades. This attempt to be more 'market orientated' tended, however, to bring the school more frequently into conflict with the University which questioned proposals for admissions that did not seem to place a premium on academic ability.

The schools have increasingly used face-to-face selection methods, which enable some assessment of personal qualities thought difficult to discern otherwise. Interviews are held with those who survive an initial weeding out process which pays attention to career inclinations and 'managerial potential' as well as to the candidates' intellectual abilities. A one-day selection conference has also been used at Manchester for some years, during which an observed group discussion is held. Applicants are given an unseen topic to debate and are expected to display their social and group skills. It is also worth noting that both schools show an interest in the candidates' social backgrounds. At Manchester they are asked at the interviews about their fathers' occupations, whilst at London the application form includes a question which requests details of 'father's business'.

INSEAD's selection policies

By the standards of many academic institutions offering post-graduate courses, the entry requirements to INSEAD have always been notably high. The details of selection policies and methods of selecting candidates to the PGP have varied somewhat over the years, but the main lines have remained the same. In general, successful applicants to INSEAD must hold university degrees or equivalent professional qualifications. Students should be between twenty-four and thirty years of age, have at least one or two years of professional experience in a business or other organization, and have fulfilled their military obligations. Some exceptions to the graduate rule were made, however, provided candidates had at least five years of professional experience. From 1959 to the mid 1960s, candidates were not required to have completed their national service obligations, nor was professional experience necessary, although many students did have this. When these requirements became mandatory, the average age of the students rose, and by the late 1970s many of the recent students had five to ten years professional experience. In 1970–71, selection procedures became more demanding because of the additional requirement of a good score in the 'Princeton Test'.

The language requirements of INSEAD have always been extremely tough. Until 1973, tested fluency (written) in all three of the Institute's official languages – English, French, and German – was an entrance requirement. In 1973, after much argument within the school, German was made a leaving, rather than an entrance, requirement because it was felt that candidates from many European countries and outside who were potential students were, in effect, being asked to be quadrilingual and that this was perhaps unreasonable. It is notable, and this distinguishes INSEAD's students markedly from those at London and Manchester, that at least half of 1977–78 class were fluent in or had a good working knowledge of all three official languages. There was also thought to be a significant number competent in four or more and, as an INSEAD report pointed out, 'the language skills of INSEAD graduates are impressive by any standards and have always been one of their distinctive and valuable assets'.

Each candidate filled in a long and detailed application form (virtually identical to the Harvard Business School form), giving family, educational, and employment background information as well as career aspirations. Even more important the candidate was invited to write an assessment of his or her own major personal strengths and weaknesses (of both intellect and character) and to describe two events in his or her life, outside work or education, that had been of particularly great significance to the development of his or her personal maturity.

This form of selection represented an effort by the school to assess the potential of the 'whole man'. Thus, while intellectual capacities as evidenced by educational qualifications obtained were important, they were only one element. An attempt was made to form qualitative judgements about the 'management calibre' or 'leadership' potential of the candidates. Attention was paid to evidence that the candidate had been active in student societies, especially those involving the organization of fellows and fund-raising. During the interviews, attempts were also made to assess the degree of student motivation for INSEAD by reference to some expressible, if not detailed, career plan. By this battery of complementary methods of assessment of a candidate's suitability for an academic preparation for a career in business, INSEAD attempted to reconcile the demands of the academic postgraduate degree and the realities of the demands of business careers.

The effects of selection

THE BRITISH SCHOOLS

Because the MBA courses offered by the business schools are both post-graduate courses and ones that prepare students for careers in management, the pool of potential applicants consists predominantly of graduates who have already begun careers in business or who have the intention of doing so.

This pool is likely to reflect the social biases that are present in graduate population as a whole and, if no other factors were influential, we might expect about a quarter of the applicants to have been the sons of manual workers. However, within the graduate population the type of career selected is itself related to social origins (Kelsall et al. 1974) those from high-status backgrounds being most likely to aspire to careers in administration, management, and the established professions. We would therefore expect the backgrounds of graduates who had entered business to be biased further in the direction of those from high origins. These differential preferences for managerial careers, together with the differential chances of realizing such aspirations, serve to reduce the representation of those from lower origins among graduate managers to a level below that found for graduates as a whole. Some indication of the likely composition of the pool of potential applicants to the business schools can be obtained from the data reported by Kelsall, which showed that for those male graduates in 'general management'[2] six years after graduation, 19 per cent were sons of manual workers and 56 per cent sons of those in professional or 'intermediate' occupations.

To assess the effects of selection for entry to the British schools, data on the characteristics of successful applicants were compared with those of rejectees. Information was collected for three years' applications at each school only, less information being available for Manchester than for London. In particular, the occupations of the fathers of rejected applicants to MBS are not known; unlike London, this information is not sought on the application form. *Table* 6 (1) and *Table* 6 (2) compare successful and unsuccessful applicants with the graduate population in terms of socio–professional origins (LBS only) and secondary and higher education. The comparison in terms of socio–professional origins is fairly crude because of the different classification systems used, but the relatively strong attraction of business schools for graduates from managerial and administrative backgrounds is apparent. Although comprising about a sixth of all

Table 6 (1)   Socio-professional origins of university graduates, applicants, and entrants to LBS (percentages)

	Adminis-trative, managerial	Profes-sional, technical	Clerical, sales	Manual, agri-cultural
Fathers of university entrants, 1968*	14	30	28	28
Fathers of applicants to LBS, 1969, 1971, 1973	51	23	13	14
Fathers of entrants to LBS, 1969, 1971, 1973	52	25	12	11

* For notes on source, see *Table* 5 (2)

graduates, they consistuted half of the applicants to LBS in the selected years. Graduates from professional backgrounds, on the other hand, were under-represented amongst applicants, probably because of the greater likelihood of their pursuing professional careers, as were those in the clerical and manual working groups. The latter are particularly likely to take up teaching careers (Kelsall, Poole, and Kuhn 1974). Although the clerical and manual groups may enter industry or commerce just as frequently as those from higher origins, they seem less often to obtain managerial positions, perhaps preferring, and being preferred for, more highly specialized technical and scientific jobs. Thus the pool of applicants, although skewed in the direction of the

Table 6 (2)   Type of school attended and institution of first degree of university students, applicants and entrants to LBS/MBS (percentages)

	Independent school	Oxford or Cambridge
University students 1974	16[1]	10[2]
Aplicants to LBS, 1969, 1971, 1973; MBS 1971, 1973, 1975	43	25
Entrants to LBS/MBS (years as for applicants)	53	39

[1] Adapted from Table C1, *UCCA Statistical Supplement to the Twelfth Report, 1973–74*, p. 9. Figure refers to accepted male home candidates, England and Wales.
[2] Adapted from Table 7, DES, *Statistics of Education*, Vol. 6, 1974. Figure refers to full time students at undergraduate level, England and Wales.

upper groups when compared with graduates as a whole, probably broadly reflects the social and educational composition of graduates in management.

A comparison of the educational backgrounds of graduates in general and applicants shows a considerable increase among the latter in the proportion having attended an independent school (i.e. a fee-paying school, whether a member of the HMC or not). Similarly, Oxbridge graduates are over-represented amongst those who apply. This is of course commensurate with the differences between the composition of the graduate population and the applicants in terms of social origins. It is, however, very difficult to know the extent to which these educational characteristics have been important influences on the decision to apply for graduates who choose managerial careers.

Turning to the characteristics of those who were admitted as against those who were not, the schools' selection had little effect on the chances of entry for those from different socio-professional origins, for although the lowest group did least well in this respect, on the whole each group was represented broadly in accordance with its contribution to the applications pool. The predominance of those from high social origins at the schools seems, therefore, to have been more a function of pre-selection than of school selection. The strongest influence on the chances of entry was the applicant's score on the admissions test (Princeton Test) which, together with the extent of previous work experience, accounts for a high proportion of the selection decisions, neither of these attributes being significantly related to social origins.

The type of school and university attended was, however, an important influence on the chances of entry. Fifty-five per cent of applicants from independent schools were admitted but only 35 per cent of those who had not received this type of education. Similarly, over two-thirds of graduates from Oxford or Cambridge were accepted but only one-third of those who were not. An educational background of this kind seems to have been particularly important for those from the lowest social origins. Of the members of this group who had been to Oxford or Cambridge, for example, three-quarters were admitted in comparison with two-thirds of those from higher origins. It is difficult to explain why this should be so, because of the interrelations between characteristics such as work experience, Princeton Test score, type of school attended, and type of university, each of which had a significant relationship with successful or unsuccessful application. It would seem that, overall, the importance of 'academic' attributes for entry served to equalize the chances of entry for those from different social origins, leaving relatively little room for differences in personality which might be assessed in terms of 'management potential' to take effect.

FRANCE

The social origins of the French alumni were, as we have seen, much higher than even those of the *grandes écoles* graduates. The direct effect of INSEAD's selection process was, however, rather similar to that of the British schools, in that the origins of those selected showed little difference from those of the unsuccessful applicants.

Table 6 (3)   Socio-professional origins of accepted and rejected INSEAD applicants (selected years: percentages)

	Patrons	Liberal professions	Cadres moyens	Clerical, manual	Total
Accepted	54	52	43	49	50
Rejected	46	48	57	51	50
(Base)	(251)	(182)	(211)	(118)	(762)

As *Table* 6 (3) shows, the sons of the *patrons* were most successful in gaining admission, those from the liberal professions and *cadres supérieurs publics* almost equally so, but the differences between the four groups are not very substantial.

The type of higher education received (commercial, engineering, etc.) had little effect on the chances of admission, although the type of higher education institution attended did. Graduates of *grandes écoles* were four times as likely to be admitted as graduates of the faculties, and those who had attended the most prestigious *grandes écoles* were more successful in securing a place than those who had not. The pre-eminent position of the École Polytechnique is reflected in the fact that not one of the *polytechniciens* who applied to INSEAD failed to secure a place. By comparison only 61 per cent of those who graduated from other prestigious Parisian *écoles* were admitted and 56 per cent of those from lesser French or foreign institutions. Similarly, 69 per cent of the graduates of the top Parisian commercial schools and 62 per cent of those from provincial Écoles Supérieurs de Commerce ('Sup. de Co.') were admitted, but only 38 per cent of those from 'Sciences Po'. Work experience and the possession of foreign language skills were crucially important influences on the chances of selection, and in practice almost entirely reflected the Institute's formal demands.

Overall, the selection policies and practices of all three schools had relatively little effect on the social compositions of their student bodies. Rather, the characteristics of the student bodies are determined as a result of a lengthy process in which the decisions of the schools are but the last stage. Previous education and career orientation serve effectively to structure the pool of applicants so that the schools choose from a group which is already highly skewed in terms of social origin, and thus unavoidably acquire a student body similarly skewed.

The student's decision to attend business school

Although the decisions of the schools play a critical role in determining who attends, there are a number of decisions that the potential business graduate must himself take if he is to stand a chance of entry. He must, of course, know of the existence of business schools, and, in particular, he must learn of them early enough to enable him to take on the costs of attendance, which generally increase with age, and to obtain full value from the benefits. He must have some idea of what an MBA can do for him and be able to relate this to his aspirations, and to his expectations of their realization, in such a way that attendance at business school is seen to be worthwhile. In all this, social background plays an important role, as can be seen in relation to those who succeeded in entering the schools.

Hearing of the schools

Age on entry to INSEAD and to the British schools varied consistently with social origins. At each school the sons of the upper groups were younger, and this is linked to the ways in which they heard about the schools. *Patronat* sons and those of top managers have grown up in a business milieu, hearing talk of business from their earliest days. They learn about business education opportunities first and take advantage of them earlier than those from other backgrounds.

In France, the essential mechanism for the sons of the *patronat* and *cadres supérieurs* is the 'grapevine', the network of personal sources of information from members of the family, classmates, and ex-students of the Institute who are often also family members and friends. The students from the upper groups in business were considerably more likely to have this kind of privileged access to new and useful information than were the others, who had to rely much more on formal means of communication such as newspapers, brochures, notices, and talks by INSEAD staff members.

Hearing of the Institute early seems also to be associated with entering it younger, and more quickly. Analysing the number of years elapsing between students' first hearing of INSEAD and entry to the course shows that nearly half the *patronat* sons went to INSEAD within one year of 'realizing' its existence, whereas less than a third of sons from other backgrounds did so.

Family influences also affect the decision to attend. Nearly a quarter of the sons of business owners and top managers were advised by their families to attend INSEAD, whereas virtually none of the others had that kind of advice. Privileged access to information and the importance of family advice accentuate the advantage of belonging to a business family. Younger entrance to a business school such as INSEAD means that the advantages of having an MBA can be obtained earlier and therefore less time is wasted on an 'unsuitable' or 'dead end' career.

Of the British alumni, about half first heard about business schools while they were at university and a further third first heard about them later while they were working. However, 10 per cent first heard about them when they were at school, and these were heavily concentrated in the business owners and top managers group. Members of this group had in general heard of and applied to business schools earliest, followed by the middle managers group, and then the professional/administrative group. The lowest socio-professional group both heard about and applied to business schools latest of all, only 5 per cent having heard at school whilst 38 per cent had learned of business schools only during their work years. This indicates that just as at INSEAD, the British students with business backgrounds, and especially those whose fathers were in top positions in business, benefited from an earlier awareness of the schools than the others and had a better opportunity of integrating attendance into a career plan.

The means by which the British students heard about business schools also varied in a similar way to the French at INSEAD. Almost two-thirds of the business owners' and top managers' sons heard about business schools from 'personal' sources, such as parents, relations and friends, rather than from more 'institutional' ones, such as notices and talks, the latter being most frequently used by the least endowed group.

The influence of parents on the decision to apply to INSEAD particularly for the sons of the *patronat*, does not appear quite so markedly in the case of the British students, but the same trends are apparent. Only 12 per cent of the British indicated that their parents had influenced their decision to apply to business school. In the top business group, however, this percentage was doubled and was also markedly higher for the professional/administrative group than for the rest. Both these high-status groups were particularly conscious of the need for their sons to acquire additional cultural capital if their positions were to be maintained or improved. The lesser importance of parental influence for the British as compared to the French probably reflects the traditionally weaker links in Britain between higher education and success in business careers.

Many students had considered several business schools before making their choices. Those who had done so perceived a hierarchy of schools, with American institutions, and Harvard in particular, being seen as particularly prestigious and particularly likely to give valuable experience. Knowledge of this hierarchy again varied with social origins, the business groups, and in particular the top business group, having been most likely to have considered applying to foreign schools and actually to have done so. It is not clear why those who applied to schools abroad did not go to them, but the students frequently mentioned financial problems, even in the case of the top groups. Although this may in some cases simply disguise a failure to obtain a place, it would confirm the view that, even though they come from high origins, these students are not the highest of the high. It is interesting that the sons of business owners were particularly likely to have applied to foreign schools but were also particularly likely to have mentioned financial problems, perhaps explained by the problematic personal relations which often exist between business owners and their sons, several examples of which were vividly described to us in the course of interviews with the students.

Motivations

Knowledge of business schools is not, of course, sufficient in itself to lead to a decision to apply to business school. To understand why the students wanted to attend it is necessary to look more closely at their biographies to see how their social circumstances, their educational histories, and their work experiences interlock in such a way as to make attendance seem worthwhile. To obtain detailed information on the students' perceptions of their past and future careers and the circumstances that led them to attend business school, a lengthy series of interviews was conducted with students still at the schools at the time of the study. At INSEAD, the interviews covered one year's intake whilst two cohorts were interviewed at each of the British schools, a very high coverage being obtained throughout.

MOTIVATIONAL PATTERNS OF THE BRITISH STUDENTS

To summarize the reasons given by students for wanting to attend business school, five motivational categories were devised. Each student's reasons were coded into as many of these categories as were applicable, and where a single type of motivation seemed predominant each case was also allocated to one of the five categories. Such a procedure is fraught with difficulties; in a fifth of the cases the reasons given fell outside the five categories, and for almost half it was impossible to confidently assign a predominant motivation but some broad comparisons can be made. The five types of motivation were: transitional, accelerational, clarificational, compensatory, and family business entry.

Transitional motives were expressed by students who had entered business before attending business school and who had encountered, or anticipated encountering, blockages in their careers. They often referred to these in terms of barriers within firms between specialist, technical positions and managerial positions that prevented them from 'getting on'. For them, attendance at business school was seen as a way of making a transition from specialist to manager, and hence from an unpropitious career path to one that would lead to higher and better things. One student, for example, had left university with a science PhD to run a research team in a mining company. He had soon become dissatisfied with his prospects.

'It was a very specialist post. We were promised management development but no-one got out of the laboratory without leaving the firm. I decided I must leave so as to develop my potential. I looked for jobs elsewhere which were outside research, but people wanted to employ me in my old capacity. The PhD worked against me and at interviews they saw my main future in the lab., and couldn't guarantee a training for general management. So I thought I would have to retrain and began thinking about business school. I wanted to make the transition from specialist to generalist because there was a sense of frustration with my specialism and a contraction in research work.'

Those with accelerational motives were more concerned with speeding their passage along a path that already seemed satisfactory. For them, the importance of business school was less in terms of getting on to the 'right' track than of going faster along the track they were already on. They saw the MBA as helping them to 'short-circuit the system' or 'jump several rungs up the ladder'. The following is a typical example of what these students said.

> 'I came to business school because I wanted an accelerated leap into management rather than having to wade through six or seven years of managerial experience. I also want a highly increased salary and status in the organization and among my peer group.'

Another said:

> 'I could either climb up a company or go to business school and start at a higher level earlier. The MBA will help me to get where I'm going quicker. I want to be in a big organization somewhere near the top eventually. The MBA will open doors more quickly and get me to a higher level faster.'

Clarificational motives were those that stressed the importance of business schools for providing a broad understanding of the business world and the possible role of the student within it. Those expressing this type of motivation frequently entered the schools without work experience or with work experience in a non-business field.

Being at business school was essentially a prelude to a business career, rather than a means of solving problems that had arisen within a business career. These students were often occupationally 'lost' and hoped to find themselves during the course of their business school studies.

> 'I didn't like the idea of being a public servant or working for a local authority. I thought I might do a higher degree, and I'd already done an optional course in management in case I wanted to go into town planning. I didn't really consider going straight into work. I got the idea of going to business school and was washed along by it and that's how I ended up here.'

> 'The idea of earning a lot of money in business appeals to me, though I hate to admit it. I don't really know what I want to do, I want to keep my options open. I've no idea at all at the moment about my career. In fact it has become less clear since I've been here. I can't say much more about my long term ambitions – I wish I could.'

> 'The most valuable thing I will get out of business school is purely and simply the qualification. That's probably *the* most valuable thing. I don't know why exactly as I'm not sure what I will do with it, but I'm certain it will be valuable eventually.'

For those with compensatory motives, the overriding attraction of business school was its status as a university institution offering the chance of obtaining a degree, and so making up for some perceived deficiency in their educational biographies. Although only seven students were classified as having predominantly compensatory motives, these reasons were mentioned overall by about 10 per cent, scattered across the main social groupings. Such students had typically not taken first degrees at universities, having attended polytechnics or taken accountancy articles, and they mentioned how they felt they had 'missed out' by not going to university, referring to their need to be 'stretched', to test themselves and to prove themselves academically. At the extreme, career ambitions were subordinated to the academic attractions of business school. One student turned down what he regarded as a very attractive job to take up a business school place, to compensate for what he felt had been his second-rate experience at a secondary modern school and polytechnic.

'I felt I'd been on the scrap heap after A-levels and I didn't want to be in that position again. My choices had always been blind. When I was offered a place at business school I thought, "I have always had second best in schools and university but now I have got to the top in at least one thing".'

The final motivational category, family business entry, is self-explanatory in that this referred to those from family business backgrounds who saw attendance at business school as a way of equipping themselves to take over the family firm. Of these there were very few. Almost two-thirds of the main motives given were transitional or accelerational, and even where no main motive could be attributed, these types of motivation occurred very frequently. Thus a significant proportion of the students saw the need for business school in terms of a desire to 'get on'.

The three main types of motivation – transitional, accelerational, and clarificational – were closely related to the extent of the students' previous work experience. Transitional reasons were more likely to be given as the students' length of work experience increased, with three-quarters of those who had had at least five years' experience offering these sorts of reasons. This suggests that the longer a person worked the more likely he was to become aware of the limitations for advancement from his existing career path. Accelerational reasons were more likely to be given by the younger and less experienced who had not, as yet, had time to encounter serious obstacles to their progress. Neither transitional nor accelerational reasons were cited by

students without any work experience. As might be expected, clarificational reasons were given predominantly by those without previous
experience, although there were a number who had worked before
business school, usually outside the business field.

Career ambitions

The students' career ambitions were often closely intertwined with
their motivations to attend business school, since the majority saw the
schools as providing solutions to career problems. Frequently, however, the immediate impetus to attendance arose from the student's
current work situation and the reasons given did not always refer to
longer-term aspirations. Students were therefore asked not only about
their reasons for going to business school but also about their 'ultimate'
career ambitions, that is, the sort of position and size of firm in which
they wanted to be in the long term. The results of this inquiry are
summarized in *Table* 6 (4).

Table 6 (4)   Ultimate career ambitions of the British students
(percentages)

Top management, large firm	17 ⎤
Top management, small/medium firm	21 ⎬ 48
Top management, no size given	10 ⎦
Middle management	6
Running own firm	29
Other	7
Don't know	29
(Base)	(204)

Percentages do not total 100 due to multi-coding

Slightly less than half of the students gave their long-term career
ambitions as 'the top', 'top management', 'board level', 'managing
director', or similar, and less than a fifth specifically mentioned a large
firm in this context. Relatively few of the students seemed to be aiming
deliberately for positions at elite level, at least in terms of the industrial
sector. It is possible that those mentioning small to medium-sized firms
were thinking mainly in terms of financial institutions, but, even then,
only a third of the students could be said to be aiming for elite entry in

the industrial and financial sectors together. The single most frequently mentioned option was 'running my own firm', and although the business owners' sons found this a particularly attractive possibility, it was often mentioned by students whatever their social background. On the whole the students could be said to be fairly ambitious, in the sense of wanting to get to the top, but often seeking to realize these ambitions either in smaller firms or in their own businesses (Hughes 1977; Willig 1970). Some, however, had very high aims indeed, as in the case of the student who declared himself to be a future Chancellor of the Exchequer!

The following statements of career ambitions were fairly typical.

'If I was going to work for my last firm [a giant nationalized industry] I could say exactly – director level. But I can't say really. Something nice in an industrial company at director level. I would prefer a small to medium-size organization. Most people here would say that. They have mostly experienced large organizations. But I wouldn't really mind . . . I have tried a large organization and survived.'

'Managing director of a small to medium-sized firm within five years. I'm unsure of the long term because I want to be a managing director fairly early. I don't much want such a position in a large firm as it offers very few advantages over the small.'

'Either be in a large firm working my way up through it, or having a firm of my own. That would be an achievement, I think, having employees. It's the idea of not working for anyone myself but having people working for me.'

'At a fairly senior level fairly quickly or else the investment of coming here, which is considerable, isn't worth it. It must be a small company. That's where my interests lie and where I'd have the best chance.'

'The higher the better. I want to be the driver of the industrial car, not the engineer.'

'As far as I can go without collapsing and ending up in an asylum.'

Too much weight should not, of course, be given to these statements because the students were often tentative about their ambitions, and it would be surprising if they did not change subsequently. Nevertheless, they do give some clues to their career intentions at this early stage of their work histories, and show them to be, on the whole, an ambitious group.

Information on the students' career ambitions was generally collected from the interviewees at the time of their arrival at business school, and does not, therefore, take into account the effect of the experience of being at the schools. For one year's entry, however, students were interviewed both at the time of entry and again just before they left, which enables some estimate to be made of the impact of having been at the schools.

Although the number involved in this analysis is rather small (n=41), some tentative conclusions can be drawn. The proportion willing to declare their long-term ambitions increased after business school, as one might expect, although a quarter still said they did not know. The proportion mentioning the 'top' rose by a quarter, and the number saying the top in a large firm doubled. Thus the levels of ambition that have been identified at the start of the students' time at business school may be taken as underestimates of the position at the time of leaving. It seems reasonable, however, to suppose that on leaving only a minority have their sights set firmly on the highest positions in the largest firms.

Social origins, motivations, and ambitions

Before looking at the motivations of the different social groups, it is necessary to take into account any differences in the extent of work experience and concomitantly age, because of the close relation this has with the students' motives for attending business schools. Amongst the British interviewees, a fifth had not worked before business school, with little variation across the social groups other than in the case of the business owners and top managers. This group was a little more likely to have worked before business school (84 per cent compared to 77 per cent for the other groups) although the average length of experience was lower (3.7 years as against 4.3 years) which reflects the tendency for owners' sons to spend short periods in the family firm before leaving for business school. The three other main groups were very similar to each other in terms of length of experience. Those whose fathers were in clerical or manual occupations were least likely to have worked before business school (70 per cent worked) but had the longest average length of experience if they had done so (4.6 years). In general, however, the extent of previous experience is similar for the four social groups, so any variations in the predominant patterns of motivation cannot be wholly attributed to this factor.

SONS OF BUSINESS OWNERS AND TOP MANAGERS

Business owners' sons

Because of the importance of sons of *patrons* at INSEAD and the rather special position in which the sons of business owners find themselves, we treat the British business owners' sons as a distinct group.

There were thirty owners' children (including two daughters) among the 204 British interviewees, a very similar proportion to that found for the alumni. Nineteen of these were attributed a 'main' motivation of whom two-thirds were regarded as transitionals or accelerators, which is similar to the situation for the students as a whole.

Only three of the business owners' children mentioned possible entry to the family firm as the main reason for attending, with another two mentioning it as a subsidiary factor. Rather, these students tended to see business school as a way of escaping from the family firm to bigger and better things, particularly if they had themselves worked in the family business. One student, who had spent two years as managing director of his father's manufacturing company, said:

> 'I want to open up opportunities for myself outside the family business. I want extra security in an uncertain economic climate, something to fall back on rather than depend on the continued existence of the family business. I've definitely not come to qualify myself better to run the family's firm – if anything it's because it will help me to keep my options open to get away from it.'

Another said:

> 'To move into a non-family, larger organization it's useful to have a better grounding in more areas. I want to leave the family business and go into wider industry. There are conflicts within the family firm and the problem of not being able to do your own thing.'

Because those who had worked in their family's firm had often done so at a high level (they were frequently company directors), they tended to have high aspirations, but recognized the limited value of their experience for rapid advancement outside the family business.

> 'Working in the family business has given me experience of the small firm, but business school can provide a knowledge of the business world in general. The MBA will enable me to work for large companies with a degree of competence I wouldn't otherwise have had. It will give me the ability to get on, because my current

background is in small business. In the immediate future I want to be in general management in a large firm. I want the sort of decision-making control in a large firm that I've already had in a small one. I'm ambitious and I want promotion as fast as possible. I think it's unlikely that I will return to the family firm.'

In four cases the father no longer owned the family firm, so that pursuing a career in it was not an option, but for the rest, two frequently mentioned reasons for discounting this possibility were 'family frictions' and 'lack of scope' in the family business. When asked why he did not intend to pursue his career in the family firm, one student said: 'To preserve family relations. It doesn't work to work for a member of the family.'

Students often mentioned the lack of independence they felt in the family business and the need to 'make it on one's own' rather than building on what father (or sometimes grandfather) had already created. This attitude was clearly reflected in their career ambitions, as almost half of the business owners' children stated that having their own business was their ultimate goal, which is twice the proportion of the other students. Their ambitions outside the field of business ownership were also high, as over half said they wanted to be 'at the top' although only three students expressed a preference for a 'large' firm. In general the owners' children saw their career goals in terms which were related to their family background – at 'the top' in a small to medium-sized firm or their own company. In this sense, attendance at business school can be seen as helping many of the business owners' children to reproduce, in a very direct manner, their fathers' positions as owners of *their own* business or as controllers of firms of similar standing.

Top managers' sons

The motivations of the top managers' sons were generally similar to those of the business owners' children, with the obvious exception of the irrelevance of a family business as a career influence. Nearly two-thirds of them gave transitional or accelerational reasons for attending business school, whilst a further quarter had clarificational motives.

Their career ambitions were generally high. Over half of those who could give long-term career goals mentioned the 'top' – board level, managing director, or senior management – slightly more than for the business owners' children because of the latter's preference for starting their own firm. However, relatively few students said they were aiming for the top of a large firm, the largest group (30 per cent) specifying a 'small or medium-sized organization'. The desire to reach the top was expressed by one student like this:

'I want to get into senior line management, and I want to get there as quickly as possible. If I wasn't progressing fast enough through the organization there would be a lot of frustration. This might lead me to start a company of my own. How fast I progress is the principal factor in my ambitions so the size of the company isn't so important to me.'

Another said:

'I'd like to be at the top. I'd like to have succeeded in my career, to have progressed at varying rates, but to have progressed. I wouldn't like to have to take any sideways or backwards steps. I think I am fairly ambitious, inasmuch as when I am moving in one direction I like to keep going forward. I did think before I came here that I would go into a large organization because you'd be very much away from the muck and brass of it and could get into an office environment where you could really get to grips with the theory and out of the practicalities of the system and get away from the dirt, sort of thing. But I don't really think you can get away from it, so it doesn't really matter all that much which you do.'

The sons of professionals and administrators

Like the sons of the business owners and top managers, those of higher professionals and administrators gave transitional or accelerational reasons in over half the cases that could be classified. However, almost twice as many (43 per cent) of these students had clarificational motives as any of the other social groups. This was despite the fact that they were just as likely to have worked before business school as the middle managers' sons and the least endowed group, and had the same average length of experience as the others.

The explanation for this can be found in the type of work experience these students had had before business school, for they were almost twice as likely to have been working in professional services as the sons of the business groups and seven times more likely than the sons of the least endowed. They had also had less stable work experience before business school, with nearly half having changed 'industrial' sector between their first employment and their last employment before entry, whereas only about a fifth of the other students had done so. Nearly a third had begun their careers in the professional services and the same number were in this field at the time of entering business school, although half of these had moved into this field from other sectors.

This group, therefore, contained a greater proportion of those who, although having worked, were not working in business immediately before going to business school. These students seemed principally to have been oriented to 'professional' careers but had come to realize that they would not get on fast enough in their present fields. In general the professional/administrative sons were more uncertain of their business ambitions as the following case illustrates:

Mr Jones   The son of a senior civil servant, Mr Jones attended grammar school and took an upper second in science at a large redbrick university. Like many of his fellows he had no ideas about careers while at school. 'I didn't even think about it. I assumed I was going to university and that was it.' Even in his final year at university he was unclear about careers:

> 'Until December of my final year I gave no thought to it. Even then I was lost and confused. I went around randomly pulling out brochures. I wanted to travel but that was all. I quite enjoyed my subject so I thought I would do a PhD, but I applied to about fifteen firms for a bizarre assortment of jobs from personnel to research. I also applied to business school, both London and Manchester, but I was rejected by both. A friend of the family had done an economics degree and tried to persuade me to go to an American business school, but I wasn't strongly motivated. I had offers to do a PhD but I was thinking about a business career. Of the fifteen firms I applied to only one offered a job.'

Mr Jones took this job as a research worker with a large manufacturing company. He thought he would be able to do 'academic' research there, but soon became dissatisfied. 'I was dissatisfied by Christmas. The work wasn't what I expected. The premises were grotty and I was working with unpleasant materials [asbestos] and it was dirty and repetitive.'

He decided to re-apply to business school and this time he got a place, but he was also offered a job abroad and, as he wanted to travel, he decided to go. He managed to defer his application, but after two months abroad he found his work permit would not be renewed and returned to Britain.

'I thought perhaps I wouldn't mind trying accountancy so I wrote to ten firms and got some offers. I joined one of the major firms and might have stayed if I really liked it. I would have gone to business school sooner or later anyway. The ACA with the MBA is a good qualification and I still might go on to qualify in accountancy.

I came to business school because I didn't know where I was career-wise. I thought business school was a good place to go to sort myself out. I had thought of teaching and I still am.

The MBA will certainly place me several steps up the ladder. Being here gives me a chance to find out what I want to do and get towards it. I want to be successful. Perhaps I will work for myself at some stage, maybe in consultancy, but its probably just a fancy. Perhaps I will be a partner in an international banking-oriented firm.'

These attitudes may be contrasted with those of one of the business owners' sons: 'I suppose I'm a capitalist at heart. I have no desire to do anything other than further my own ends in business or finance of whatever kind, and I have no desire to go into teaching or whatever.'

The relative career uncertainty of the professionals' sons is reflected in their views on their long-term career goals. Thirty-five per cent of the professionals' sons did not know about their ultimate career ambitions in comparison with 20 per cent of the middle managers' sons, 18 per cent of the top managers' sons and 13 per cent of the owners' sons. However, half gave their long-term goals as the 'top' and were more likely to refer to the top in large firms than the other groups which, given that this is objectively the least realistic expectation, is consistent with the professional sons' relative lack of business experience and business knowledge from their families.

To summarize, the sons of the professionals and administrators had similar career aspirations to the top business group, though they tended, in particular, to think of themselves at the top of large firms. On the other hand, they were particularly likely to be unclear about their career ambitions. As with many other students, they had frequently encountered blockages to their career progress during their work experience, and saw business school as a means to switch to more promising pathways and go more quickly along them.

The middle managers' sons

The twenty middle managers' sons are too few to allow more than a brief summary of their position in relation to the other groups. Over half gave transitional or accelerational reasons for attending business school and a further third had clarificational motives. Their career aims were generally high, thirteen of them mentioning 'the top', and six of these indicating large firms. In these terms they were fairly similar to the sons of the professionals.

The sons of the least endowed

Nearly a third of the interviewees were the sons of 'lower' professionals, small proprietors, clerical or manual workers. These students were the most likely of all to give transitional or accelerational reasons for attending business school, but at the same time they were the least likely to aim for 'the top' in their long-term ambitions, only a third of them doing so. The members of this group were the most likely not to know about their long-term career ambitions (38 per cent) and the most likely to be unclear about their career ideas (52 per cent).

In some cases their road to business school had been hard indeed, as Mr Williams's story indicates.

Mr Williams   Mr Williams entered business school at the age of twenty-eight, a married man with no children. He came from a railway family, his father having been a turner on the railways, his grandfather an engine driver. He attended a secondary modern school in the North of England and took five 'O' levels, obtaining four. He left school at sixteen years of age and took a job.

> 'There was never any encouragement to do anything else and I hadn't enjoyed the time at school, so it was fairly obvious the thing to do was to get a job, and again this was a bit difficult as all the jobs seemed to ask for five O-levels and I only had four. So you were limited. The insurance companies didn't want you, the building societies didn't want you, and the banks didn't want you. So after a struggle I ended up with the Corporation. It wasn't necessarily a choice of mine, it was really a question of it was the first job that came along.
>
> I knew I didn't want any sort of manual, technical jobs. I wanted something on the administrative, clerical side. It was sort of institutions that really captured the imagination, more so than the engineering works.
>
> I think its been my attitude to all jobs. Qualifications count for a lot and I know they don't help you once you're *in* the job but they certainly go one hell of a long way to *getting* you the job. As I was fairly ambitious, I could see that with four O-levels I wasn't exactly heading for the board of ICI. So I thought a degree would be useful

and would probably be beneficial, probably more so than at eighteen, and, you know, I fancied three years on the state as well.'

Mr Williams decided to take A-levels and apply for university.

'My parents were upset that I was leaving more than anything. They felt the job at the Corporation was a good steady job and I wouldn't do much better. To throw it all up and go to university for three years was a bit stupid in their opinion. So I never got any encouragement to go. And, of course, I was the youngest of the family so my mother was a bit upset because the other three had left, you see. But I think the main feature was that they never encouraged me to go, I was never pressurized into going. It was always my decision, what I wanted. You see, to a certain extent they thought I was being a bit silly. But they were very good. They just said, get on with it and do your own thing.'

Having been rejected by five of the six universities he applied to, Mr Williams took a lower second in economics at a plate-glass university. He then looked for a job.

'I must admit I was a bit perplexed. I hadn't really any idea. I think I'd gone off the idea of the institutions to a certain extent. I think really where I went wrong was that I tried for too many things because I didn't really know what I wanted, and rather than trying to narrow the field down a bit and go for certain types of jobs, I was going for all sorts . . . I don't know if my interview technique wasn't too good. I went for a tremendous lot of interviews, but I didn't seem to get a lot of response, not even to the point of getting second interviews. I didn't really know how to approach the problem.'

Eventually Mr Williams joined a large company as a graduate trainee, and within a year he became the assistant manager of the firm's largest branch. But he became disillusioned when promises of promotion to 'executive' status came to nothing. Having heard about business schools while at university, he decided to apply.

'I discussed it with the wife. We'd bought our house and everything. I knew, obviously, our standard of living would drop, and she was going to be affected as much as anybody. She was quite pleased that I was going back because she'd always been a bit homesick. I think since we've been married we've been a long way from her part of the world and I think to a certain extent she was itching to get back.'

Mr Williams saw attendance at business school as a chance not only to get an MBA but also to build on and specialize in his previous experience. Mr Williams characterized his ambitions as follows:

> 'I'd like to be in a high position. I'm fairly ambitious. I would say I'm very ambitious. Plotting my life out over a few years, I think the thing that's motivated me has been this striving for success, and whenever success doesn't appear to be on the horizon then I'm moving into something else to try and achieve it. I think that'll always be me . . . I can't see myself ever saying I've got as far as I want to go and that will be it. Possibly, if and when things are getting to the point where you're having to sacrifice your home life for your business life, that might be a different matter altogether. There's got to be some degree of moderation between your ambition and how it affects you as a person. I think I'd like ultimately to run my own business. Nobody likes being told what to do. I could be very happy running a small outfit of my own.'

The comments made by these students about their career ambitions have a distinctive tenor which is worthy of notice, for although, like the professionals' sons, they were frequently unsure of their long-term goals, they were much less sure of how far they might go and more ambivalent in their feelings about the *desirability* of getting to the top. Comments such as the following were almost unique to this group:

> 'I'm not super ambitious and I wouldn't want to be managing director of Shell. Perhaps it would be too much responsibility. Perhaps I will end up in middle management. I don't want to be so preoccupied with the job that other things in life don't count.'

> 'I'm not the most ambitious person and I won't feel very dissatisfied if I don't get to a particular post. I'll just play it by ear.'

> 'It's hard to assess – I keep reassessing the end position. At first I was vaguely pessimistic of my capabilities though I now feel more confident. But I would hedge if promotion meant overwork and neglecting my family, which probably means being in middle management.'

> 'I want to retire very early. I don't want to work for the rest of my life.'

> 'It's hard for me to say because I don't think in those terms. My main motivation is to go for a job-style that I find appealing rather than to realize any grandiose ambitions. It's job-style or satisfaction that really matters to me, not ambition.'

For this group the imperative of 'getting on' pressed less strongly than for the others, perhaps because they had already 'made it' in their own eyes and could afford to think more broadly of the quality of their lives. On the other hand they may simply have been least aware of the 'benefits' of getting to the top.

The motivations and ambitions of the French students

Interviews were carried out with fifty-eight of the sixty-one French participants who entered INSEAD in 1973; because of the small numbers involved, the students were not allotted to categories along the lines of the British analysis. A similar pattern of high aspirations coupled with career blockages was found among the students, particularly in the case of the top social groups; almost two-thirds of the interviewees came into this category. For the French students, however, the pressure to 'live up to expectations' was much more evident, arising from the more rigid and explicit system of educational ranking in France and the relatively close linking of educational attainments to the occupational system. The often expressed influence of parents on educational and career decisions stems from the very visibility of these linkages and hierarchies, since it becomes apparent much earlier in France than in Britain whether one is, or is not, *en route* to an 'appropriate' social destination.

As was shown earlier, the majority of the INSEAD students, although having had the best form of higher education at the *grandes écoles*, had often failed to secure entry to the very best of those schools. The interviews showed that their educational 'choices', at every level, had been strongly conditioned by their awareness of the interconnecting hierarchies of institutions, qualifications, and occupational opportunities, and that these 'choices' had often been of a highly instrumental kind. Nearly half the students interviewed seemed to have had a wholly instrumental approach to their higher education, always choosing what was 'necessary' for the sake of 'getting on', and a further quarter included instrumental considerations among their reasons for their educational decisions. Usually brought up in families of high socio-economic status, their early education had largely been chosen by their parents, and even their higher education had been strongly influenced by their families. The students had been led to hold high expectations of their career prospects, and their awareness of the social and economic hierarchy, derived most frequently from the socio-economic position of their parents, had made them acutely aware of where they stood in career terms.

Of these students, only nine had attended engineering schools in Paris and only six had been to the very best of these. Similarly, only eight had been to one of the top Parisian commercial schools, so overall less than a third could consider themselves part of the *crème de la crème*. Most of them had either attended lesser *écoles* in the provinces or abroad, or had been 'relegated' to the university faculties. There is considerable emotional shock associated with these misfortunes; although in the eyes of the bulk of the population, their achievements would be considered as hallmarks of success, for those of high origins anything less than the top seemed like failure. Most of the students expressed disappointment, often bitterly, at their lot, and although many had managed to rationalize their sense of inadequacy, it often loomed large in their minds.

Such feelings are reinforced in France by the publication of league tables of salaries commanded by graduates of various top institutions. The edition of *L'Expansion* for June 1974, for example, gave salary figures for the *cadres débutants* showing graduates of Polytechnique at the top, followed by those of the École Centrale (Paris), École Nationale Supérieure d'Electricité (Sup. Elec.), École Nationale Supérieure d'Aéronautique (Sup. Aéro.), Télécommunications and Mines (Paris, Nancy, and St Etienne), and of three major Parisian commercial schools (HEC, ESSEC, ESCP). These were followed by holders of doctorates in economics, graduates of the smaller engineering schools, commercial schools and 'Sciences Po', and holders of a *maitrise* from the business faculty (Dauphine) in Paris, and finally graduates of the university departments. Lists such as these make it relatively easy for the ambitious young Frenchman to see precisely what the stakes in the educational game are in a way that is impossible in Britain.

As most of the interviewees had had some work experience, they had had an opportunity to savour the reality of these figures, and at the same time could see how attendance at INSEAD would serve to improve their prospects. The same *L'Expansion* figures showed that the salaries of INSEAD graduates were much higher than even those of graduates from the major engineering *grandes écoles*. The salary range for *Polytechniciens* was 43–54,000FF per annum (c. £4,300–£5,400), but for INSEAD graduates it was 52–75,000FF per annum (c. £5,200–£7,500). For the ambitious, attendance at INSEAD must have seemed a tempting proposition.

A high salary is of course only one possible focus of motivation. The interviews showed that responsibility and power were also important considerations, the students often emphasizing these factors in relation to the jobs they wished to have. Their descriptions of their work experience reflected a concern with the 'slowness' of their promotion paths and the likelihood of being side-tracked into the more technical and less managerial aspects of their firms, as well as an awareness that the more responsible posts, with their attendant privileges, tended to be reserved for those with different educational backgrounds. Many specifically attributed their attendance at INSEAD to the disappointments they had suffered in their work careers, the majority saying that they would have looked for a change of job even if they had not been able to gain admittance to the Institute.

The reasons for dissatisfaction at work varied, but a number of themes recurred. 'I found I was blocked,' said one student. 'The firm was very small' said another, 'and I soon found I had done everything that was available.' The jobs were often too limited or repetitive, or too technical and boring. Frequently, there were 'human relations' problems: inability to get on with the boss, or a change of superior leading to a discord in working relationships. Changes in economic conditions had sometimes closed down the opportunities, promising career routes suddenly changing or disappearing altogether as a result of company mergers or enforced 'rationalization'. A few students had, in fact, been made redundant along with other employees.

In some cases 'the problem' was expressed in a general way. Thus one engineering graduate said:

'The market for engineers (*ingénieurs*) has weakened and there is less need for them . . . in short, one must appreciate that an engineer is not, after all, a polymath, and that one does not systematically develop from an engineer to a *cadre*, and above all that engineers do not necessarily become managers. It was this that led me to think of going to business school.'

Others were more specific, relating their lack of promotion and success directly to educational qualifications that did not fit in with the promotional policies of their firms. One began abruptly by saying that 'the first thing to say, and the first fact to establish, is that I had to move'. He went on:

'I realized that people identify closely with their qualifications, and with an INSEAD diploma one gets on. In companies, qualifications themselves help a little, but when it comes to a high-level position it is in general the 'old boy networks' which count even if people don't admit it, and I saw in my firm that graduates of ENA and Polytechnique were very well placed and those of Centrale also. But those from HEC did much worse, and people like myself did very poorly.'

Another student linked his feelings of disappointment about the sort of higher education institution he had attended to his disillusion with the internal promotion policies of companies, which effectively meant that the privileges of education were carried over in to privileged progress through the firm.

'I could see that I needed something extra . . . it is important to say that in France people are obsessed by the level of their qualifications . . . and it is quite painful, when it happens that one has failed to get into a so-called *grande école*, to then find oneself not really inferior but left with the impression that one has not done as well as other people, and is somehow an idiot or stupid. It is certain, nevertheless, that the difficulty of the entrance examination does impose a degree of selection, and I would not pretend that I have the mathematical ability of a *polytechnicien*, but I also believe that what makes the difference afterwards is the different cultural milieux (*formation*) of the schools themselves. There is no doubt that in the French *grandes écoles*, students are educated into a way of seeing things which enables them to behave differently in the environment they enter afterwards. From the moment you tell someone he will be a manager (*dirigeant*), that he is destined for responsibility, he behaves completely differently from someone to whom this has not been said, and that, I think, is important. So, very often, someone who graduates from a French *grande école* is quickly associated with positions of power, and is promoted rapidly and develops quickly . . . There is, in that, a phenomenon which places everyone else in an inferior position at least to some extent. I believe that from now on the only solution is to defend oneself and to take action.'

Hence this student's attendance at INSEAD.

Many, then, were dissatisfied and were able to give a fairly clear account of the reasons for this and of their expectations of INSEAD. Like the British, however, they were usually rather less clear about the careers they wanted afterwards and about where the most fruitful opportunities might lie. Just as the British had only rarely moved from school to university with any specific career ends in view, so the channelling of the French by family and school into the *grandes écoles*, and especially the engineering *écoles*, had prevented the students from developing strong occupational identities held by them as their own.

'My father imposed my studies on me for many years because he wanted me to be in his image and afterwards I was obliged to operate a reconversion strategy first through a doctorate in Economics and then through INSEAD because at last I can do as I like. He (the father) forced me to prepare the Arts-et-Métiers as he had done himself.'

The crucial importance of ability in mathematics in relation to entry to the most prestigious *grandes écoles*, and the obsession with diplomas mentioned by the student above, had tended to lead to a narrow concentration on 'beating the system' in which personal aspirations had been frequently forced into second place. The 'choice' of higher education had thus often hinged less upon the desire to follow a particular vocation than on success or failure in mathematics, and once out in the world of work the students had often found themselves dissatisfied not only in career terms, but also in a more immediate way in terms of the content of their jobs. In much the same way as some of the British students had hoped for some clarification of the nature of their 'true' occupational talents at business school, so many of the French students hoped that attendance at INSEAD would both awaken and develop their hidden strengths. 'If you like, in France, people admire the *grandes écoles* but when you come from one they tend to think that you can do nothing but equations. INSEAD is an excellent means of ridding oneself of being the victim of that prejudice.'

The students talked relatively easily about themselves and their biographies, but it was almost impossible to get them to talk in any but the vaguest terms about their future career plans. Many said they would prefer a large firm to a small one, or vice versa, the preference often being the opposite of the firm they had worked in prior to going to INSEAD. Some said they wanted to start their own firm, but few had a concrete project or scheme in mind. Most, however, though not all, said they were aiming for posts in general management (*direction générale*), probably in a small to medium-sized firm, and in this they were strikingly similar to the British.

7 The 'switchboard effect': jobs before and after business school

For both the British and the French students, acquisition of a post-graduate degree from an established business school represented a means of changing direction. The sense of that change, however, varied somewhat between the two countries as did the significance of the use to which the degree could be put. Many of the French students at INSEAD saw the diploma primarily as a means of compensating for their lack of the 'best' educational background which would enable them to compete on equal or better terms with graduates of the *école polytechnique* and *école centrale*. Attending INSEAD was for many students, particularly those from the *patronat*, a way of acquiring a valued educational qualification that seemed to ensure easy access to the top stream of managerial posts; access that might have been much more difficult for those who only had diplomas from schools not quite at the top of the French higher educational systems.

On entry to the school, they therefore saw the INSEAD diploma largely in terms of its place in the hierarchy of educational qualifications giving good value on the managerial labour market. Associated with the wish to 'improve' the quality of educational achievement, however, was also the wish to broaden educational qualifications. A number of the students recognized that, with the 'technical' diplomas they possessed, they were destined to occupy technical positions rather than managerial ones. As engineers, they would be on the production or perhaps management services side and find it hard to leave them. Indeed, the more competent they became in their technical positions the less inclined their employers seemed to be, or were thought to be, to move them. At the same time, during the 1960s, the increasing corporate size, product diversity, and consumer orientation of many companies in France was making the functions of marketing and finance more important. These seemed to many to be the new routes to the top. For engineers, therefore, who entered INSEAD in increasing number from the mid 1960s, acquisition of an MBA seemed to offer possibilities of 'conversion' from the production side to the commercial side of companies, a side that seemed to offer more opportunities for rapid promotion.

In contrast, many of the British students expected to switch employment sectors as well as functions by attending business school. The relative lack of importance of higher education qualifications for business careers in Britain, and in particular the much weaker stratification of educational institutions in relation to job opportunities in management, did not allow students to believe that simply acquiring a further degree would in itself lead to a privileged position in business. What possession of the MBA did for many British graduates was to signify commitment to a business career and to provide more relevant managerial and commercial skills than did their first degree. These skills enabled business-school graduates to move away from their previous area of employment to ones perceived as more central to the business world. Specifically, the MBA allowed graduates in technical subjects working in production, research and development, and management services departments in industry to change managerial functions and/or sector of employment. For most of British business graduates who had had some work experience before going to business school, the qualification offered the opportunity of transferring from relatively disadvantaged jobs and sectors to more lucrative and expanding fields.

In particular, the low status and pay of qualified engineers in British industry as seen in several reports (Department of Industry 1977; Gerstl and Hutton 1966; Glover 1976) was perhaps felt most keenly by those graduates from upper business and professional families who took engineering degrees during the 'science boom' of the 1960s and subsequently worked in production and engineering departments in manufacturing industry. It was these 'relatively deprived' graduates who could be expected to see business schools as offering a means of escape from their specialist technical training into more 'managerial' jobs and, as we have seen, they constitute the largest single degree subject group of business school entrants in Britain. Associated with this desire to move away from technically specialized work was the wish to leave the production function, which has traditionally been under-paid (British Institute of Management 1977; Council of Engineering Institutions 1977 : 3) in favour of 'cleaner' managerial work with a more professional image such as finance or planning (Leggatt 1978). As Granick (1972 : 226–27) points out, functional mobility in many British companies is low (but cf. Gunz 1978) and if broader experience is desired it is usually necessary to change employers. A business school qualification could well be helpful in enabling such movements.

Some graduates who had been working in non-business spheres and who wished to move into managerial posts also used the MBA as means of doing so. Those especially who had not experienced as rapid upward mobility as they thought appropriate seemed to be attracted to business school as a means of acquiring a head start in a novel employment sector. In general, then, business schools function more as career-switching institutions in Britain than in France, where possession of an additional diploma from a highly regarded school is accepted as an important factor in determining career chances in business. The contrast, however, should not be drawn too sharply, for many of the French felt that they could obtain fast promotion only by switching career paths.

Employment experience before business school: Britain

Two-thirds of the British students at LBS and MBS had worked for more than one year, mainly in business, so they had a considerably greater experience of the business world as employees than had the French. The way the British schools enabled graduates to switch jobs is seen from their last pre-business-school employment and from the way in which their pattern of job changes differed from that of other graduates. The available evidence indicates that the MBA does allow graduates to move into relatively 'new' types of employment although the sort of movement is partially dependent upon the nature of the pre-business-school posts held.

These posts can be analysed along two major dimensions: sector of employment, such as manufacturing, retailing, government service (*Table* 7 (1)), and managerial departments or function, such as produc-tion, finance, or research and development (*Table* 7 (2)). Not all sectors of course, have the same set of departments, and indeed many firms

Table 7 (1) Degree subject and employment sector of first full-time job of British business school entrants

Employment sector	Arts	Economics	Social science	Sciences	Maths	Engineering	Other[1]	%
				Degree subject %				
Manufacturing	50	48	82	83	67	74	42	66
Financial and business services	16	14	9	0	8	1	9	6
Professional services	10	21	9	7	8	8	17	11
Government and other services	13	0	0	4	0	1	16	5
Other[2]	10	17	0	7	16	16	14	13
%	11	12	3	22	4	35	13	
(N)	(38)	(42)	(11)	(75)	(12)	(117)	(43)	338

[1] Includes PPE, law, business studies, and combined degrees
[2] Public utilities, construction, conglomerates, and retail and distribution

Table 7 (2) Degree subject and functional department of first full-time job of British entrants

Function				Degree subject %				
	Arts	Economics	Social science	Sciences	Maths	Engineering	Other	%
Finance	11	23	0	4	18	1	23	8
Marketing	39	31	37	22	18	13	26	22
Production	3	6	18	26	9	37	3	22
Research and development	0	0	0	19	0	14	3	12
Management services	14	11	18	10	36	8	14	12
Other[1]	33	29	27	18	18	27	31	36
%	9	12	4	23	4	37	12	
(N)	(28)	(35)	(11)	(68)	(11)	(112)	(35)	300

[1] Includes engineering, audit clerks, trainees, personnel, and planning

differ in how the main functions are labelled, but most of our respondents were able to locate themselves in one of the major categories. Most graduates in science and engineering enter manufacturing industry and so, given the dominance of scientists and engineers among the British alumni, it is not surprising to find that two-thirds of them had their first full-time job in manufacturing industry. In this respect British business-school entrants are not proportionately substantially different from graduates in general (Department of Industry 1977).

A substantial minority took their first job in the professional services sector, especially those with first degrees in economics. A few were employed in engineering consultancies, but most were working in accountancy and law firms as junior clerks. Few took their first job in the financial services sector but the dominance of arts and economics graduates in this field should be noted, particularly in view of the substantial proportion of MBAs who subsequently work there (Business Graduates Association 1973; Zehnder 1975).

The importance of the subject of the first degree held is clear from consideration of the functional department of first full-time employment. Scientists and engineers dominated the group who worked in production departments and research and development laboratories. Graduates in the arts and in economics tended to work in marketing departments with a substantial proportion of economists in the finance function, mostly in the service sector. The functions occupied varied too by sector: nearly all those who worked in marketing, production, management services, and research and development were employed by manufacturing firms while two-thirds of those in finance functions were working in the services sector.

Only a quarter of the British business school entrants had worked for more than one employer before going to business school, but the extent to which this sub-group had changed type of job indicates possible occupational mobility patterns before acquiring the MBA. It can be seen from *Table* 7 (3) that although there were no major changes in the overall proportions of business graduates in each sector between their first and second full-time jobs before going to business school, there was substantial mobility between sectors, with outflows balanced by inflows. Less than three-quarters of those whose first job was in manufacturing firms, for example, took their second job in that sector, but a roughly equal number moved to that sector from the service sector, thus leaving the general proportion in manufacturing practically identical. Similarly, although only a third of those who began their working life in the professional services sector remained there

Table 7 (3) Employment sector changes of British business school entrants before going to business school: first and second full-time jobs (percentages)

Second full-time job	Sector of employment First full-time job					
	Manufacturing	Financial services	Professional services	Govt. and other services	Other[1]	%
Manufacturing	70	40	48	25	15	52
Financial services	10	0	8	25	15	11
Professional services	10	40	32	25	15	18
Govt. and other services	3	0	4	12	10	6
Other	7	20	8	12	10	14
%	31	4	21	7	17	118
(N)	(60)	(5)	(25)	(8)	(20)	

[1] Public utilities, construction, conglomerates, and retail/distribution

with their second employer, others moved into this sector, leaving the general proportion in it only 3 per cent lower. In total, just under half of those taking their first job in manufacturing, financial, or professional services took their second job in a different sector. This suggests a considerable degree of career uncertainty translated into mobility between the different major sectors of the economy. The business school entrants who did change employers before going to LBS or MBS move disproportionately from the professional services sector. Inversely, few of those who began in manufacturing industry changed employers.

Some functions lost more than others. While marketing, management services, and finance groups retained high proportions of those who changed employers before business school, the production and research and development functions 'lost' about half of the graduates who began in them. Usually, as with employment sectors, these 'losses' were almost compensated for by other graduates moving into those two fields. Finance, however, was unusual, in that no one moved into the finance function from marketing, production, research and development, and development or management services when they changed firms. This may indicate that the finance function is difficult to enter for those with only a first degree, and, as we shall see, an MBA undoubtedly facilitates such a move.

The effect of pre-business-school mobility is slightly to reduce the proportion of British entrants still in manufacturing industry and in production and research and development departments at the time of entry to business school. In spite of this, the manufacturing sector is still clearly predominant. Just under two-thirds of the British entrants to LBS and MBS were in manufacturing at the time of entry while very few, under a tenth, came from the financial and business services sector. Within manufacturing, more entrants came from marketing departments than from production and only a tenth were still working in research and development laboratories just before going to business school. A considerable minority came from firms in the professional services sector, but over three-quarters of these were in clerical, not managerial, posts. Thus, despite the predominance of scientists and engineers among the British business school entrants, a majority had already left traditional technical fields by the time they went to LBS and MBS as can be seen from *Table* 7 (4).

Last employment before business school: France

Rather more than half of the French alumni of INSEAD had acquired

Table 7 (4) Characteristics of British business school entrants' last pre-business-school job: employment sector and functional area

Functional area	Employment sector %					
	Manufacturing	Financial and business services	Professional services	Govt. and other services	Other[1]	%
Finance	4	50	10	0	7	9
Marketing	25	3	0	11	14	22
Production	21	0	0	0	24	16
Research and development	10	0	6	0	2	7
Management services	14	13	0	0	7	11
Other[2]	14	23	27	18	31	18
Unclassified[3]	6	10	56	71	14	17
%	62	8	13	5	13	
(N)	(221)	(30)	(48)	(17)	(42)	358

[1] Public utilities, construction, conglomerates and retail/distribution
[2] Engineering, market research, personnel, planning, trainees
[3] Nearly all of these were clerks or in positions which could not be classified in a similar way to managerial departments in industrial firms

some professional experience in business before entering the Institute. On the whole, however, they had not worked for very long periods. Around a third of the sample had worked for two years or more but two-thirds had worked for one year or less and a number of those had chosen specific jobs with entry to INSEAD in mind. They had, for instance, chosen to work in Germany to improve their German to INSEAD admission standard rather than choosing a particular company or field of activity with a longer-term career in mind. Others, even though accepting a job with INSEAD entry in mind, would have stayed in it 'had it worked out'. Because of those complicating motivations, even for first jobs, it is less meaningful to compare 'before and after' INSEAD careers than it is for the British. Moreover, the proportion of the French at INSEAD who had worked varied considerably over the years.

For the first decade, the Institute did not make employment experience an entry criterion, although a number of the early entrants had worked. Even after the change in policy, selectors of candidates seemed to feel that one or two years of work in business was an especially appropriate period for benefiting from what INSEAD offered.

More recently, not only have considerably higher proportions of entrants worked in business, they have also worked for a much longer period of time, reflecting perhaps a further change in admission policies.

Although much of the direct business experience among the French alumni in the sample was brief, their background and the experience they did acquire, nevertheless sufficed to give them fairly clear notions about recruitment and promotion policies. As we saw earlier, *patronat* sons in particular had 'family' experience of the business world that compensated for a lack of direct experience in understanding the workings of companies as they affect chances of different careers. At the same time, these sons are especially well placed to hear of changes in such opportunities and to assess the value of a business-school diploma for changing direction. The increasing proportions of engineers at INSEAD witnessed the growing realization of the limitations on careers in 'engineering', at least for those not equipped with certificates from the best *grandes écoles*. Even though these students have not worked, or have only worked for short periods, they may be understood as changing professional direction.

Just under half of the French entrants to INSEAD who had worked beforehand for a year or more came to the Institute from manufacturing companies – mostly in the capital goods industries. The next largest proportion, over a fifth, had been working in service companies, nearly all in consultancy. The only other notable area was mining and construction (10 per cent). The relatively high proportion coming from consultancy may be due to the predominance in this area of North American companies, which often insist on an MBA for senior posts. However, it should be borne in mind that the numbers are quite small for the French entrants, with only just over two-fifths having worked full time before going to INSEAD.

Employment after business school: Britain and France

The weak connection between the higher education system and the business world in Britain suggests that British MBAs are likely to be given advisory or staff posts rather than full managerial responsibilities immediately upon graduation, thus witnessing the hostility to formal educational certification of managerial expertise evidenced by British business over the past forty or fifty years. The qualification may provide access to jobs in novel sectors but it is unlikely in itself to lead directly to major managerial responsibilities. Thus, two-thirds of the British business graduates who had worked before going to business school started their post-MBA employment either as trainees or in staff advisory posts.

The novelty of the kinds of jobs British MBAs enter after business school, compared to their first full time jobs, can be seen from *Table 7* (5). Relative to their first full time job, the jobs of the fully-fledged MBAs differed quite considerably both in employment sector and in functional department. In particular, the proportions entering the financial and business services sector and the corporate planning and personal assistant functional roles had increased considerably.[1] Far fewer business graduates entered manufacturing firms and jobs in the professional services sector and a much higher proportion entered the City and management consultancy firms. Internal changes within the residual 'other' category of employment sector are also interesting: while the public utilities employed over half of the first degree entrants in this category, the diversified companies which could not be located in one of the standard industrial classification categories took most of the MBAs in this sector, many of these in corporate planning or personnel assistant roles. So graduates with MBAs did take jobs in rather different types of industry than when they had only their first degree.

The functional area of employment of MBAs shows similar changes. In particular, while marketing, production and engineering account for

Table 7 (5) Employment sector and functional area of British MBAs' first post after business school

	Employment sector %					
Functional area	*Manufacturing*	*Financial and business services*	*Professional services*	*Govt. and other services*	*Other[1]*	*%*
Finance	22	50	6	17	20	30
Marketing	23	7	0	0	4	13
Production	8	0	0	0	0	4
Research and development	0	0	0	0	0	0
Management services	4	0	6	0	10	4
Corporate planning[2]	21	7	0	67	31	18
Management consultancy	0	23	0	0	0	8
Other[3]	21	13	87	16	35	23
%	47	33	4	2	13	
(N)	(172)	(120)	(16)	(6)	(49)	363

[1] Public utilities, construction, conglomerates and retail/distribution
[2] Including personal assistant roles to top managers
[3] Engineering, market research, personnel, purchasing, trainees and internal consultants/project managers

over a half of the first full time jobs taken before entry to business school, on leaving business school over a half of the MBAs took jobs in finance, corporate planning, or management consultancy. Less than a twentieth went to work in production departments and none of the MBAs joined technical development departments. British business school graduates then, obtained substantially different sorts of jobs from those held by entrants who had worked before going to business school, and these differences are probably at least as great for university graduates as a whole.

Only about a third of Kelsall's 1960 graduates were working in industry or commerce (1974 : 211) and other surveys such as that by the Department of Industry in 1977, show that most such graduates are engineers or scientists in production, engineering, or development departments. It thus seems clear that the British business schools do produce graduates who are able to obtain quite distinct jobs.

Although the French graduates from INSEAD showed a similar unwillingness to enter production departments, they did join manufacturing firms to a greater extent than the British MBAs as *Table* 7 (6) shows. The importance of business service firms – mostly in management consultancy – for the French business graduates is emphasized by this table, which also indicates that the banking and insurance companies are not nearly such big recruiters of MBAs as in Britain.

Table 7 (6) Employment sector and functional area of first post-INSEAD jobs of French business graduates

	Employment sector %			
Function	Manufacturing	Financial and business services	Other[1]	%
Finance	20	10	6	15
Marketing	52	13	41	37
Production	5	3	12	5
Consultancy	0	58	0	21
Other[2]	23	16	41	22
%	54	37	9	
(N)	(102)	(69)	(17)	188

[1] Includes commerce, construction, mining, agriculture and food
[2] Includes research, administration and general management

Within manufacturing, the dominance of marketing departments is clearly demonstrated and again, contrasts strongly with the British data. The increasing attraction of marketing, especially the North American approach, as a key to management success in many French companies during the 1960s may be largely responsible for this dominance (Bourdieu, Boltanski, and de St Martin 1973; Table Ronde 1978). The apparent lack of any clear French equivalent to the corporate planning role may reflect the slower movement towards divisionalization and concomitant growth of head office staffs in France (Dyas and Thanheiser 1976), together with different managerial career structures and greater acceptance of educational qualifications as indicators of managerial competence in many French firms (Granick 1972). In terms of overall proportions in a given employment sector, the French INSEAD graduates did not show as much change in their jobs before and after business school as did the British.

It seems, then, that the British schools do lead to greater changes in job type than does INSEAD and, in the case of corporate planning, could almost be said to have created a good 'fit' to a new kind of managerial role. The greater use of educational diplomas in French business as a means of stratifying managerial cadres, and hence closer links between the higher educational systems and patterns of management organization, probably means, however, that INSEAD graduates are easier to 'fit' into established hierarchies and be given direct responsibilities than their British counterparts. This is especially likely where a functional area – marketing – is expanding and the MBAs are seen as possessing the latest techniques and skills.

Relations between pre-business school and post-business school employment

So far we have considered how the overall proportions of MBAs entering particular employment sectors and functional departments differ from those of most first degree graduates entering industry. We now turn to a more detailed discussion of how the business schools enable particular groups of entrants to change sector and/or function as well as to increase their salaries.

Possibilities of entry to some of the 'new' types of jobs obtained by British MBAs were related to previous business experience. In some sectors great importance was given to the type and extent of such experience while in others it was regarded as irrelevant. The banking sector, in particular, appeared to regard the quantity of pre-business school work experience as largely irrelevant, for nearly a third of the

British MBAs joining banks had not worked previously, compared with under a fifth of those joining manufacturing firms. Professional accounting was similar to banking; nearly half of those taking jobs in professional service firms as a whole had had no previous work experience. Almost all the MBAs were joining accountancy firms as audit clerks with a view to obtaining the professional accountancy qualification. This desire by some of the youngest MBAs to acquire a further financial certificate suggests that the MBA alone, without previous business experience, was not considered quite sufficient to obtain important jobs in the finance field where alternative, longer established diplomas exist and are regarded as the primary professional qualification. Given that many senior managers in finance departments are chartered accountants this relative self-devaluation of the MBA may not be unreasonable.

In contrast to these two sectors, almost all of the MBAs joining management consultancy firms had worked before going to business school and three-quarters had been working for two or more years beforehand. Indeed, one well known consultancy firm had decided not to recruit any new MBAs unless they had had over two years previous business experience. The other major 'new' field of employment for business graduates, corporate planning in manufacturing and con- glomerate firms, had roughly the same proportion of MBAs without previous work experience as all other functions – just under a fifth. However, it was noticeable that MBAs who took corporate planning or personal assistant posts in highly diversified companies tended to have rather more experience than those elsewhere. In general, though, business graduates entering advisory fields in manufacturing firms, such as management services and market research, tended to be younger than those moving into finance or marketing departments, as might be expected given the predilection of British business for experience over educational certification.

The French graduates from INSEAD did not show such marked differences in terms of job type and length of pre-business school experience. While the younger business graduates tended to join marketing sections in multinational consumer goods firms to a greater extent than did those with at least a year's previous business experience, there were no such differences for MBAs working for management consultancy firms, nor for the relatively few joining banks. Length of experience *per se*, then, did not seem to play the same role for French business graduates as for the British, presumably again because of the greater importance of educational diplomas *per se* in France.

Further differences between first post-business school employment of the French and British MBAs can be seen when we examine the proportion who 'returned' to the same employment sector after graduation. *Tables* 7 (7) and 7 (8) show that in general the French business graduates who had worked previously switched sectors after graduating much less than did the British. In particular, while only half of the British entering from manufacturing firms joined companies in that sector after business school, over three-quarters of the equivalent group of French MBAs returned to manufacturing industry.

Amalgamating consultancy, banking, and other financial services into one sector and contrasting that with industry, we can see that the French in general remained more frequently in their initial employment sector than did the British. Whereas just over half of the British MBAs returned to the same field they were working in before business school, nearly two-thirds of the French did so. The figure for sector change by the British before entry to business school is roughly similar to that after graduation, except that more MBAs left manufacturing after their management degree. This suggests that although the MBA does assist those wishing to change employment sector, it does not do so independently. Business schools alone do not make young managers leave manufacturing industry; rather, they are used by such entrants to obtain a qualification which may help them to do so.

The switching function of the British business schools is even more clearly shown by comparing functional departments occupied before and after obtaining the MBA.

Considerable movement out of production, research and development, and management services departments occurred. In addition to finance departments, corporate planning and consultants also 'gained' MBAs relative to pre-business school employment, but marketing, curiously enough, did not. Indeed, marketing seems to play a largely transfer function for the British. Many of the MBAs entering business school from production departments joined marketing ones when they graduated rather than finance or consultancy. In contrast, only a quarter of those coming from marketing returned to that function, with almost as many moving to corporate planning roles. Students coming from finance departments seemed to differ considerably from other entrants with work experience in that nearly a half returned to the same function. Over a fifth moved to management consultancy but relatively few took corporate planning roles. This could indicate perhaps, that students with financial experience are more able to obtain high-level posts than MBAs coming from other departments. In sum, British business school graduates seem to be able to use the MBA successfully

Table 7 (7) Employment sector of British MBAs from LBS and MBS before business school and upon graduation

First employment after business school	Last employment sector before business school %						
	Manufacturing	Financial services	Consultancy	Professional services	Govt. and other services	Other[1]	%
Manufacturing	51	31	29	50	50	51	49
Financial services	23	46	66	20	25	10	22
Consultancy	9	19	0	9	0	4	10
Professional services	3	0	0	5	0	0	2
Govt. and other services	1	.0	0	3	12	3	2
Other	14	4	5	13	12	32	15
%	62	6	2	13	3	13	
(N)	(176)	(16)	(7)	(38)	(8)	(37)	282

[1] Includes agriculture, retail/distribution, construction, public utilities and conglomerates

Table 7 (8)   Employment sector of French MBAs from INSEAD before
going to business school and upon graduation

| First employment sector after INSEAD | Last employment sector before INSEAD % | | | | |
	Manufacturing	Financial services	Consultancy	Other[1]	%
Manufacturing	77	0	47	38	56
Financial services	9	67	7	0	12
Consultancy	11	33	33	15	19
Other	3	0	13	46	13
%	51	9	22	19	
(N)	(35)	(6)	(15)	(13)	69

[1] Includes commerce, construction, mining, agriculture, and food

as a means of changing employment sector and/or functional department, especially from the more traditionally 'technical' fields that have
relatively low prestige and rewards in much of British industry, into
novel areas of employment that appear to offer more. In this, their
motivations for entry to the schools seem to be appropriate to the
opportunities offered.

Certainly business graduates do seem to improve their financial
rewards by going to business school. Most MBAs gained considerably
higher salaries upon graduation. While part of these increases is due to
inflation, especially in the later years of our study, nonetheless, the
MBA does seem to add substantially to one's earning power as well as
enabling sector and function mobility. For instance, two–fifths of those
entering in the earlier years earning under £2,000 more than doubled
their salary by obtaining the MBA.

The British business schools, then, appear to function largely as
switching institutions for those in certain fields of employment who
wish to move into more lucrative and 'managerial' ones, whereas
INSEAD serves a largely 'topping up' educational function for French
graduates who have not succeeded in obtaining diplomas from the
'best' of the *grandes écoles*, so that they can improve their careers in
their chosen areas. This need not mean, of course that in either country
the business schools enable the ambitious young graduate to move
rapidly to top management posts in large-scale industry. Indeed,
placing MBAs in many of the staff posts that are usually offered to

MBAs leaving business school can be seen as an attempt by some businesses to control them, since it is by performance in line management posts that a manager's 'track record' is established, as many alumni themselves mentioned. The ability of business graduates to move rapidly into 'profit responsible' positions and thence up managerial hierarchies will be discussed in the next chapter.

8 Getting ahead: careers in industry and services

According to the London Business School graduate course brochure, 'graduates expect to hold a substantial position with full profit responsibility within five years of graduation' (London Business School 1978:6). Similar views have been expressed in the course brochures of the Manchester Business School and INSEAD and by MBAs themselves in numerous surveys. INSEAD indeed advertises itself as the 'School for Leading Europeans' (Business Graduate Association 1973; Hughes 1977; Willig 1970). However, such ambitions are not always fulfilled in practice and the mere possession of an MBA seems unlikely to guarantee a speedy rise to top management posts in the major corporations of Britain or France, not least because it would imply a devaluation of business procedures of managerial training and promotion in favour of those institutionalized in the higher education system.

The combination of high ambitions among many business school graduates, the difficulties of fitting these graduates into long managerial hierarchies in large firms, and the frequent emphasis on 'experience' and 'track record' in line management posts as the major criteria for making promotion decisions suggest two developmental points. On the one hand, where big business does recruit MBAs they will tend to do so for staff advisory posts initially; on the other hand, ambitious business graduates may move away from the big firms' employment field to areas where general management responsibilities may be given to younger managers. In particular, they are likely to move to smaller firms and to those that are less formally structured than the very large, vertically integrated oligopolies. A further inference from the preference for experienced managers for promotion to top management is that MBAs who work in large firms will not move rapidly into senior management if they remain in predominantly advisory positions. In addition, in seeking senior posts they compete with non-MBAs who have more traditional background qualifications and in some sectors, these young managers may be preferred to those with the new type of diploma. Consequently, not all business graduates will develop careers in big business and those who do so successfully will have particular qualities and experience that enable them to be seen as different from, and superior to, non-MBAs.

The tendency of many large firms to recruit newly qualified MBAs to staff posts was shown in the last chapter. Here we focus on the subsequent business careers of the early graduates of the three schools who were in their mid-thirties at the time of the surveys, specifically examining those who had graduated at least five years before the surveys were conducted. The median length of post-business school work experience was seven years for the 192 British and eight years for the 105 French business graduates considered here.

Employment mobility of business graduates: employment field and firm size

We start with the sort of employment field graduates are working in after some years of post-business school work experience. 'Employment field' is here used in a rather different sense to 'employment sector' as used in the previous chapter, in that we distinguish between large industrial firms – including those in the construction and distribution industries as well as conglomerates – large and/or economically important financial institutions, small firms, management consultants, the self employed, family firms, and the public service sector. The extent to which alumni remain in large firms is of interest here because of the tendency of the major companies to recruit their senior management internally (Clements 1958 : 114–15; Guerrier and Philpot 1978; Leggat 1972 : 56; Melrose-Woodman 1978). Business graduates who opt out of the big company field are unlikely to be able to return to top posts in dominant firms at a later stage of their business career. Consequently, in so far as the business schools do, in fact, produce potential business elite members they are likely to be restricted to those who remain in large firms.

It can be seen from *Table* 8 (1) that the drift away from industry, noted previously for those who had worked before business school, continued after graduation. Just over two-thirds of the British alumni who joined large industrial firms upon graduation were still working in such firms at the time of the survey. Although a few graduates had joined large companies from other type of firms, the overall proportion of British alumni in major industrial companies had fallen from 60 per cent at graduation to 45 per cent at the time of the survey. The reverse was true for those working for major financial institutions, nearly all of whom were still employed in such firms. The movement away from dominant companies then, was almost entirely a movement away from large manufacturing firms, mainly to small firms. Overall, the proportion of the British business graduates working in small firms had almost doubled at the time of the survey, which suggests that many of those seeking general management posts and 'profit responsibility' did so in relatively minor companies. A further point to be noted is the comparatively small proportion of alumni remaining in management consultancy firms. Over half of those who joined such firms when they left business school had moved to other sorts of jobs when the survey was conducted. This indicates the transitional nature of management consultancy for business-school graduates, many of whom use the contacts obtained there to find other posts.

The movement away from large industrial firms is even more marked for the French graduates from INSEAD. Nearly half of those who had joined such companies when they graduated had left this field at the time of the survey. Including major financial institutions in this category, while three-fifths of the British alumni were still in large companies at the time of our study, only half of the French were. Furthermore, while the City seems to function as a 'sink' for the British, in that once alumni had taken jobs there they tended to remain in that sector, the French exhibited a considerable degree of mobility out of banking – including moving into large-scale industry. Traditionally, the banking system has been much more closely linked to industrial firms in France than it has in Britain (Aldcroft and Richardson 1969: 165; Kennedy 1976; Morin 1974) and French companies rely more extensively on borrowing from banks for new investment funds (Carré, Dubois, and Malinvaud 1973: 166–94) than do British ones. Mobility between financial and industrial firms may, therefore, be easier and more common in France. Moreover, as can be

Table 8 (1) Employment field changes of British business graduates[1]

Current (1976/7) employment field	First employment after business school (%)							
	Industry[2]	City[3]	Small firm[4]	Consultancy	Self-employed	Family firm	Public sector	%
Industry	69	0	12	22	40	0	8	45
City	5	82	6	0	20	0	0	16
Small firms	13	14	62	11	0	0	0	16
Consultancy	4	0	0	44	0	0	0	4
Self employed	6	0	19	0	40	0	0	7
Family firm	2	0	0	0	0	100	0	3
Public sector	2	4	0	22	0	0	91	9
%	60	15	9	5	3	2	7	
N	109	28	16	9	5	3	12	182

[1] Alumni of LBS and MBS who graduated from business school at least five years before the survey
[2] Firms employing over 2,000 people
[3] Major banks, insurance companies, etc.
[4] Includes minor banks and stockbrokers as well as industrial firms employing under 2,000 people

seen from *Table* 8 (2), there was greater mobility into large industrial firms from small companies in France than in the UK. This may partly be a consequence of using 1,000 employees as a cut-off point for large firms in France, as opposed to 2,000 in Britain, but it may also reflect greater mobility between employment fields for business graduates in France. Certainly fewer INSEAD alumni were still in the same employment fields that they joined upon graduation than were the British business graduates.

In general, then, the early careers of business graduates in Britain and France show a move away from large firms to small firms and self employment and, for the French, a return to the family business. If this pattern is continued it seems that these business schools are not going to produce general managers for the major firms in the international economy in the sense that most of their graduates would assume such posts largely as a consequence of attending business school. The schools, in fact, probably intensify a desire on the part of many students to 'be the boss', rather than become 'organization men' (Whyte 1956). Indeed, their own programmes and publicity material seem to emphasize such components of the entrepreneurial ideology at the same time as claiming to produce 'team builders' and 'cooperative decision makers,' which often results in mutual disillusionment between MBAs and large companies. Partly reflecting conflicts and divisions within the business world, business schools manifest both entrepreneurial legitimations of capitalism and the more 'managerial' ideologies of large multinational firms.

Employment field and salaries

Whichever of these two views MBAs choose to emphasize and to identify with, they all shared a desire for a substantial salary and a belief that the qualification[1] would lead to a well paid job.

This belief was correct for the early graduates of the business schools considered here. Almost half of the British graduates were earning over £10,000 a year in 1976/7 while the median annual income of the French graduates from INSEAD was 124,000FF.

How much these high salaries can be attributed to the MBA degree alone is difficult to determine in the absence of similar information about a suitable control group. However, some idea of how much more managers with MBAs than managers in general was obtained by examining surveys of managerial salaries in Britain and France. In a 1976 study of some members of the British Institute of Management, Melrose-Woodman found that of those aged between thirty-six and

Table 8 (2) Employment sector changes of French business graduates[1]

Current (1974) employment field	First post-INSEAD employment field (%)							
	Industry[2]	Big banks[2]	Small firms	Consultancy	Self-employed	Family firm	Other[3]	%
Industry	59	14	25	22	0	0	0	41
Banks	0	50	0	11	0	0	0	8
Small firms	14	21	56	11	0	0	0	21
Consultancy	9	0	0	44	0	0	0	10
Self-employed	7	0	12	0	100	0	0	9
Family firm	7	7	6	11	0	100	0	9
Other	2	7	0	0	0	0	100	3
%	55	14	16	9	3	2	1	101
N	56	14	16	9	3	2	1	

[1] Alumni who graduated from INSEAD at least five years before the survey
[2] Firms employing over 1,000 people
[3] Public field and employers' association

forty-five half were earning less than £7,000 a year (1978:42). Similarly, a 1977 management salary survey (British Institute of Management 1977) found a median salary for managers of all ages below the level of director of under £9,000. The relative youth of the British alumni compared with the managers in these surveys further emphasized their well-paid status.

The salaries of French managers were considerably higher than those of managers in Britain (Beaudeux and Rouge 1978; Granick 1972). Each year the business journal *Expansion* publishes tables of managerial salaries in relation to educational qualifications and firm size and sector. These tables show that a graduate of one of the top engineering schools can increase his salary by 20 per cent by going to INSEAD (Beaudeux and Rouge 1978:161). In 1974, the year of the INSEAD alumni survey, the same 'league tables' showed that the mean salary of top managers who had graduated from the best engineering schools in their late thirties was 98,000FF, which was distinctly less than the figure found for the INSEAD alumni who were slightly younger. Graduates from elite commercial schools in top posts earned slightly more than those from engineering schools but still less than the INSEAD graduates. In general, then, the MBA seemed to have helped considerably in obtaining highly paid jobs in Britain and France.

In both countries, managerial salaries varied between employment fields and MBA earnings follow a similar pattern. In Britain the movement to small firms led to substantially lower salaries being earned. Over half of the MBAs in small firms were earning under £9,000 a year while only 38 per cent of those remaining in large industrial companies earned so little. Similarly, as *Table* 8 (3) shows, alumni in family firms, self employment, and the public sector were paid relatively low salaries. The highest incomes were found among those in consultancy and major financial institutions.

In France, too, the large banks paid high salaries but the other differences found in Britain were not replicated. *Table* 8 (4) indicates that small firms paid rather higher salaries to INSEAD alumni than did large industrial companies, while consultancy led to rather low financial rewards. In general, the distinction between large and small firms did not seem to be as marked in France as in Britain, at least for INSEAD graduates, and those who developed careers in small companies in order to acquire senior posts at high salaries seem to have been successful. Given the size of these firms, though, it is improbable that these alumni will move into top positions of dominant national or international companies.

Table 8 (3) Employment field and current (1976–77) salaries of British Business Graduates at least 5 years after graduation

Salary (£'000s)	Employment field (%)							
	City	Industry	Small firms	Consultants	Family firms	Self employed	Public services	N
<7	0	13	17	0	20	50	27	23
7–7.9	8	12	21	0	0	10	20	19
8–8.9	15	13	17	0	40	10	0	20
9–9.9	19	10	12	12	0	0	27	20
10+	58	52	33	87	40	30	27	75
N	26	69	24	8	5	10	15	157

Table 8 (4) Employment field and current (1974) salaries of French business graduates at least 5 years after graduation

Salary (FF 1000s)	Employment Field (%)							
	Big banks	Industry	Small firms	Consultancy	Family firms	Self employed	Public service	N
51–80	0	13	5	20	0	0	0	8
81–110	29	31	25	30	37	45	0	30
111–150	14	36	40	40	37	36	50	35
151+	57	21	30	10	25	18	50	24
N	7	39	20	10	8	11	2	97

Thus, while the MBA does seem to lead to a substantial salary at a relatively young age, it does not encourage all business school alumni to develop careers in major economic institutions and to constitute a 'high flying' echelon within them.

Business graduates in big business

The improbability of business graduates in small firms or management consultancy moving to top management posts in dominant companies leads to an analysis of the early careers of those alumni remaining in large firms, so that the contribution of the business schools to the reproduction or change of the business 'elite' can best be understood. In the rest of this chapter, therefore, we focus on the careers of the 63 per cent of the British alumni and the 49 per cent of the French alumni who were working in large industrial and financial companies at the time of the survey. This group of business graduates contained some MBAs who, although not yet in management posts, seemed to be in the recruitment stratum for such jobs. This subgroup consisted of alumni in senior management posts in large companies in their thirties, who could be termed 'high flyers'. The rest of the business graduates in major firms, who were in less promising positions, we called the 'non-high flyers'. Not all high flyers would become top managers, of course, but they were the business graduates, we suggest, from among whom future top managers with MBAs would be selected. They formed the group that has been most successful in obtaining important managerial posts with major responsibilities at a relatively young age.

The job descriptions provided by the alumni formed the basis for distinguishing the high flyers. These descriptions covered the number of subordinates they had, to whom the alumni reported, their job title, responsibilities and general information about the work involved. We considered business graduates to be in senior management if they fulfilled the following conditions:[2]

1   Their position was no more than two management levels below the main board (one level below in the case of the smaller merchant banks). Thus, divisional board directors and/or function heads in divisions would be included but not usually their immediate subordinates unless the division was so large as to constitute a major firm in its own right.

2   The position was not purely advisory but involved some responsibility for allocating resources and taking decisions.

3 The position involved control of a number of managerial sub-ordinates and not simply two or three assistants.

4 The post was not one of more than two identical positions. This excluded works managers where there were a number of such managers all reporting to the production director.

5 The post was not a narrowly technical position but included some general management responsibilities.

Some of the examples of the position which fulfilled these conditions are: assistant general manager of a large British clearing bank, director of a major bank, managing director of the transport subsidiary of a multi-national agri-business company, financial controller of the international division of a large British engineering group, director of a large trade and transport group, finance director of a major subsidiary of a multi-national vehicle firm, main board director of a conglomerate, director of a major engineering subsidiary of a multi-national holding company.

In order to mitigate the effect of age upon the distinction between high flyers and non-high flyers we only considered business graduates who were in their thirties. We also left out most of those graduates from MBS who left after one year with a diploma rather than continuing to obtain the two-year MBA. As we have already mentioned, evidence concerning salaries indicate that one-year business graduates do not advance as fast as two-year MBAs and certainly the proportion we considered to be high flyers was much lower (24 per cent) than that of MBAs (46 per cent).[3]

Applying these criteria showed that there were ninety-six British business graduates remaining in big business and forty-six French MBAs from INSEAD. Twenty-six of the British were working for major financial institutions and seventy were in large industrial companies. Because the City of London has traditionally been regarded as a distinct field of employment and separate from manu-facturing industry (Ferris 1960), the British business graduates in financial institutions are here examined separately. Only seven of the forty-six French MBAs worked in large banks, so they were included with those in industry. There were, then, three groups of business graduates working in big business to be considered: twenty-six British alumni in major financial institutions, seventy British alumni in major industrial companies, and forty-six French alumni of INSEAD in large firms.

A higher proportion of the British alumni in industry were found to be high flyers than those in financial firms. Only 27 per cent of British alumni in the City were judged to be in senior management posts whereas 40 per cent of the British graduates in industry were considered high flyers. This difference might be due in part to the younger age of the former, their mean age being one year less than those in industry. It is more likely, though, that the rather exclusive ethos of the City and the relatively 'flat' administrative structure of some merchant banks were more important factors. Nearly half of the British graduates in major financial institutions worked for merchant banks, which have fewer employees than the big clearing banks and relatively few top management positions. The proliferation of technically based managerial positions in these firms created a number of positions of middle management posts for which MBAs specializing in financial analysis might be thought appropriate but the proportion of executive positions above this level is fairly low, thereby limiting promotion possibilities to senior posts. Consequently, although business graduates in major financial institutions were better paid than those in industry, they might not have been able to move into senior management posts so easily.[4]

Almost half of the forty-six INSEAD alumni remaining in large firms were considered to be in senior management. Although this overall proportion (46 per cent) was higher than that found for the British business graduates, the French alumni were older and had been working for slightly longer since graduation. In contrast to the British alumni, most of the small number of the French who were still working in big banks were high flyers (five out of seven) while only two-fifths of those in large industrial firms were in senior management posts – the same proportion as the British graduates in industry. While this difference may be an artefact of the small number of alumni being considered, it may also reflect differences between the role and ethos of large banks in Britain and France. It is also possible that French banks are less the special preserve of the 'mafia' from the top engineering schools than are some large industrial firms.

Overall, the proportion of business graduates considered to be contenders for membership of the business elite in either country is rather low. Only 23 per cent of the total British alumni and 21 per cent of the French, whose early business careers we analysed here, were judged to be in senior management positions in major firms in their thirties and so possible members of top management of dominant economic institutions in the future. The three business schools would scarcely be said, then, to be producing the future business elite let alone monopolising access to it.

Work experience and early career success in big business

Given the preference of British industry for 'experience' over high-level educational qualifications, we would expect the nature of managerial jobs held by British business graduates to be more important in distinguishing high flyers from the non-high flyers than for the French alumni. In the remainder of this chapter we discuss relations between the work experience of business graduates before and after business school and their relative early career success in big business. In the following chapter these relations, especially those found for the alumni in British industry, will be discussed in the context of educational backgrounds and family characteristics.

In general, the sort of post likely to lead to favourable opportunities for MBAs would be one which combined a broad range of activities requiring a number of skills which could not easily be matched by non-business graduates, together with visibility to top managers. Specialist expertise may distinguish the MBA from other graduates in some functions, but excelling simply at one task, such as market research, and doing it for too long, is unlikely to lead to line management jobs (Beaudeux and Rouge 1978; Table Ronde 1978). The ambitious business graduate has to demonstrate the capacity for successfully undertaking a set of managerial tasks that are not readily reducible to a technique, and that require working with senior managers so that he or she can show an ability to work with people in a 'team'. Largely technical functions – such as some jobs in management service departments – are not likely to provide such opportunities because their 'managerial' content is not high. On the other hand, advisory posts dealing with investment strategy and planning may be useful, as they involve close contact with top managers and require broad consideration of a number of areas and not simply financial techniques. Equally, previous work experience in a purely technical function – especially engineering (Gerstl and Hutton, 1966; Glover 1976) – may not be as helpful to rapid advancement after business school as that in a more commercial or managerial job such as marketing.

High flyers and non-high flyers in major British financial institutions

The financial sector in Britain has been traditionally distinct from industry and other fields, and has developed a separate ethos and culture (Lupton and Wilson 1959; Spiegelberg 1973). When recruiting MBAs, banks and insurance companies pay little attention to their previous work experience – unless it has been in banking – and are likely to take younger business graduates than do large industrial firms. It is experience in financial companies that counts rather than management jobs elsewhere. As one 'high flyer' in a merchant bank said: 'Despite their business qualifications they (MBAs) still need specific training in banking.' And another high flyer in a clearing bank said: 'Banking is a craft industry still and your background is very important – that is, a proper background in banking. You still need to take the professional examination to get on within the bank whatever your previous training.'

Sheer longevity in financial firms, then, was a major factor in becoming a high flyer in this sector. All the high flyers in our survey had worked in banks or insurance companies for five years or more, whereas all the business graduates who had moved to banking after an initial job in industry were non-high flyers. Another factor that distinguished the high flyers was their reliance on personal contacts to obtain their current job. Only two of the seven successful alumni used the placement services of the schools and none relied on the press. In contrast, six non-high flyers found their present employers through the placement services and three had used press advertisements, so nearly half of the non-high flyers had relied on impersonal means of contact. As Granovetter (1974) has pointed out, managers tend to use personal contacts more than other qualified groups in changing jobs and this tendency is likely to be even stronger in the City where trust and personal knowledge are so important to making deals (Ferris 1960). A shared social background is also helpful in establishing successful contacts and the City is well known for its restrictive recruiting practices (Spiegelberg 1973; Whitley 1973), which are also manifested in the case of business graduates, as will be seen in the next chapter.

High flyers and non-high flyers in British industry

(A) TYPE OF FIRM

We suggested earlier that diversified and divisionalized companies might be attractive to business graduates, since they could offer general management opportunities at an earlier age than could functionally organized firms. In this survey it proved difficult to allocate the firms in which business graduates were working to one of the categories of diversification and managerial control structure indicated by observers such as Channon (1973), so that a systematic analysis of the type of managerial structure in relation to career success was not possible.

Some firms, for example, could not be allocated to one of the categories based on the Standard Industrial Classification because they were involved in more than one industry and so were highly diversified. These companies, and those in transport and trading that are also notably diversified, were coded in the 'other' category. Although only twelve of the seventy alumni were working in such firms at the time of the survey, seven of these twelve were considered high flyers, a much higher proportion than that found within any other industry group. At the other end of the diversification scale, only one of the ten alumni remaining in firms entirely in the chemical industry was a high flyer, so some connection between diversification and early career success of MBAs might be inferred.

The ownership of firms was another characteristic that was related to the early career success of business graduates. Nearly all the high flyers were working for British firms while over a third of the non-high flyers were in foreign companies. While this is due in part to the fact that six of the fifteen non high flyers in foreign multi-nationals worked for the same firm, even when these alumni are removed from the analysis there is still a tendency for MBAs in foreign-owned companies not to progress as fast as their counterparts in British-owned firms. Most of these foreign firms were US multi-nationals, so this result was partly a function of their size in that the managerial hierarchies were longer.

(B) TYPE OF JOB AFTER BUSINESS SCHOOL

The major factors relating to early career success in large industrial companies concerned the type of job obtained after business school and the nature of work done before going to business school. In particular, working in a corporate planning function or as a personal assistant to a top manager after graduation was associated with being a high flyer in a large firm. Previous work experience in a marketing department was also beneficial. Exactly half of the high flyers had worked either as corporate planners or as personal assistants when they left business school. In contrast, only a fifth of the non-high flyers had done so. In addition, a further five of the twenty-eight high flyers had moved to such posts after their first job. In all, just over two-thirds of the British alumni who had early career success in large firms had worked in those positions that provide opportunities for high-level contact across the major departments and visibility to members of the firm's top management. In contrast, only a quarter of the non-high flyers had had experience of such posts and five of these were still in corporate planning sections. In general, remaining in the same functional area was not helpful to rapid promotion, nearly all of the MBAs who did so were non-high flyers. This result is similar to some other surveys of top managers (Granick 1972 : 226; Melrose-Woodman 1978) although not all observers agree with the overriding importance of functional mobility (Fidler 1977).

By way of contrast to the success of the MBAs entering corporate planning posts, those who joined finance or marketing departments in industry after business school did less well. In marketing, only a quarter of those choosing it as their first job became high flyers and in finance less than a fifth. Indeed, two of the four high flyers who did start their post-business school career in marketing jobs subsequently moved to corporate planning posts. Why these two functional areas should appear to be so unrewarding for business graduates is difficult to ascertain, but it may be related to the nature of the competition provided by other managers in these functions.

In finance departments, the long-standing high professional status of chartered accountants in Britain (Berridge 1978; Johnson 1973) and their perceived relevance to financial management[5] in large firms (Hannah 1976 : 88–90) may place MBAs without accounting qualifications in competition with an already entrenched and professionally certified group of managers who consider their skills to be readily transferable and capable of letting them move into more generalist posts (Guerrier and Philpot 1978 : 38–9). In this function especially, the MBA degree is not the unique high status vocational qualification and may, indeed, lack credibility when compared to the more clearly professional certificate.

Marketing, on the other hand, does not have a generally recognized professional qualification of the same stature as the chartered accountant but here, too, there is stronger competition for the business graduate to contend with than in some other areas. This competition results more from social factors, for the sales or commercial side of British business has always attracted the public school boy or Oxbridge Arts graduate (Acton Society Trust 1956, 1962; Clements 1958; McGivering et al. 1960; Melrose-Woodman 1978; Leggatt 1978). Managers in this field tend to come from high-status family and educational backgrounds which give them as much, if not more, social capital than many MBAs. Companies, too, show some scepticism as to how much of the work in this area is 'technical' and generalizable across industries as distinct from being social, and essentially specific to an organization. As one early graduate from a British school who joined a multinational consumer goods firm said, the marketing instruction he

received was not very useful because the company was more sophisticated at marketing than were the business school staff.

The combination of the relatively non-technical nature of the
activity and the higher social status of many managers in marketing
may reduce the perceived stature of the MBA degree in this field and so
result in slower progress for many business graduates.

(c) TYPE OF JOB BEFORE BUSINESS SCHOOL

In total contrast to the negative relations between working in finance
and marketing departments *after* business school and career success is
the strong connection between having worked *previously* in these areas
– including accounting – and becoming a high flyer. All the British
business graduates who had worked as accountants and/or in finance
departments before going to business school became high flyers –
mostly by moving to corporate planning posts. Similarly, although not
so strongly, over half of the alumni who had previously worked in
marketing became high flyers. Business graduates who came to
business school specifically to move out of the more technical areas
such as production, engineering, and management services, did not do
nearly so well. All but one of the British alumni who were in production
departments before business school were non-high flyers as were all the
five who were in management services departments. Even when they
moved to corporate planning sections these alumni did not have early
career success.

The business graduates who had worked in the more managerial or
commercial areas *before* business school did better than those who were
restricted to the more technical fields where contact with other
managers and people outside the organizational unit was limited
(Acton Society Trust 1956 : 27). Accountants, in any case, already had
one relevant professional qualification before going to business school
so they possessed extra 'cultural capital' in the eyes of many large firms.
Also, given the suspicions some firms still have about university
graduates, the accounting qualification may have implied commitment
to the business world and a basic grounding in applicable techniques
(British Institute of Management 1968; Sorrell 1966). Previous
experience of commercial and similar functions was also helpful in that
alumni had some exposure to managerial norms and practices and
contact with middle managers before going to business school. They
were, therefore, likely to be more commercially orientated than MBAs
coming from technical fields and to have the social skills required for

working with senior managers and in project teams (Leggatt 1972 : 107–19).

Particular combinations of pre- and post-business school work experience seem crucial to the early career success of business graduates in British industry. To examine this we brought together previous work experience in marketing, finance and accounting, planning and consultancy posts under the general title of 'managerial' experience. Alumni who had worked only in production, engineering, research and development, management services, and other fields before going to business school were combined with those who had not worked previously in the 'other' category. Post-business school jobs were then divided into those in corporate planning or personal assistant roles and the rest. It can easily be seen from Figure 8 (1) that the combination of some 'managerial' experience before business school and a corporate planning job afterwards nearly always led to a senior management job by their mid-thirties for these business graduates. Only one of the eight alumni with this combination was not a high flyer.

At the other end of the scale, only seven of the thirty-three alumni without either of these desirable types of work experience became a high flyer, so the relation between the type of jobs held by British business graduates and their early career success in large industrial firms was quite strong. Previous experience in a managerial post seemed to be rather more beneficial for early career success than post-graduation work in a high-level staff post, but the small numbers involved make any clear-cut conclusion about their relative importance difficult to draw here. In general there did not appear to be any strong connection between having had a managerial sort of job before business school and obtaining a post as a corporate planner afterwards, although previous experience in production or engineering was clearly not associated with moving to such jobs.

(D) FORMAL AND INFORMAL CONTACTS

Finally, as in the case of the City, personal contacts were important to joining a firm where rapid upward progress could be made. Over two-thirds of the British high flyers used informal channels to find their current employer rather than going through the school placement services or the press. In contrast, exactly half of the non-high flyers had found their present company through formal means. Use of the press seemed especially disadvantageous; only ten MBAs had found their current jobs through press advertisements and eight of these were non-high flyers. Again, the high degree of personal contact and collabor-

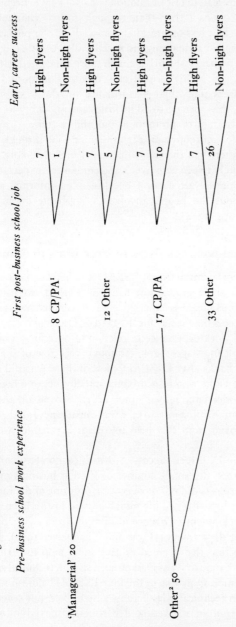

Figure 8 (1) Pre-business school work experience, first post-business school job, and career success in industry for British business graduates in large firms

[1] Corporate Planning and/or Personal Assistant to a top manager
[2] Includes those who did not work before going to business school

ation required at senior management levels suggests that recruitment to posts that may lead to fast promotion is most likely to occur through personal connections rather than through formal channels (Clark 1966 : 109–10). The less technical and specialized the post, the more important are personal qualities and social skills. As Offe (1976 : 64–6, 79) points out, managerial work is much more concerned with people than with things or highly structured symbols. The more difficult it becomes to assess individual performance on the basis of purely technical skills, the more personal qualities and an ability to fit in will be used as indicators of promotion and ability (Offe 1976 : 64–98; Sorrell 1966; Slocum 1966 : 240–45). Obtaining a job through personal connections rather than through impersonal media is more likely to lead to a closer fit between employer's and employee's expectations and so to greater mutual satisfaction because more informal and tacit information about the people involved is available on both sides (Granovetter 1974 : 13–45).

High-flyers and non-high flyers in large firms in France

Most of the French alumni from INSEAD who had been at work for at least five years since graduation had not worked extensively beforehand. Previous business experience was thus much less relevant to early career success than it was for the British. One major area of post-business school work experience in relation to becoming a high flyer was employment in a large bank. Although very few of the French alumni entered banks after INSEAD, most of those who did did very well. Six of the eight who joined banks initially became high flyers, including two who later joined other firms. Second on the list of apparently favourable first jobs to take was consultancy; all three of the alumni who moved from this field into large companies were high flyers.

In contrast to the career success of British corporate planners and personal assistants, the small number of French business graduates who took similar posts did not do very well; only one of the four could be considered a high flyer. This might be due to the later and less widespread development in France of divisionalized companies with central planning departments (Dyas and Thanheiser 1976).

The one function that seemed to give some help to early career success in French industry was marketing; a start in technical sales was a definite hindrance. Only one of the four INSEAD alumni who took their first jobs in technical sales became a high flyer, but seven of the sixteen who began in marketing departments moved into senior management posts at a relatively young age. This proportion, though, is not as high as might be expected given the apparent prestige of marketing in French business in the 1960s. (Bourdieu, Boltanski, and de St Martin 1973; Dyas and Thanheiser 1976:36; Table Ronde 1978).

It is only slightly greater than the proportion of INSEAD graduates starting in other fields who became high flyers in industry (44 per cent compared to 39 per cent). Certainly, compared with the clear success of the alumni who began their post-business school careers in banks, the connection between a marketing background and becoming a high flyer in industry seems less than strong. In general, there do not seem to be the same sorts of close connections between types of work experience and early career success for the French MBAs as were found for the British. Parental backgrounds and educational experiences were more directly relevant, as we shall see in the next chapter.

Conclusions

The combination of prestigious post-graduate business schools claiming to educate the future general managers of major firms, the ambitions of their students, and the reluctance of many firms to share their control over appointments to senior management posts with the educational system, has resulted in a substantial proportion of the early graduates from the three business schools discussed here moving out of large firms into small businesses and, for a few, self employment. The likelihood, therefore, that these schools will provide most of the future business leaders of Britain and France seems remote. Rather, they enable graduates to switch career paths and employment fields and obtain well rewarded posts in business. A few may become members of the big business elite, but the MBA as such seems to be only one factor among many leading to such positions.

9 Capital and careers: links between backgrounds and career paths

The diversity of careers followed by the alumni from INSEAD, LBS, and MBS, and, in particular, the tendency of some to opt out of big business, lead to consideration of the ways in which their previous educational and family backgrounds are related to career choices and success. As we have already seen, career expectations were linked to parental occupations; fields of post-business school employment can also be expected to vary between different groups of business graduates. Similarly, the rate of advancement up managerial hierarchies of MBAs in large firms is likely to be related to particular educational and family characteristics, both directly and indirectly, through the sort of work experience and job types that prove to be favourable to early career success in big business. Finally, the extent to which business schools may alter the constitution of the business elite can be partially assessed by a comparison of the high flyers in major firms to the existing set of top managers and directors. If, in fact, the MBA does become an important credential for access to the managerial posts that function as a springboard to top management positions, is this going to change the sort of people who dominate big business, or, rather as the proponents of the 'reproduction' thesis argue, merely lead to a reinforcement of existing recruitment patterns? In this chapter, then, we examine the connections between type of higher and secondary education, parental occupation, and employment choices and consequences for the early graduates of the three business schools.

Employment field and higher education

The subject studied for one's first degree, and the institution where the degree was obtained, remained important for career choices and opportunities even after the acquisition of an MBA. The effects of taking a degree in science, engineering, or economics at Oxbridge for British alumni are clearly shown in *Table* 9 (1). Business graduates with first degrees in science or engineering overwhelmingly remained in large industrial firms, and so followed a similar pattern to that found for most first-degree graduates in these subjects (Department of Industry 1977; Kelsall, Poole, and Kuhn 1974). In contrast, business graduates with first degrees in economics disproportionately joined financial institutions as did, to a lesser extent, alumni with degrees in arts and the other social sciences. The business school qualification enabled economics graduates to develop careers outside industry to a far greater extent than it did for scientists and engineers.

An Oxbridge degree also assisted mobility to fields of employment that were different from those previously joined. The financial sector, small firms, and management consultancy attracted business graduates with degrees from Oxbridge, whereas those who had graduated from other universities tended to develop careers in large industrial firms. The consequences of obtaining a first degree from Oxford or Cambridge were in part linked to the subject of that degree. Most of the engineers considered here did not go to Oxbridge, while more scientists and alumni with 'other' degrees had attended one of these two universities.

Oxbridge qualifications seemed to be especially important for scientists and engineers with MBAs wishing to work in financial institutions. All the British alumni considered here who were in the City, and who had degrees in these subjects, had obtained them at either Oxford or Cambridge. This suggests that the prestige associated with having attended one of these institutions outweighed the disadvantages of taking a degree in a 'technical' subject. It is possible, of course, that the experience of being at Oxbridge heightens awareness of job opportunities in such firms and of their attractiveness. The strong connection between having a first degree in engineering and working in large industrial firms was echoed in France. In particular, attendance at the two most prestigious engineering *grandes écoles*,

Table 9 (1)   Current employment field of British business graduates in relation to first degree subject and institution

| | Institution of first degree | | | | | | | | |
| | Oxbridge | | | | Others[1] | | | | |
Current field	Economics[2]	Sciences	Engineering	Other[3]	Economics[2]	Sciences	Engineering	Other[3]	Total
City	7	5	3	3	6	0	0	2	26
Industry	7	14	3	4	9	7	16	6	66
Small firms	3	5	2	5	2	3	4	0	24
Consulting	2	1	1	2	0	1	1	0	8
Family firms	1	0	0	1	1	1	0	1	5
Self-employed	0	1	1	2	2	1	2	3	12
Public Sector									
Industry	2	0	0	3	0	1	1	0	7
Teaching	0	0	1	0	1	2	2	2	8
Total	22	26	11	20	21	16	26	14	156

[1] Including Polytechnics but excluding accountants
[2] Including joint degrees with other subjects
[3] Arts, sociology, politics, law, and business studies

Polytechnique and Centrale (Paris), was associated with remaining in large firms, as shown in *Table* 9 (2). Over three-quarters of the INSEAD graduates with diplomas from these schools were in this field compared to a half of those from other engineering schools and just over a third of those from the commercial schools.

Significantly, the engineers in France did not join large banks. In fact, banks attracted most the alumni who had been to the Institut d'Etudes Politiques ('Sciences Po') in Paris. Three of the seven INSEAD graduates developing their early careers in banking had been to Sciences Po and a fourth had attended both Sciences Po and HEC. These two institutions form part of the *écoles de pouvoir* (Bourdieu, Boltanski, and de St Martin 1973) and are known to attract students from high stratum families. They are particularly attended by people from Parisian business and financial families and Sciences Po also attracts many students with fathers in the top echelons of the civil service. These two schools together represent the most socially and educationally prestigious undergraduate commercial and adminis- trative schools in France. It is also striking that only 14 per cent of the French MBAs with diplomas from them were still working in large industrial firms at the time of the survey. The early division in which manufacturing industry is associated with an engineering diploma and the service sector is associated with a degree in commerce, or economic and political sciences, seems to be followed in later career decisions. The INSEAD MBA here appears to reinforce initial orientations rather than to function as a mechanism for change of employment field.

Career choices, degrees, and family backgrounds

(A) BRITISH BUSINESS GRADUATES

In addition to one's subject and institution of higher education influencing career choice, we suggested earlier that students from particular families would use the business schools to effect a conversion from the father's occupation field to different, more promising ones. We described in Chapter 7 how the MBA enabled many British students to move into the major financial institutions from other sectors – especially those who had already been to public school and/or Oxbridge. *Table* 9 (3) similarly shows how half of those currently in the City came from business-owner or top-manager families – and more than a quarter of MBA sons of business owners developed careers here. Nearly all (eleven) of the thirteen British business graduates from these

Table 9 (2) Institution of diploma and current field of French business graduates

Current field	Engineering schools Paris			Other Eng.	Sciences Po	Commercial schools Paris			University	Abroad	Total
	Polytechnique	Centrale	Mines			HEC	ESCP ESSEC	Other Comm.			
Banks	1				3	1			1	1	7
Industry	3	3	1	13	1	2	8	4	3	1	39
Small firms	2	1		6	2	1	3	3	1	1	20
Consultants				3	1	3	2	1			10
Family firms				1		4		2	1	1	9
Self-employed			1	3	1	1	2	3			11
Other					1	1	1				3
Total	6	4	2	26	9	13	16	13	6	4	99

[1] Where more than one institution was attended, the one with highest prestige was used

Table 9 (3)   Current employment field of British business graduates in relation to father's occupation and distribution of first degree

Current field	Oxbridge						Other[1]				Total
	Father's occupation										
	Owners	Top mgrs.	Other mgrs.	Prof.[2]	Other[2]	Business owners	Top mgrs.	Other mgrs.	Prof.[2]	Other[3]	
City	7	4	3	2	2	1	1	1	3	2	26
Industry	2	5	6	6	8	6	3	12	9	12	69
Small firms	3	4	3	4	1	1	2	1	2	4	25
Consulting	0	2	1	2	1	1	0	0	1	0	8
Family firms	2	0	0	0	0	3	0	0	0	0	5
Self-employed	1	1	0	2	0	4	1	1	0	2	12
Public Sector											
Industry	0	0	0	3	1	0	1	0	0	1	6
Teaching	0	1	0	0	0	0	1	1	1	4	8
Total	15	17	13	19	13	16	9	16	16	25	159

[1] Including polytechnics and accountants
[2] Higher professions, senior military officers, and civil servants
[3] Lower professions, small businessmen, clerical and manual workers

two types of families did not have fathers active in the financial services sector and so can be considered to be converting into it by going to business school. Rather than using the qualification to move into large, multi-national firms, then, this group seemed to be reproducing a well established pattern of mobility in Britain away from manufacturing industry towards older established and more prestigious fields (Coleman 1973; Stanworth 1980).

Furthermore, this group was already well endowed with cultural capital before going to business school: 85 per cent had been to Oxbridge and 77 per cent to public school. This combination of business background and prestigious education at all levels seems crucial for certain careers, even for MBAs, and the lack of one such characteristic can constrain career opportunities. Thus, for instance, all of the sons of business owners who were in the City had been educated at both Oxbridge and public school. In contrast, six of the eight alumni from similar families who entered large industrial firms did not have first degrees from Oxbridge. In the case of the business owners' sons, the positive relation of an Oxbridge education to financial institutions can be seen especially clearly.

As well as rejecting industry, the sons of business owners seemed to reject large firms in general, with a substantial proportion working for small firms or running their own businesses – with a few of course returning to the family firm. Given greater access to economic capital than is presumably available to any other occupational group, it is not surprising that business owners' sons should set up their own firms, although it is not clear why Oxbridge-educated ones preferred to work for other small firms rather than striking out on their own. In general, then, British MBAs who are the sons of business owners seem to use the qualification as a means of transferring into the financial services and small firm fields rather than into large manufacturing firms – especially those MBAs with the most prestigious educational background.

The sons of top managers behaved rather differently. Most had a degree from Oxbridge and some of these joined financial institutions, but nearly a third of the group developed careers in large firms in industry. Indeed, whereas an Oxbridge degree seemed to turn MBAs from business-owner families towards the City, it was more associated with an industrial career for this group of British alumni. This contrast, though, was partly a product of the subject of first degree taken. Three of the five with Oxbridge degrees who remained in industry had taken degrees in science or engineering and another had been sponsored on the MBA programme by his employer – an oil company – with whom he remained after graduating. Further contrast between this group and those who came from business-owner families was the greater tendency of the latter to start their own business while the former preferred to join small firms. In addition, none of the owners' sons took jobs in the public sector, yet three of the alumni from top managers' families did so.

British business graduates from other occupational backgrounds did not move into major financial institutions to the same extent as the sons of owners and top managers, largely because they did not have degrees from Oxbridge to the same extent and/or had not as often been to public school. However, even when they had been to Oxbridge, they did not seem to pursue careers in the City as much as did the top business groups.

For the sons of higher professional and senior administrative fathers, this might be because alternative careers in the public services and management consultancy seemed equally, if not more, attractive. As can be seen from *Table* 9 (3) they constituted the major group of the small number of British MBAs in these occupations[1] and, assuming that something of the professional and/or public service ethos of their father's job had rubbed off onto them, these business graduates could be seen as having used the MBA as a means of acquiring lucrative and attractive jobs in management that were not too dissimilar to their fathers' occupations.

However, the relative dominance of these service sector posts by the sons of higher professional and senior administrators should not obscure the fact that nearly half of the business graduates from such backgrounds were pursuing a managerial career in large industrial firms – a higher proportion than that found for the top business groups. So, many of these MBAs had used the degree to switch from their father's employment sector to well paid jobs in industry.

In contrast, most MBAs who were from managerial families, but not top ones, returned to large industrial firms. Indeed, they formed the highest proportion of any group taking jobs in industry, with only a few moving into the City or joining small firms. Family knowledge of the business world seemed here to encourage MBAs to work in large firms, although the negative effect of a first degree from Oxbridge is again noticeable. Over half of this group who went to Oxbridge did not remain in large firms, while three-quarters of those with first degrees from other universities did develop careers in big business.

Similarly, over half of the business graduates from backgrounds less well endowed with social and cultural capital developed careers in industry. Again, the effect of an Oxbridge degree in turning MBAs away from large industrial firms is noticeable although not as marked as in the case of business owners' and other managers' sons. Business graduates from lower social status backgrounds who did not go to Oxbridge were strongly attracted to jobs in the education sector, this group including half of the eight MBAs working in business schools or management departments. Indeed, only one of the eight had been to public school, suggesting that perhaps the public educational system that had enabled their own vertical mobility was an attractive goal to aim at.

(B) FRENCH BUSINESS GRADUATES

Particular combinations of family background, institution of higher education, and subject studied were also influential in the selection of career paths by the French alumni. The relationships occurred however in different ways, reflecting, perhaps, the different 'tramlines' of early educational choices and the different tertiary education system, coupled with the much greater prestige of an engineering diploma in France, especially one from the top *grandes écoles*.

The sons of the *patronat* did appear to use the MBA as a means of converting from their fathers' fields of activity, which were often in declining industries. Only a quarter returned to family firms and none of the rest took jobs in the same industry or geographical areas as their fathers. They did not move, however, into the financial services sector to the same extent as the British. Only three of the thirty-four *patronat* sons considered here joined banks after obtaining the MBA. Instead they developed careers in large manufacturing firms: nearly half of those not returning to the family firm were working in industry at the time of the survey. A few were working in small firms or had started their own businesses and so could be said to have opted out of big business. Most of these opting out from the *patronat* had not managed to enter one of the major Parisian *grandes écoles*, as can be seen from *Table* 9 (4), and they may have been influenced by the tendency of large firms in France to rely on prestigious first degrees for recruitment and promotion decisions. An INSEAD MBA may not be considered to make up completely for the lack of a first diploma for this ambitious group.

Over a third of the small group of INSEAD alumni who were sons of top managers were working in large firms, a similar proportion to that found for their British counterparts. Rather than moving to financial institutions and small firms, however, the rest of this group were

Table 9 (4) Institution of diploma, father's occupation and current (1974) field employment

	Institution of diploma																
	Ecoles de Pouvoir										Other schools and institutions					
	Top engineering schools[1] Father's occupation					HEC + 'Sciences Po' Father's occupation					Father's occupation					
Current (1974) employment field	1[3]	2	3	4	5	1	2	3	4	5	1	2	3	4	5	6[4]	Total
Major firms[2]	3	0	2	1	1	4	2	0	1	1	8	2	5	10	3	1	44
Small firms	0	1	0	1		1	0	0	1	1	3	0	3	4	3		18
Consultants						2	1	1				3	1	1		1	10
Family firms						3				1	5						9
Self-employed	1					1	1				3	0	3	2	0		11
Other										2		1					3
Total	4	1	2	2	1	11	4	1	2	5	19	6	12	17	6	2	95

[1] Polytechnique, Centrale, Mines de Paris
[2] Including banks
[3] For key to classifications see Table 9 (3)
[4] Wealthy but not connected to business

largely working in management consultancy firms. This was especially so for those with first diplomas from provincial *grandes écoles*.

The French alumni who were sons of higher professionals and senior administrators had not had quite such a prestigious tertiary education as their British counterparts. Only a fifth had been to one of the *écoles de pouvoir*, although a further third had attended one of the two major Parisian commercial schools, ESSEC and ESCP, usually considered only slightly less prestigious than HEC. This group did not move to jobs in consultancy and the public sector as much as their British counterparts. Indeed, over half of them developed careers in big business, including two in banks. They also constituted a substantial proportion of those in small firms. Presumably many in this group had already committed themselves to careers in business by training in a commercial school and considered the INSEAD diploma as additional cultural capital to improve their chances relative to those of alumni of HEC and 'Sciences Po.'

INSEAD graduates who were sons of *cadres supérieurs* and *cadres moyens* also attended schools just below the top in terms of prestige. A slightly greater proportion, though, followed their fathers in attending engineering schools as opposed to commercial ones. Not all continued along the same path into manufacturing firms, however; just under a half went into industry. A fifth, all from the less prestigious schools, had set up their own businesses which was the highest proportion doing so of any occupational category. A further fifth had joined small firms and, like most of the business owners' sons, this group had been to provincial schools for their first diploma. For these sons of *cadres* it appears that those with the highest prestige first diploma were more likely to stay in the larger industrial firms, perhaps for them the INSEAD qualification was not as successful a conversion device as the ones who did not go to the top schools had expected or perhaps their motivations for attendance at INSEAD were accelerational rather than 'conversionary'.

Almost none of the French alumni came from manual worker or routine clerical family backgrounds. Rather more had fathers who were in the semi-professions or who ran small businesses. This group, as a whole, were educationally very highly selected. It included the highest proportion of graduates from the *écoles de pouvoir*, especially HEC and Sciences Po and most of these were the sons of small businessmen, artisans, and shopkeepers. This sub-group was noticeably less inclined to work in industry. Two of the five with diplomas from a major commercial school were working in the public sector and it is clear that for this small group, which possessed considerable cultural capital before entering INSEAD but low social and economic capital, large industrial firms were relatively unattractive. The one business graduate from this family background who went to a top engineering school later went to a major US graduate school after INSEAD, thus acquiring even more cultural capital, and later developed a highly successful career in industry.

Overall, the majority of the French business graduates from INSEAD did not come from an *école de pouvoir* and were seeking to add to their relatively low stock of cultural capital. Although nearly three-quarters of those from the most prestigious engineering schools remained in large firms, only a third of those from HEC and Sciences Po did so. Nearly a quarter of the business owners' sons returned to their fathers' firms, while almost half of the rest were working in major banks and industrial firms and had converted to a different field of activity. The relative success of this conversion in terms of rapidly acquiring senior management posts will now be examined.

Career success in big business and the distribution of social and economic capital

Although only just over half of the British and French MBAs considered here were still working in large firms at the time of the survey, it is this group who are important in considering whether the business schools are, in fact, training the future general managers of the largest companies, as distinct from producing well paid managers of small or medium-sized businesses that have relatively little economic impact. The existence of some MBAs already in senior management posts in major firms in Britain and France allows us to examine the extent to which particular social and economic background characteristics are associated with the rapid rise of these MBAs. This should in turn provide evidence towards ascertaining whether the business schools function largely to reproduce privileged access to important positions in business by dominant groups, or to offer some assistance to less well endowed groups. Insofar as the high flyers from business school are potential future members of the business elite, they can be compared with current members of this stratum to see whether they come from distinctly different family backgrounds and have followed distinct educational paths.

Career success in the City

The well known connection between the top public schools, Oxbridge, and top positions in major financial institutions in Britain (Whitley 1973, 1974) reappears here. Over three-quarters of the MBAs in such firms had attended public schools, and four of the others went to Oxbridge. Nearly all had thus attended at least one of these relatively exclusive sets of educational institutions. In contrast, just under two-thirds of those working in large industrial firms had been to public school, and, as we saw earlier, an Oxbridge degree was negatively associated with a career in industry. The relatively low extent of pre-business work experience of most MBAs in the City and its apparent lack of relevance to career success suggest that it is in this sector that relations between educational backgrounds, family status, and career success should be most clearly observable.

In Figure 9 (1) we illustrate the interrelations between these factors for the twenty-six business graduates in major financial institutions. It can be seen that all seven of the high flyers had been to public school and most had fathers who were business owners or top managers. None of those who went to direct grant or grammar schools were high flyers, nor were the sons of the lower status groups progressing very rapidly. Where social origins and secondary school were the same, higher education seemed to make some difference. All five of the high flyers from business owner families went to Oxbridge and three had degrees in economics. All the non-high flyers from this background had also been to Oxbridge but only two read economics and their grades were slightly lower than those of the high flyers. The apparent importance of degree subject for success in this sector is confirmed by an examination of the sons of higher professionals, administrators, and army officers. The only member of this group who achieved early career success had an upper second in economics. In contrast, a degree in science or engineering does not help in the City. None of the engineers were high flyers and only one of the five business graduates with science degrees had early career success there. In general though, subject and class of first degree were of only minor importance for early career success in financial firms compared to family background and secondary school attended.

In conclusion, while the MBAs may have enabled some of the sons of lower status families to join banks and other financial institutions, they had already been to public school, and in two cases to Oxbridge, and the qualifications did not apparently lead to rapid upward progression. Consequently, it seems unlikely that, as far as this sector is concerned, business graduates will alter the high degree of social reproduction among holders of top positions. There is no indication that the MBA is as important as one's parents' occupation and one's

Figure 9 (1) Career success in the City and background characteristics of British business graduates

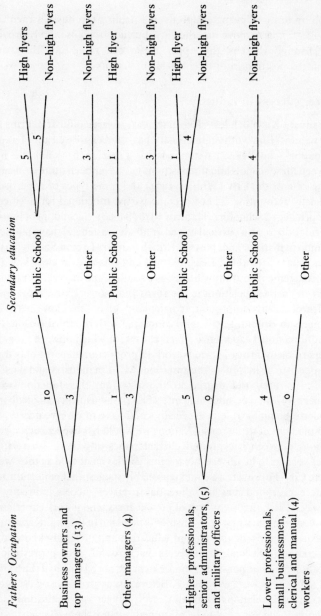

school in terms of being a high flyer. Enabling top businessmen and managers' sons to move into the City, business schools merely provide the channel whereby the upper strata can reproduce their own privileged position in different fields of activity.

Career success in industry

The situation is much less clear in the case of large industrial firms for four reasons. First, although industry has often expressed a preference for public school boys (Acton Society Trust 1956, 1962) the link between these schools and top positions has never been quite as clear as in the case of the City (Whitley 1974) and some types of expertise – especially accounting – have become partial functional replacements for a privileged schooling (Hannah 1976: 89–90). Second, people with Oxbridge degrees in particular, and graduates in general, have not been common in management posts in British industry (Acton Society Trust 1956, 1962; Clark 1966; Leggatt 1972) and it is not yet clear how the top management stratum will alter as a result of the increased graduate intake to business positions in the 1950s and 1960s. Third, the subject of degree seems important, particularly given the low status of engineers in Britain. Lastly, and connected with the third reason, the type of functional experience affects the rate at which upward progress occurs in many firms. Previous work in production departments does not appear to be helpful to the ambitious MBA in industry and most of those who used the degree to transfer from this function were engineers. Moreover, obtaining one's first post-business school job in a corporate planning role is especially conducive to career success.

In the light of these considerations we would not expect such direct relations between background characteristics of MBAs and relative career success to be observable for this employment field as they were for the City. However, we could reasonably suggest that education and family background may be influential in career success indirectly in two ways. First, the 'right' sort of pre-business school work experience and obtaining one's first post-business school job in the 'right' area may be related to a particular type of education and/or family knowledge and contacts. Second, a business background and a prestigious education may compensate to some extent for not having had the 'right' kind of business work experience. Before discussing these two suggestions, though, relations between degree subject and institutions and early career success need to be examined because these characteristics affect the influence of other background factors.

Although the career success of MBAs in general was not strongly associated with degree class, over half of those with firsts were high flyers while only a quarter of those with thirds progressed quickly. Academic prowess was thus not entirely irrelevant. However, attendance at Oxbridge seemed to outweigh the lack of a good degree. Seven out of the eight business graduates with third class degrees had been to Oxbridge but only one of those with firsts. The lack of correlation between degree grade and prestige-awarding institution obscures any direct relation between the latter feature and early career success. Nonetheless, as *Table* 9 (5) shows, more Oxbridge economists and, especially, arts graduates did become high flyers than non-Oxbridge ones, and the three Oxbridge engineers did less badly in industry than engineers with degrees from other universities. The relatively poor performance of the Oxbridge scientists seems to be associated with their poor degree grades; they were from equally high-status backgrounds and had been as often in the more commercial business functions before going to business school as other MBAs. Finally, it is worth emphasizing the lack of early career success of business graduates who took their first degree in engineering – including those who were in non-production departments at the time they entered business school. Although many had fathers in managerial positions and most (three-quarters) had been to public school, the vast majority of engineers did not progress rapidly after business school. The MBA enabled them to move out of engineering and related fields in large industrial firms but did not add sufficient cultural capital to overcome the disadvantages of the degree.

Most of the engineers had not taken their first degree at Oxbridge and did not work in the more commercial and managerially visible field before going to business school. The relative importance of each of these factors in the early career success of business graduates in British industry is, therefore, difficult to clarify. In Figure 9 (2) we illustrate the interrelations of these three characteristics and their bearing upon success. It can be seen that the only engineer who moved to a marketing job before business school became a high flyer, but he also went to a major public school, and his first post-business school job was in corporate planning. It is not clear, therefore, how much his career success can be attributed to this single feature alone.

For the non-engineers, the type of pre-business school job seems more important for quick success than does the institution of first degree; the proportion of high flyers from Oxbridge is lower than that of the non-engineers from other universities. This is partly because many of the Oxbridge scientists had third class degrees. Possession of an engineering degree is not, however, enough to account for the

Table 9 (5) Degree subject and institution and career success of British business graduates

	Oxbridge				Other university				
	Economics	Science	Engineering	Other	Economics	Science	Engineering	Other	
High flyers	4	2	1	3	4	5	3	1	23
Non-high flyers	3	12	2	1	5	0	12	5	40
	7	14	3	4	9	5	15	6	63

Figure 9 (2)   Institution and subject of degree, last job before business school, and career success in industry

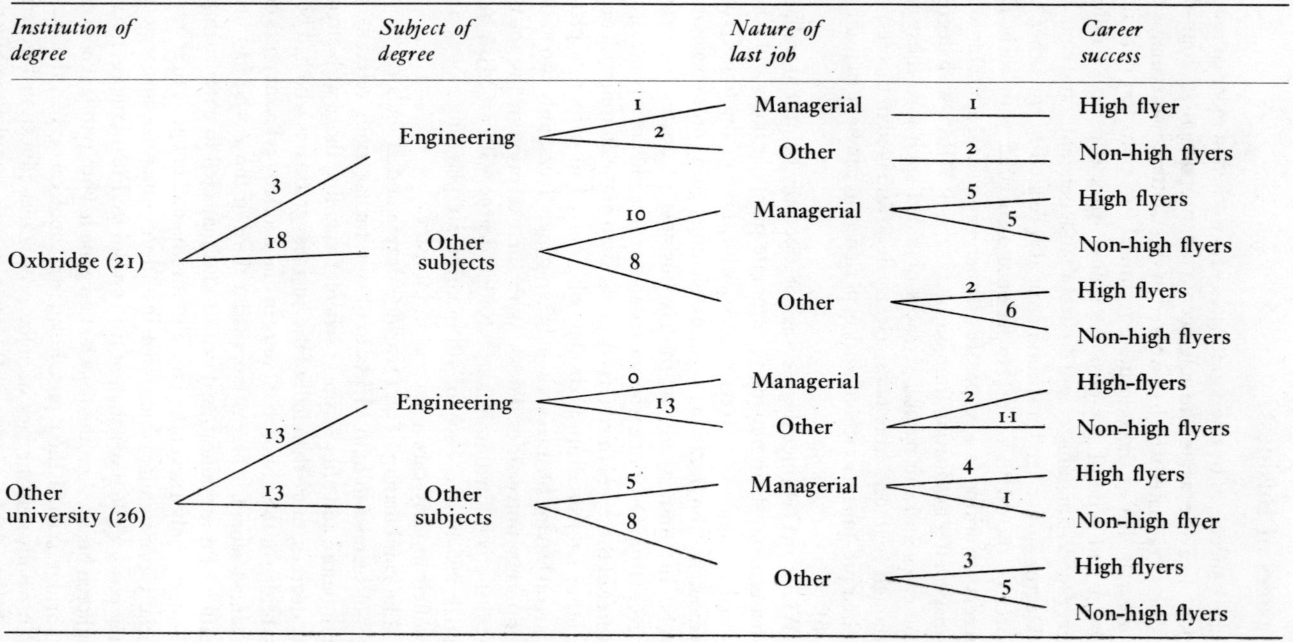

Column headings (left to right):

Institution of degree — Subject of degree — Nature of last job — Career success

Oxbridge (21)
- Engineering — 3
  - Managerial — 1
    - High flyer — 1
    - Non-high flyers — 2
  - Other — 2
    - High flyers — 5
    - Non-high flyers — 5
- Other subjects — 18
  - Managerial — 10
    - High flyers — 2
    - Non-high flyers — 6
  - Other — 8
    - High-flyers — 2
    - Non-high flyers — 11

Other university (26)
- Engineering — 13
  - Managerial — 0
    - High flyers — 4
    - Non-high flyer — 1
  - Other — 13
    - High flyers — 3
    - Non-high flyers — 5
- Other subjects — 13
  - Managerial — 5
  - Other — 8

relative success of business graduates who worked in more commercial fields. Leaving aside the engineers, the proportion of high-flying business graduates who had worked in these latter areas remains twice as great as that of those in more technical functions. So both degree subject and type of pre-business school work experience influence career success in industry and do so both independently and conjointly.

Degree subject and institution are also related to the other major aspect of the MBA's work experience associated with early career success – working as a corporate planner or personal assistant to a top manager after graduation from business school. MBA's with degrees in economics and the natural sciences obtained such jobs most easily, although engineers were not so clearly disadvantaged in this respect as in their pre-business school work experience, as can be seen from *Table 9* (6).

Whilst an Oxbridge degree was not especially helpful overall, it did assist economists in moving to corporate planning posts and was also related to their early career success, with three of the four Oxbridge economists who began in corporate planning going on to become high flyers. In contrast, five of the six business graduates with science degrees from Oxbridge who started in this area did not advance quickly – three of these had third class degress. Both of the alumni with degrees in other subjects from Oxbridge who moved to corporate planning posts on leaving business school became high flyers; only two of the six from other universities did so. With the exception of the scientists, then, the combination of an Oxbridge degree with an MBA and an initial post-business school job in corporate planning almost always resulted in early career success in industry.

The combination of an Oxbridge degree and attendance at public school seemed to help MBAs to obtain 'managerially relevant' posts both before and after business school. Excluding those with engineering degrees, more than half of the business graduates who had been to Oxbridge or to public school were in managerially relevant posts before business school, whereas less than a third of those who had been to neither of these educational institutions managed to enter such posts. Similarly, only a seventh of the alumni who had not gone to at least one socially prestigious educational institution obtained corporate planning posts while nearly half of the rest did so. Furthermore, ten of the eighteen business graduates who had gone to both public school and to Oxbridge started their post-business school careers in this field. It seems both that the lack of some prestigious educational experience could negatively affect an MBA's career path, and the combination of public school and Oxbridge could considerably aid it. Parental

Table 9 (6) First degree subject and institution in relation to the first post-business school job of British business graduates

| | Institution of first degree | | | | | | | |
| | Oxbridge | | | | Other | | | |
First job	Economics	Science	Engineering	Other	Economics	Science	Engineering	Other
CP/PA[1]	4	6	1	1	2	2	5	22
Other	3	8	2	3	7	3	10	41
	7	14	3	4	9	5	15	63

[1] Corporate planning or personal assistant to top manager.

occupation did not seem directly connected to either pre- or post-business-school jobs but obviously could indirectly affect them through the education system.

So far, we have largely concentrated on those business graduates who had advantageous features in their careers. To discuss possible ways in which background characteristics could compensate for the lack of these, we will now examine connections between career success, education, and family status for those without these features. Only six of the twenty-eight high flyers had neither had a managerially relevant job before business school nor had taken a corporate planning/personal assistant job upon graduation, while twenty-six of the forty-two non-high flyers did not have these beneficial career features.

For this group, who had not had useful work experience, a business background seemed to help. Four of the six high flyers came from business families but under half of the twenty-six non-high flyers did so. Almost all the high flyers had been to public school; but just over half of the non-high flyers without favourable work experiences had attended such institutions. For early career success, then, background features do play an important part for those MBAs who have not had particularly beneficial work experiences. Of special note here is the negative effect of coming from a non-business family and attending a local authority grammar school. Only one of the eight business graduates with both these characteristics became a high flyer while four of the eleven sons of managers or business owners who had been to public school did so.

In summary, the early career success of business graduates in British industry was related to particular features of their pre-business school jobs and first post-business school position. These aspects were in turn related to the subject of the first degree and, to a lesser extent, the grade of that degree. Job types were also related to educational backgrounds in that attendance at a fee-paying secondary school and Oxbridge continued to improve chances of working in positions favourable to early career success. Business graduates without either of these educational experiences did not move to advantageous jobs. In addition, family knowledge of the business world and attendance at a public school were directly associated with early career success in the case of MBAs who did not have especially useful previous work experience. Thus, while career success in British industry was not so directly connected to the family and educational backgrounds of business graduates as it was in the City, indirect connections certainly were important and while the additional cultural capital of the MBA probably did help some of the least endowed alumni to progress quickly, the general effect was by no means redistributive of privileged opportunities.

Career success in French industry and banks

The relative lack of pre-business school experience of most of the French alumni from INSEAD, and the apparent lack of any particular first job being especially favourable to early career success in France mean the relations between family, educational experience, and career success in industry can be examined directly. Figure 9 (3) shows that although educational success, in terms of attending a high prestige institution for one's first diploma, is by no means irrelevant to career success in large French firms, it is not quite as important as one's father's occupation. Two-thirds of the sons of business owners in larger firms became high flyers, although over half had not been to an *école de pouvoir*; while just over a third of the alumni from other families had such early career success. Indeed, the proportion of owners' sons who became high flyers was much the same whether or not they had been to one of the 'best' schools. For this group, the INSEAD diploma seemed to compensate for the relatively low status first diploma.

For the other business graduates in large firms, though, the importance of having a prestigious first diploma was more marked. While half of those with such diplomas had a successful career at an early stage, only a third of the business graduates with less prestigious qualifications advanced quickly. In particular, the importance of an engineering diploma from one of the top three schools seemed especially advantageous for this group while HEC and 'Sciences Po' appeared to be better value for the sons of business owners. This was largely because early career success was related to the nature of the industry worked in and to the type of first diploma. Graduates from HEC or 'Sciences Po' were more successful in banking, commerce, and consumption goods industries than they were in capital goods firms. On the other hand, graduates of the three top engineering schools did better in the latter firms and worse in the more market-based industries. Even engineers from the top schools who went to INSEAD as a means of transferring out of heavy industry progressed more slowly than alumni from the top commercial schools. Equally, capital goods firms seemed to prefer INSEAD graduates who already had a prestigious engineering diploma.

One further point about types of cultural capital should be mentioned here. All four alumni in large French firms who had obtained a post-graduate degree – not usually in business – from a

Figure 9 (3) Career success, father's occupation, and institution of first diploma of French business graduates

Father's occupation		Institution of first diploma		Career success
Business owners (15)	3	Polytechnique, Centrale, Mines	1	High flyer
	4	HEC, Sciences Po	4	High flyers
	8	Other	5	High flyers
Cadres dirigeants (4)	0	Polytechnique, Centrale, Mines	1	High flyer
	2	HEC, Sciences Po	1	High flyer
	2	Other		
Cadres supérieurs and *Cadres moyens* (7)	2	Polytechnique, Centrale, Mines	1	High flyer
	5	Other	1	High flyer
Higher professions and senior military officers (12)	1	Polytechnique, Centrale, Mines	1	High flyer
		HEC, Sciences Po		
	10	Other	3	High flyers
Wealthy but not in business (1)	1	Other	1	High flyer
Other (5)	1	Polytechnique, Centrale, Mines	1	High flyer
	1	HEC, Sciences Po	1	High flyer
	3	Other	1	High flyer

university in the USA became high flyers, and two of these could be regarded as being relative failures in terms of the hierarchy of French educational institutions. None of these, incidentally, had business-owner fathers.

The additional cultural capital conferred by a foreign higher degree seemed to outweigh to some extent the lack of a highly prestigious French diploma. In addition, the one business graduate who obtained his first degree from Cambridge university also became a high flyer. Thus although those who escaped the verdicts of the French education system by taking diplomas in Belgium or Switzerland did not advance particularly quickly, alumni with British or American qualifications did achieve early career success.

The importance of one's father's occupation in progressing rapidly to senior positions in large French firms for INSEAD graduates suggests that business owners' sons' 'conversion strategies' have paid off. Whatever their previous educational accomplishments, most of them were able to move away from their fathers' firm and industry to important, usually salaried, positions elsewhere by going to INSEAD. In this sense the business school functioned as a system of social reproduction for the *patronat*. This does not mean, though, that they are necessarily going to become members of the international managerial elite that we discussed in Chapter 2. Indeed, only three of the ten high flyers from business-owner families were currently working for international companies while seven out of the other eleven high flyers were doing so. Of course, owners' sons may move to important positions in multi-national firms in the future but they were certainly not much in evidence there at the time of the survey. Indeed, if some INSEAD graduates are to become part of an international business elite, those that do seem likely to come from families with relatively little direct ownership of economic capital.

Business schools and business elites

The relation between father's occupation and success in large firms for business school graduates is most marked for those working in the City in Britain and for the French alumni of INSEAD. Indirect connections through the educational system have also been outlined for the British graduates in industry. However, in a few cases the educational system in general, and business schools in particular, do seem to have enabled sons from non-business families, including those in the lower professions, artisans, and manual working class, to achieve considerable career success in big business. In the light of this – and of the claims made at the time of the establishment of the British business schools that they would enable the best of the young talent available to fill major managerial positions – it is worthwhile comparing the back ground features of the high flyer business graduates with those of current top managers and directors of large firms.

Although there have been a number of studies of the social backgrounds of French top businessmen and *cadres* (Birnbaum *et al.* 1978; Bourdieu, Boltanski, and de St Martin 1973; Delefortrie-Soubeyroux 1961; Hall and de Bettignies 1968; Monjardet 1972) most studies of British business elites focus more on educational background than on father's occupation and published data do not always include this information. In Britain attendance at a private fee-paying secondary school – especially one of the major ones – is generally taken as evidence that one has a successful father, although the latter's employment sector is usually unknown. Where the family background of managers in Britain has been studied, it is often restricted to a particular geographical area and/or covers a wide range of firm sizes (Clements 1958; Clark 1966) so that the elite, in terms of economic resources controlled and incumbency of top positions, is difficult to identify.

(A) THE FINANCIAL ELITE IN BRITAIN

Studies of the major financial institutions in Britain by Lupton and Wilson (1959) and Whitley (1973) did not systematically examine family status, but investigation of kinship connections, especially through the aristocracy, suggested that many directors came from 'top' families. The importance of family connections in acquiring top management posts in major British banks is further attested by Leslie (1978) in a *Financial Times* article on Barclays Bank. The crucial importance of attendance at a major public school to becoming a director of a large bank or insurance company is shown by the fact that 35 per cent of such directors in 1971 had been to Eton (Whitley 1973). Public schools in total contributed four-fifths of the total number of City directors in that study. In comparison, all the MBA high flyers in the City had been to public school and two of the seven had been to one of the 'Clarendon Nine' schools. Consequently, it seems unlikely that even if all future directors of major financial institutions were to be business-school graduates, their secondary education would be typical of the total population.

Similar results are obtained for tertiary education. Omitting the 35 per cent of 1971 directors of major private City firms who did not go to university, Oxbridge clearly dominates, for 90 per cent of those with degrees had been there. Business graduates who have succeeded at an early age in the City are not quite so limited to Oxbridge – only five of the seven had degrees from these two universities. In general, though, the available evidence suggests that MBAs who succeed early in these firms have had practically identical educations, with the exception that fewer went to Eton than did existing incumbents.

(B) THE INDUSTRIAL ELITE IN BRITAIN

British industry is not quite so restrictive in its recruitment practices as are the financial institutions. In 1953 Copeman found that two-fifths of the directors of large companies had fathers who were themselves directors or executives. A further quarter came from professional or administrative families. A 1970 survey of British managers in all sizes of firm found that just under a third of the directors were sons of managers (Leggatt 1978) and over half came from all middle-class families. In comparison, 29 per cent of the business graduates who were high flyers in British industry came from top business families and over half were from managerial backgrounds in general. A further 29 per cent had fathers in the higher professions, senior civil service, or military, so again, if top managers of major British industrial firms went to business school in the future it seems unlikely their social composition would be fundamentally altered. Indeed, the social basis of recruitment could become more restricted.

Similar results occur when secondary school and university are considered as can be seen from *Table* 9 (7). Copeman (1955 : 101) found that over half of his directors had been to public school and the Acton Society Trust study of *Management Succession* in companies employing over 10,000 people in 1956 found both that a third of the top managers had been to public school (1956 : 9) and that 40 per cent of these managers who had been to a major public school were top managers. Other studies (e.g. Melrose-Woodman 1978 : 15) suggest the proportion has dropped since the 1950s but much of the variability in results can probably be attributed to differences in definition of the top stratum and variations in firm size and/or peculiarities of sample selection. In any case the percentage of business graduates with early career success is clearly more similar to the higher figures although only a tenth went to a major public school.

The comparison of business graduates' university education with that of directors and top managers in industry is complicated by the considerable number of the latter group who did not go to university.

Table 9 (7) Educational backgrounds of senior British managers and directors and 'high flyer' business graduates in industry

	Secondary school						
	Copeman[1] (1955)	Acton Society Trust[2] (1956)	Clements[3] (1958)	Heller[4] (1973)	Leggatt[5] (1978)	Whitley[6] (1974)	MBAs[7]
% Public School	58	33	45	71	36	65	61

	University						
	Copeman	Acton Society Trust	Clements	Heller	Leggatt	Whitley	MBAs
% with degrees	36	33	45	49	28[9]	57	86
% of graduates with Oxbridge degrees	56	23[8]	55	59	14[10]	70	42

[1] Directors of large companies
[2] Top managers of large companies
[3] Top managers of 4 big firms in the North West
[4] Survey of Directors of top 200 firms
[5] Directors of firms of all sizes
[6] Directors of 50 largest British firms
[7] LBS and MBS graduates in senior positions in large firms in their 30s
[8] Of all graduate managers, not just top managers
[9] Senior managers, mostly in large firms
[10] Of all graduate managers in firms of all sizes

Only 36 per cent of the British Directors in Copeman's study went to university and only a third of the top managers in the Acton study had degrees (Acton Society Trust 1956:8). However the BIM study claimed that 98 per cent of its top businessmen had been to university (Melrose-Woodman 1978) which perhaps says more about response bias than about top managers in major British companies. As with the variations found in the percentage attending public schools, many of the differences between the studies concerning those going to Oxbridge can reasonably be supposed to derive from difference in procedure and definition. The figure for the alumni is, however, lower than that found in the majority of the other studies cited in Table 9 (7) which may, if and when these business graduates move on to main boards, slightly alter their composition. In general, however, these comparisons clearly imply that business schools are unlikely to create a new meritocratic stratum of top managers drawing from all levels of society, indeed if the MBA does become important as a filter for top management posts it may result in even more socially and educationally restrictive recruitment practices than are currently in evidence.

(C) THE FRENCH BUSINESS ELITE

The French business elite is more similar to that of the City than to that of British industry, recruiting overwhelmingly from top business groups. INSEAD, as we have seen, is equally restrictive, so the background features of the future top managers with MBAs are not substantially different from current incumbents of elite posts. In the 1950s Delefortrie-Soubeyroux (1961 : 51) surveyed the *dirigeants* of the major French firms and found that two-fifths had fathers who were business-owners or top managers. A further 45 per cent came from professional, administrative, and managerial families. As Monjardet (1972) has pointed out, though, this study included a number of *cadres supérieurs* and owners of smaller firms so may not be sufficiently restrictive in its definition of the business elite. In his own study of the *Présidents-Directeurs Généraux* (PDG) of the one hundred largest French firms, including state controlled ones, he found that three-fifths were sons of business owners, bankers, etc. and a further 36 per cent came from professional and managerial families. Thus virtually all of the chief executives of France's largest companies came from the upper strata. A slightly later study of the owners and PDG of the larger banks and industrial firms as listed in *Who's Who* in 1974 found that nearly half were sons of owners and managing directors (Birnbaum *et al.* 1978:98). As an INSEAD study itself has shown, firm size plays a considerable role in explaining such differences (Hall and de Bettignies 1968). In nearly all cases the larger the firm, the more socially selected is its top management group. While not all the INSEAD high flyers in our study were in the hundred top French firms, they were mostly in the top five hundred by turnover and their fathers' occupations show a similar configuration to those found for the current elite. Just under half were sons of business owners and a further tenth came from top managers' families. The 'openness' of a managerial elite based on the INSEAD diploma is therefore unlikely to be especially marked.

Similarly, the relation between family background and the prestige of first diploma for the successful INSEAD alumni differs little from that obtained for the current business elite. Generally it seems that the sons of business owners in France who succeed to top posts in the major firms have been to lower prestige schools, or sometimes have had no higher education, than the *patrons* and PDG who came from non-business-owner families who have frequently been to the École Polytechnique (Birnbaum *et al.* 1978:129–42; Bourdieu, Boltanski, and de St Martin 1973; Delefortrie-Soubeyroux 1961:62–9; Monjardet 1972). As we saw earlier, INSEAD high flyers who came from top business families had not, on the whole, been to one of the top three engineering schools but a third of the rest of the high flyers had done so. While there was little difference among the sons of business owners as to whether they had been to an *école de pouvoir* previous to INSEAD and subsequently became high flyers, additional cultural capital did appear to assist other INSEAD graduates. The general relationships between education and family found for the current top managers of French big business thus appear to hold for successful INSEAD alumni in the larger firms, so again, the business school seems to function as an aid to social reproduction rather than as a channel for upward mobility.

10 Masters of business?

This study has explored the changing relationships between the higher
education system and the business world in Britain and France as these
can be seen in the new links between institutions of business education
and patterns of recruitment and promotion to superordinate posts in
industry and commerce. Alone among the major occupational structures in modern Europe, business careers have never been 'bureaucratized' in the sense that career entry and promotion possibilities became
tied exclusively to possession of educational diplomas. While for
medicine and law an educational certificate is the only means of
acquiring a licence to practice, and while the senior posts of the central
civil service have frequently come to require (*de facto* or *de jure*
according to the country) a particular educational past, business, like
the military, has largely eschewed making use of external criteria of
suitability in assessing applicants for 'officer' posts.

In the decades after 1945, however, a series of high-level schools
appeared in Europe whose *raison d'être* was to provide an education in
the discipline of 'management' or of 'business administration'. The
claims made for their purposes and competence by the schools
themselves, and their location at the highest levels of the education
system, seemed to suggest that major businesses had recognized the

need to 'professionalize' their management and to recruit and promote individuals chosen initially on the basis of externally 'proved' competences. The use that 'business' now seemed to be prepared to make of the education system might be interpreted as heralding a fundamental shift in the attitudes of the controllers of business who had hitherto insisted on the autonomy of managerial practices and the necessity of managerial knowledge and experience gained within specific enterprises.

Major changes in the industrial structures of the more developed European countries which occurred after the Second World War may be seen as having stimulated changes in attitudes. The domination of many industries by a small number of very large firms operating on a multinational scale led to the development of new methods of market management and control. These, in turn, became linked to the development of new products and processes, which themselves became an integral part of overall corporate strategies and plans. As giant firms' activities grew in diversity and complexity, new managerial skills were seen by many as necessary. New functional departments developed and novel forms of managerial organization were instituted to integrate diverse activities and to permit the development and implementation of general corporate policies. These changes, many of which originated through the introduction of American capital and management techniques, seemed to demonstrate the need for distinct managerial expertise which could, at least in part, be instilled by the educational system, and especially by new institutions modelled on the most prestigious North American business schools.

These institutions, though, have sought to do more than simply inculcate the latest managerial techniques to fit their products for specialist roles in large firms. To attract students, to secure finance from business, and to encourage employers to recruit their alumni, they have presented themselves as 'elite' schools and their products as the 'high flyers' of the business world. The three business schools considered in this book have aimed to produce general managers capable of overseeing the work of specialists in the interests of the enterprise as a whole. Familiar with skills of functional specialists, the MBAs are expected, at least according to the schools' literature and curricula, to rise rapidly to positions of general responsibility in which they integrate and co-ordinate the activities of functional departments and specialist advisory services. The schools, then, have offered a credential that they see as appropriate for access to general management positions in modern European businesses. By implication, although it is not usually directly stated, this certificate is designed to replace or supplement simple organizational experience or other educational qualifications as the requirement for senior positions in the new industrial structures.

Not surprisingly, the current controllers of big business have not shown themselves unduly eager to accept such novel educational certification on its own as a licence to practise general management in large firms. They have been willing to recruit MBAs to highly paid jobs where their expertise can be utilized in a largely advisory capacity, thus recognizing the MBA as one kind of credential for management roles. In particular, finance and planning in Britain and marketing in France have been major areas of early employment for business graduates. But subsequent progress up managerial hierarchies to generalist posts has remained dependent on the MBAs' track records in big business, as it has for the non-MBA manager. By recruiting business-school graduates to staff posts initially and insisting on making movement to general management positions dependent on performance in the firm, employers are, in effect, asserting their autonomy from the educational system and maintaining their control over senior appointments in business. Thus the argument whether managers are 'born' or 'made' remains unresolved.

Business schools and the 'credentialization' of management

The continued reluctance of the business world to accept whole-heartedly the verdicts of the educational system, coupled with the fluid nature of managerial 'careers', suggests that the correspondence between the hierarchy of educational certificates and positions of power and privilege in the occupational system is less direct than some advocates of the credentialling thesis have implied. The expansion of the higher education system in most European countries since the war and the consequent proliferation and hierarchization of education diplomas have led some observers to see this system as a novel means of allocating jobs and employment opportunities in the upper echelons of the occupational structure. Bourdieu and his school have written of economic changes leading to organizational changes and hence new needs within business firms. They suggest that these new needs are then 'met' both by the provision (public or private) of 'appropriate' education institutions and as a result of strategies operated by families or individuals seeking to maintain (or improve) their position in the socio-economic hierarchy of society. The education system thus provides cultural capital which, at least metaphorically, they see as functioning in much the same way as economic capital. Investments in the education system are made by privileged families through their children and these are expected to 'pay off' in terms of direct access to privileged posts offering economic rewards and social advantage in the changed labour market. Economic and social resources are transmuted into cultural certificates of competence, which are then used to monopolize access to positions of authority and to legitimate continued inequalities in the distribution of authority and privilege both in the organizations concerned and in society at large.

In this 'radical functionalist' argument, the development of an enlarged system of higher education is seen as merely having altered the nature of the process by which social and economic inequality is reproduced. Changes in the occupational structure are matched – albeit after some delay and in different ways in different countries – by changes in the provision and type of tertiary education which in the long term leave the system of domination and stratification in capitalist societies much the same as before. The labour market becomes more overtly structured and hierarchical, in terms of competence certified by the public educational system, but the end results leave the same groups in control of dominating positions.

Whatever the equivalence between certain parts of the French educational system and the higher civil service, 'business' organizations are not so strongly hierarchically structured as to allow managerial careers to be organized *solely* on the basis of formally certified competences. While there are rough divisions in big business between top, senior, middle, and junior management posts, the ways these divisions are made vary considerably across firms and, *a fortiori*, across industries. Firms differ in terms of technology used, in size, in market situation, in form of ownership, in importance attached to the different functions such as marketing or production or others, as well as in internal organization. Equally, the development of 'internal labour markets' among managers in the largest firms, and the strong preferences frequently encountered for internal promotion to senior jobs discussed above, make difficult and unlikely the establishment of a more professional or 'craft' (Stinchcombe 1959) type of managerial labour market, in which management jobs of a certain rank are reserved for those who have obtained particular educational qualifications. The growth and differentiation of the managerial labour force as a whole may result in particular management jobs becoming defined in terms of technical skills which can be acquired at educational institutions, but their organization and control will remain the preserve of top management. The educational system may increasingly propose, but the controllers of the elite managerial labour market still dispose.

While it may be convenient for employers to use externally determined 'certificates' as part of the selection processes at certain levels of the organization, beyond those levels posts are seen to demand competencies not judged, or perhaps even judgeable, by the formal education system. The competition for a few crucial posts may make it expedient to refrain from too close a designation of the aptitudes demanded. As Offe (1976) points out, it is very difficult after a given level to determine job contents in a measurable way, still less to measure in accurate terms the proficiency of the persons filling them. Employers, therefore, as was emphasized in Chapters 3 and 4, insist on retaining their autonomy of choice and the power of determining, by their choices, what are the 'qualities' demanded of candidates. They insist on the importance of 'leadership', of the 'capacity' for decision-taking, of the 'maturity' of judgement. By this insistence, they effectively remove a considerable proportion of the most important posts in enterprises from the purview of the education system. Rather than generalists they want business schools to produce specialists, highly paid technicians with particular skills who are easy to place and easy to control.

Moreover, changing economic circumstances may modify businessman's ideas of what is a 'good' manager. Evidence gathered in interviews with specialists in executive search in the tightened economic conditions of the 1970s, indicates that the more traditional characteristics of a *chef d'entreprise*, nearer perhaps in tone to the English 'boss' than to the more neutral 'chief executive', are coming more and more to the fore. What is being sought is a person who can exercise strong leadership, 'be firm', 'say no when necessary'. The 'soft' management techniques and the emphasis on 'human relations' typifying a 'new' style of command may indeed already belong to a past state of economic boom and expanding markets for the dominant companies pioneering management changes. Indeed, 'management' itself may be a concept open to change from external sources and over time.

We have seen as well, in Chapters 5 and 6, that the MBAs themselves attend business school with different motivations and aspirations. There were important elements, for example, in the social backgrounds of many MBAs that were likely to lead them to withdraw from the slow and grinding competition for posts at general management levels in giant firms. There was a strong trend amongst the graduates of all the business schools considered here to hold aspirations which precluded them from the perseverance usually necessary to move towards positions on the boards of major companies. Many MBAs were ambitious, wanting to reach the top rapidly, even if this meant setting up their own companies. Relatively few of the MBAs analyzed here fell into the category of high flyers in large firms. Those who did might be considered right for such promotion because of their social and educational backgrounds, personal characteristics, and particular working experience rather than their acquisition of an MBA. Others drop out or are dropped out of the big business field; business does not seem ready to close the avenues of access to senior decision-making positions in favour of individuals with new business qualifications.

In summary, then, the material presented in this book suggests that the correspondence between the hierarchy of educational certificates and positions of power and privilege in the occupation system is less direct than seems to be implied by some presentations of the 'credentialist' thesis. On the one hand, the employers' side of the market is highly complex, presenting diverse policies across diverse fields of production, traditions, and changing economic circumstances. This multiplicity of factors makes a widely accepted and acceptable ranking and specification of managerial positions unlikely. On the other hand, the MBAs also present a diversity of interests and aspirations that do not necessarily lead them to choose the path towards the boards of dominant corporations. We may add, as well, the role ambivalence shown by the business schools themselves, in both countries, in their uncertainties concerning the types of courses they should offer and thus for the 'market' at which they should aim – current middle managers (short in-service courses) or the high flyers of the future (longer, post-graduate courses).

Educational credentials are far from replacing the emphasis given at the most senior levels to the intangible personal qualities given by nature, developed through family upbringing and through the incidental curricula of the most formative secondary and higher education years. Business education seems to be perceived by many employers as the formal sanction given to qualities obtained from quite other bases, rather than as an extra item of 'cultural capital' that systematically distinguishes its holders from those who do not possess it. It seems thus unlikely that Masters of Business Administration will become the new 'masters of business', the controllers of the corporations likely to dominate Western economies in the opening years of the twenty-first century. The education system is far from monopolizing access to particular parts of the elite managerial structure and still less of dominating promotion and selection policies and chances of access to the few positions at board level in major concerns.

By background and training most business school graduates are fairly similar to current business elites; they may also be assumed to share the same fundamental values. The schools are thus likely to provide a new generation of managers and entrepreneurs who have the same backgrounds and values as the present controllers of important firms. To the extent that MBAs become a major contingent of the recruitment stratum to elite positions in business in general or in certain particular businesses (one already has a seat on the board of a major oil company) they will constitute a social and ideological stratum as closed as that which currently exists. In France, indeed, the social origins are even more restricted than those of present incumbents.

To that degree, at least, in France and Britain, the systematization of business recruitment procedures through the use of education credentials as criteria for recruitment and promotion, will lead to continued rigidity in this employment field. The influence of the socio-economic and cultural structures surrounding the operation of the education system at every level are such that the net result of the addition of 'professional' education is to systematise the differential chances of children from any social group of reaching any given level of social and economic power and prestige. If MBAs as such are not necessarily likely to become the new 'masters of business' they are still likely to provide an increasingly important proportion of the recruitment stratum. The business schools, while novel educational institutions in many aspects of their purposes and functioning in Europe, have been absorbed into the general set of relations between education and employment dominant in the societies concerned.

The post-graduate business schools nonetheless do provide particular opportunities to their students. They offer a means of changing employment sector and/or moving into managerial positions at a fairly well-paid level. They also enable those who regard themselves as being relatively educationally deprived to make up for previous mistakes. This latter function may be especially important in countries with a strongly institutionalized hierarchy of educational diplomas, such as France, and where the schools concerned are, for the French, recognized as being equivalent, if not superior, to the 'best' national institution. This role also occurs in Britain, though mainly through the one-year programmes offered by the business schools that seem to attract many students from the business world who did not obtain a first degree (Whitley and Thomas 1980).

Moreover, for those who wish to remain within the world of business enterprises and corporations, business schools have further important functions. They link MBAs to existing incumbents of top positions through the shared value position of commitment to the ethos of private business. Passage through business school may be taken by employers as proof of that commitment, in that it involves, for example, a willingness to forego one or two years' earnings to learn the latest management skills. Even if less than a quarter of the alumni reach senior management positions in large firms while still in their thirties, business schools nonetheless produce highly-educated managers who may yet come to have an impact on organizational policies, affecting both the internal form of the business world and its relations with other activities of society.

Notes

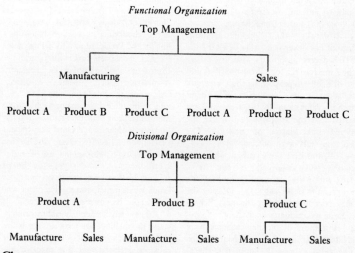

Functional Organization

Top Management

Manufacturing   Sales

Product A   Product B   Product C   Product A   Product B   Product C

Divisional Organization

Top Management

Product A   Product B   Product C

Manufacture   Sales   Manufacture   Sales   Manufacture   Sales

Chapter 2

1 This change has been diagrammed by Dyas and Thanheiser (1976 : 19) in the above way.

2 Financial management involves the allocation of financial resources, managing relations with external capital markets,

planning asset allocation, and monitoring the performance of sub-units, values of subsidiaries, and planning future acquisition and divestiture policies. Accounting, in contrast, is usually restricted to cost accounting and budgeting procedures. Marketing management is concerned with managing the 'marketing mix' of product planning, pricing, banking, distribution, advertizing, packaging, display, and research, while actually selling is considered to be only a part of this 'mix' (cf. Jalland 1973).

Chapter 3

1 An almost identical argument was later used to justify post-graduate provisions at business schools. See Earle (1965:7).
2 Several universities developed undergraduate courses in commerce during the first decade of the century, but the curricula were rather different to those which later became associated with management, and commerce graduates were generally recruited to specialist positions in industry and did not aspire to become top managers (Chester 1965:8).
3 Ironically, the London Business School has never been able to award the MBA degree despite its wish to emulate the American schools. Whilst MBS found no difficulty in persuading the University to adopt it, the University of London stolidly refused to do the same and insisted that the appropriate title for the award was Master of Science. The London staff were not, however, easily put off, and after a few years in which the course was described as the MSc. Programme they renamed it the Master's Programme (LBS 1973:11). Despite the MSc. tag, the London Business School regards its graduates as 'MBAs'.
4 A number of business schools were created after London and Manchester. The views expressed should not, therefore, be taken to have been directed only at these two institutions.
5 Details of the Schools' selection policies and methods are given below in Chapter 6.

Chapter 4

1 By the mid-1960s the 'management gap' was a phrase on many lips. Europe, it was thought, must 'catch up' on American techniques. France was the European country sending the biggest contingents to American business schools and the 'MBA vogue' caught on all over Europe (Mathewson 1976).
2 Fondation Nationale pour l'Enseignement de la Gestion des Enterprises (National Foundation for Management Education), set up by the Paris Chamber of Commerce and the French Government in 1968.
3 The Chambres de Commerce are publicly regulated and recognized bodies but are 'private' in effective control, attitudes, and activities.
4 The choice of site was delicate, given the government's decentralization plans. It was chosen because the local Chamber of Commerce gave the idea a great welcome. The English title of INSEAD is the European Institute of Business Administration.
5 On the Board, the Paris Chamber of Commerce and Industry held three seats because of its heavy financial commitment to the school since its creation. In addition to this, the President of CEDEP (a major French industrialist, R. Gillet) and the President of INSEAD's Alumni Association held seats ex-officio. Otherwise, the Board consisted of a 'certain number of personalities who bring their time, their personal relations and the caution of their firm'. Until very recent years neither Faculty, Dean, or Director General were represented as of right. Until these recent changes, the Board invited the Faculty to join its members for lunch when it met, and the Faculty knew little about its powers.
6 In case any student should misunderstand the qualification they receive at the end, the brochure hastens to insist that 'it must be stressed that this distilled experience . . . in no way substitutes for the actual business experience necessary for anyone aspiring to the higher levels of management'.
7 The Principal of the London Business

School noted in 1974, 'the troubled circumstances in which we find ourselves'. He went on to say that 'we believe in the importance of widening the range of the School's activities in management, bearing in mind that the activities of management are not confined to the private sector'. The School proposed to create a new Institute of Public Sector Management to research management in the nationalized industries, the health and education services, and local government (London Business School 1974:6).

At Manchester it is interesting to note that in the Annual Reports it is now the post-experience courses that are described first and not the post-graduate courses as was the case in the past.

Chapter 5

1 The French students included in the study were drawn from ten of the fifteen intakes between 1959 and 1973. The selected years were 1959–61, 1964–66, and 1970–73. During these years just over 400 French students attended the Institute. The data on the alumni were gathered by means of questionnaire surveys, interviews and from administrative records. The response rates for the questionnaires were: INSEAD, 43 per cent; LBS, 59 per cent; MBS, 52 per cent. Interviews were conducted with 276 British students and fifty-eight French. Data from the schools' records were obtained for most of the INSEAD and London graduates, but were not available for those at Manchester.
2 The sociological relevance of the distinction between manual workers and certain categories of white-collar workers has been discussed by, for example, Braverman (1974) and Kumar (1976).
3 We have had to make a difficult choice in counting the *cadres supérieurs* in the private sector with *cadres moyens* rather than *patrons*. The particularly distinctive status of the latter in French society does, however, make their separate treatment justifiable.
4 Halsey (1972:221) 1961–62 male undergraduates, GB, 25 per cent; Kelsall

(1974:200) 1960 male graduates, 24 per cent; UCCA (1975:9) males accepted for 1974 entry, England and Wales, 16 per cent.
5 Ideally, it would be desirable to deepen this analysis by creating a measure of the volume of capital constituted by the occupations of the family. Although we can see how little of this was possessed by those from different origins, it is more difficult to show 'how much' is held by those who have at least some, other than by reverting to individual cases. The difficulties in pursuing this topic are, however, substantial and at the time of writing have yet to be overcome.

Chapter 6

1 One of the ex-course directors at one of the British schools told us that the 'rumour machine' had served to reduce the number of applicants who were demonstrably unlikely to gain admittance.
2 Although Kelsall's category is described as 'general management', the youth of these graduates suggests that this must be taken as 'management positions' rather than the type of 'high power' position often associated with the term 'general management'.

Chapter 7

1 The graduates from MBS with a one-year diploma instead of a two year MBA did not show quite such a major movement into the financial sector or into the finance function in manufacturing firms. Only a quarter of the diplomas entered the City and management consultancy compared to a third of the two year MBAs. Similarly, under a tenth of the diplomas taking their first post business job in manufacturing were in finance departments, while over a fifth of the MBAs did so. Also, more diploma holders took jobs in marketing departments and fewer in corporate planning roles than did the MBAs. Since the MBA additionally seemed to command a higher salary on graduation, a finding similar to a BGA

(1971) survey of one and two year courses, the British business graduates' jobs discussed here will refer only to the two year MBA/MSc graduates. Aside from the diploma graduates differing from the MBAs, no substantial difference was found between graduates from MBS and from LBS so they were analysed together.

Chapter 8

1 In this section only business graduates with the two-year MBA from London and Manchester are considered. After the initial two or three years of the business schools' operation the one-year diploma from Manchester was taken by fewer and fewer students and has come to be regarded by some employers as a 'failed MBA'. The median salary of Manchester alumni with the diploma was £7,500, which is nearly £2,500 less than the median salary of alumni with the two-year MBA. The salaries and rate of career progression of MBAs from London and Manchester did not differ much between the schools and so they have been combined for the analysis of their careers. In a shorter survey of alumni from the one year programme at Cranfield Institute of Management we found that although their median age was two years higher than that of the LBS and MBS MBAs, their median salary was over £1,500 lower (Whitley and Thomas 1980). This and other aspects of the Cranfield alumni careers suggest that the one-year qualification is seen differently by employers (BGA 1971).

2 In most cases these conditions could be applied in a fairly straightforward manner. In ambiguous situations further information about companies was obtained from other sources to allow us to make reasonable judgements.

3 However there were five graduates from Manchester with the one-year diploma who were judged to be in senior management posts in major firms. These had graduated in the very early years of MBS, before the distinction between the one-year and two-year qualifications became clear. We included them in the analysis of business graduates' careers because their early career success means that they had characteristics which, coupled with the one year qualification, enabled them to compete effectively with alumni who had MBAs.

4 There is also the point that many top management posts in financial institutions are filled by people with family connections to the current Board (e.g. Leslie 1978; Whitley 1973).

5 This is despite the lack of connection between financial control and management technique and practices and the formal training of many accountants. As one business graduate who was a chartered accountant before going to business school put it: 'an accountancy training is a very rudimentary kind of thing. The management and budget accounting was dreadful'.

Chapter 9

1 Furthermore, the one business graduate in management consultancy from the clerical/manual worker group was in fact the son of a teacher at a major public school who could thus almost be considered a member of the upper professional group rather than being similar to small shopkeepers and manual workers. Indeed, one of this MBA's uncles was described as a 'peer of the realm'.

References

ACTON SOCIETY TRUST (1956) *Management Succession*. London: AST.
───── (1962) *The Arts Graduate in Industry*. London: AST.
ALDCROFT, D. H. (1970) *The Interwar Economy: Britain 1919–1939*. London: Batsford.
ALDCROFT, D. H. and RICHARDSON, H. W. (1969) *The British Economy, 1870–1939*. London: Macmillan.
ALFORD, B. W. E. (1976a) The Chandler Thesis – Some General Observations. In L. Hannah (ed.) *Management Strategy and Business Development*. London: Macmillan.
───── (1976b) Strategy and Structure in the UK Tobacco Industry, in L. Hannah (ed.) *Management Strategy and Business Development*. London: Macmillan.
ALLEN V. L. (1961) Management and the Universities. *Listener*, 13 July.
ANDREFF, W. (1976) *Profits et Structures du Capitalisme Mondial*. Paris: Calmann-Levy.
ANGLO-AMERICAN COUNCIL ON PRODUCTIVITY (1951) *Education for Management*. London: AACP.
ANTHONY, P. D. (1977) *The Ideology of Work*. London: Tavistock.
ARIS, S. (1965) *Sunday Times*, 9 September.
ASHTON, D. N. and FIELD, D. (1976) *Young Workers*. London: Hutchinson.

BACHY, J.-P. (1971) *Les Cadres en France*. Paris: A. Colin.

BAIN, J. S. (1956) *Barriers to New Competition*. Cambridge, Mass.: Harvard University Press.

BALDWIN, A. (1978) The Changing Nature of Managerial Positions and their Incumbents. Unpublished paper, Manchester Business School.

BALL, R. J. (1967) British Business Schools. *Electricity* May–June: 3–8.

BARKER, T. C. (1977) Business Implications of Technical Development in the Glass Industry 1945–1965: A Case Study. In B. Supple (ed.) *Essays in British Business History*. Oxford: Clarendon Press.

BAUER, M. and COHEN, E. (1979) *Les Politiques des Grandes Entreprises Industrielles*. Paris: CORDES.

BAUMOL, W. (1959) *Business Behaviour, Value, and Growth*. London: Macmillan.

BEAUDEUX, P. (1972) Les Cent qui font l'Économie. *L'Expansion* 55:119–32.

——— (1974) Les Prix des Cadres, 1974. *L'Expansion* 75:105–27.

BENGUIGI, G. (1967) La Professionalisation des Cadres dans l'Industrie. *Sociologie du Travail* 9(2):134–43.

BENGUIGUI, G. and MONJARDET, D. (1970) *Être un Cadre en France?* Paris: Dunod.

BERRIDGE, T. (1978) Work Experience and Career Paths of Accountants. Unpublished paper, Manchester Business School.

BERRY, D. (1976) L'Europe des 'Business Schools'. A la Croisée des Chemins. *Informations 79* (June). Brussels.

BERTAUX, D. (1977) *Destins Personnels et Destins de Classe*. Paris: Presses Universitaires de France.

BIRNBAUM, P., BARUCQ, C., BELLAICHE, M., and MARIE, A. (1978) *La Classe Dirigeante Française*. Paris: PUF.

BOARD OF TRADE (1946) *A Central Institute of Management*. London: HMSO.

BODINAT, H. de (1973) Les Écoles de Gestion au Banc d'Essai. *L'Expansion* 63:169–77.

BONZON, P. (1968) Le Défi des Business Schools: l'Opinion des Employeurs. *Hommes et Commerce* 101 and 103:187–93.

BOTTOMORE, T. (1966) *Elites and Society*. Harmondsworth, Middlesex: Penguin Books.

BOUCHET, J.-L. (1976) Diversification, Composition of the Top Management Team and Performance of the Firm. Paper presented to the EGOS Conference on the Sociology of the Enterprise, December, Oxford.

BOUDON, R. (1973) *L'Inégalité des Chances*. Paris: Armand Colin. Translated (1974) *Education, Opportunity and Social Inequality*, London: John Wiley.

BOURDIEU, P. and PASSERON, J.-C. (1970) *La Reproduction*. Paris: Editions de Minuit.

BOURDIEU, P., BOLTANSKI, L., and de ST MARTIN, M. (1973), Les Stratégies de Reconversion. *Social Science Information* 12:61–113.

BOURDIEU, P. and de ST MARTIN, M. (1978) Le Patronat. *Actes de la Recherche en Sciences Sociales* 20–21:3–82.

References 223

BOWIE, J. A. (1949) Management and the Closed Shop. *Industry*, January: 15–17.

BOWLES, S. (1972) Unequal Education and the Reproduction of the Social Division of Labour. In M. Carnoy (ed.) *Schooling in a Corporate Society: The Political Economy of Education in America and the Alternatives Before Us.* New York: David McKay.

BOWLES, S. and GINTIS, H. (1976) *Schooling in Capitalist America.* London: Routledge & Kegan Paul.

BOYD, D. (1973) *Elites and their Education.* Slough, Bucks: NFER.

BRABOWSKI, H. G. (1968) The Determinants of R & D in Three Industries. *Journal of Political Economy* 76:292–306.

BRAVERMAN, H. (1974) *Labor and Monopoly Capital: The Degradation of Work in the Twentieth Century.* New York: Monthly Review Press.

British Industry Week (1967) Business Schools in Business – But Still a Long Way To Go. 20 September.

BRITISH INSTITUTE OF MANAGEMENT (1968) *The Employment of Graduates,* London: BIM.

—— (1971) *Business School Programmes: The Requirements of British Manufacturing Industry.* London: BIM.

—— (1977) *National Management Salary Survey,* London: BIM.

BRITISH MONOPOLIES COMMISSION (1969) Recommendations to a Government. In A. Hunter (ed.) *Monopoly and Competition.* Harmondsworth: Penguin.

BUSINESS GRADUATES ASSOCIATION (1971) *British Industry's Attitudes to Business Graduates and Business Schools.* London: BGA.

—— (1971a), The Rate for the Job. *Business Graduate* 1:3–6.

—— (1973) *The Business Graduate in Britain, 1973.* London: BGA.

BURCH, P. H. (1972) *The Managerial Revolution Reassessed.* Lexington, Mass.: Heath.

BURNS, T. and STALKER, G. M. (1961) *The Management of Innovation.* London: Tavistock.

CAPOCCI, A. (1972) Votre Tête Mise à Prix. *La Vie des Cadres* 3:29–31.

CARRE, J.-J., DUBOIS, P., and MALINVAUD, E. (1973) *Abrégé de la Croissance Française.* Paris: Seuil.

CÉZARD, M. (1973) Les Cadres et leurs Diplômes. *Economie et Statistique* 42:25–41.

CHANDLER, A. D. (1962) *Strategy and Structure.* Cambridge, Mass.: MIT Press.

—— (1976) The Development of Modern Management Structure in the US and the UK. In L. Hannah (ed.) *Management Strategy and Business Development.* London: Macmillan.

—— (1977) *The Visible Hand.* London: Macmillan.

CHANDLER, A. D. and DAEMS, H. (1974) Introduction: The Rise of Managerial Capitalism and its Impact on Investment Strategy in the Western World and Japan. In H. Daems and H. v.d. Wee (eds) *The Rise of Managerial Capitalism.* Den Haag: Nijhoff.

CHANNON, D. F. (1973) *The Strategy and Structure of British Enterprise.* London: Macmillan.

——— (1976) Corporate Evolution in the Service Industries. In L. Hannah (ed.) *Management Strategy and Business Development.* London: Macmillan.
——— (1977) *British Banking Strategy and the International Challenge.* London: Macmillan.
CHESTER, T. E. (1965) Industry, Management and the Universities: Trends and Problems of a Changing Relationship. *District Bank Review* 156: 3–27.
CHILD, J. (1969) *British Management Thought.* London: Allen and Unwin.
——— (1972) Organisation Structure, Environment, and Performance – the Role of Strategic Choice. *Sociology* 6: 1–22.
CLARK, D. G. (1966) *The Industrial Manager.* London: Business Publications.
CLEMENTS, R. V. (1958) *Managers, A Study of their Careers in Industry.* London: Allen and Unwin.
COLEMAN, D. C. (1973) Gentlemen and Players. *Economic History Review* 26: 92–116.
COLLINS, R. (1971) Functional and Conflict Theories of Educational Stratification. *American Sociological Review* 36: 1002–19.
CONTESSE, J. (1961) Le Marché des Dirigeants d'Entreprise. *Entreprise* 315: 58–9.
CORNWELL, R. (1974) France: The Mask of Modernity. In A. Rowley (ed.) *The Barons of European Industry.* London: Croom Helm.
COPEMAN, G. H. (1955) *Leaders of British Industry.* London: Gee & Co.
COUNCIL OF ENGINEERING INSTITUTIONS (1977) *The 1977 Survey of Professional Engineers.* London: CEI.
CROWTHER REPORT (1959) *Fifteen to Eighteen.* London: HMSO.
Daily Telegraph (1968) Companies Facing Snags over 'Blue Chip' Graduates. 14 October.
DALLE, F. and BOUNNINE-CABALÉ, J. (1971) *L'Entreprise du Futur.* Paris: Calman-Lévy.
DALTON, M. (1959) *Men Who Manage.* New York: John Wiley.
DANIEL, W. W. (1971) *Business Education at 18+: A Survey of HND Business Studies.* London: Political and Economic Planning.
DELEFORTRIE-SOUBEYROUX, N. (1961) *Les Dirigeants de l'Industrie Française.* Paris: A. Colin.
DEPARTMENT OF EDUCATION AND SCIENCE (1974) *Statistics of Education.* London: HMSO.
DEPARTMENT OF INDUSTRY (1977) *Industry, Education and Management.* London: DOI.
DOMHOFF, W. G. (1969) *Who Rules America?* Englewood Cliffs, N.J.: Prentice-Hall.
DOMHOFF, W. G. (ed.) (1967) *New Directions in Power Structure Research.* The Insurgent Sociologist, University of Oregon.
DORE, R. (1976) *The Diploma Disease: Education Qualification and Development.* London: George Allen and Unwin.
DOUGIER, H. (1970) Diriger: un Metier qui s'apprend jeune. *Le Management*, Avril: 63–7.
DOUGIER, H. and HOUSTON, T. (1968) Europe's Business Schools: Overshadowed or Creative? *European Business* 19: 5–13.

References 225

DRANCOURT, M. (1973) Les Trois Profils du Manager. *Entreprise* **912** : 72–3.
DUNKERLEY, D. (1975) *Occupations and Society*. London: Routledge and Kegan Paul.
DYAS, G. P. (1972) *The Strategy and Structure of French Industrial Enterprises*. Unpublished PhD thesis, Harvard Business School.
DYAS, P. and THANHEISER, H. T. (1976) *The Emerging European Enterprise*. London: Macmillan.
EARLE, A. F. (1965) Address to the National Conference of the Institute of Personnel Management, 8 October.
EGLIN, R. (1977) Business Schools Come Under Fire from Action Man. *Industrial Management*, May: 25–7.
ELLIOTT, R. (1977) Fontainebleau – Still a Centre of Elitism. *Training*, September: 8–11. .
Entreprise (1962) Chef d'entreprise, est-ce un Metier qui s'apprend? 26 May: 51–7.
FAYOL, H. (1947) *Administration Industrielle et Générale*. Paris: Dunod.
FERRIS, P. (1960) *The City*. Harmondsworth: Penguin.
FIDLER, J. (1977) *The British Business Elite: Recruitment and Attitudes to Social Stratification*. University of Aston Management Centre Working Paper Series No. 64.
FINNISTON, Sir M. (1978) Creative Management. *Journal of the Royal Society of Arts* **5263** : 407–201.
FLORENCE, P. S. (1961) *The Logic of British and American Industry*. London: Routledge and Kegan Paul.
FONTAINE, J. (1977) Les Grandes Entreprises jugent les Grandes Écoles. *L'Expansion* **109** : 64–71.
FRANCIS, A. (1978) Company Objectives, Managerial Motivation, and the Behaviour of Large Firms. Paper presented to EGOS conference on Business Policies, Business Elites, and Business Schools, Paris.
FRANKO, L. G. (1976) *The European Multinationals*. New York: Harper and Row.
FRANKS, RT. HON. LORD (1963) *British Business Schools*. London: BIM.
FURSTENBURG, F. (1961) Aspects Sociologiques de la Promotion dans l'Entreprise. *Sociologie du Travail* **3**(1): 18–29.
GELINIER, O. (1972) *L'Entreprise Créatrice*. Paris: Homme et Techniques.
GEORGE, K. D. (1971) *Industrial Organisation*. London: Allen and Unwin.
GEORGE, K. D. and WARD, T. S. (1975) *The Structure of Industry in the EEC: An International Comparison*. London: Cambridge University Press.
GERSTL, J. E. and HUTTON, S. P. (1966) *Engineers: The Anatomy of a Profession*. London: Tavistock.
GIDDENS, A. (1974) Elites in the British Class Structure. In P. Stanworth and A. Giddens (eds) *Elites and Power in British Society*. London: Cambridge University Press.
GIDDENS, A. and STANWORTH, P. (1978) Elites and Privilege. In P. Abrams (ed.) *Work, Urbanism, and Inequality*. London: Weidenfeld and Nicolson.

226 References

226 References

GIRARD, A. (1961) *La Réussite Sociale en France*. Paris: Presses Universitaires de France.

GLOVER I. (1976) Executive Career Patterns: Britain, France, Germany and Sweden. *Energy World*, December: 3–12.

GORDON, R. A. and HOWELL, J. E. (1959) *Higher Education for Business*. New York: Columbia University Press.

GORGE, J.-P. (1975) 1974: La Nouvelle Vague de Restructuration dans les Groupes Industriels et Financiers. **67**:65–8.

GRANICK, D. (1972) *Managerial Comparisons of Four Developed Countries*. Cambridge, Mass.: MIT Press.

GRANOVETTER, M. S. (1974) *Getting a Job: A Study of Contacts and Careers*. Cambridge, Mass: Harvard University Press.

GUERRIER, Y and PHILPOT, N. (1978) *The British Manager: Careers and Mobility*. London: BIM.

GUNZ, H. (1978) Managerial Specialists and Generalists: Perceived Determinants of Career Success. Paper presented to EGOS Conference on Business Policies, Business Elites and Business Schools, Paris.

——— (1980) Generalists, Specialists and the Reproduction of Managerial Structures. *International Studies of Management and Organization*, October 1980:137–64.

GUTTERIDGE, T. (1973) The Hardest Job of All: Career Planning. *MBA*, October: 19–20.

HALL, D. and AMADO-FISCHGRUND, G. (1969) Chief Executives in Britain. *European Business*. January: 23–9.

HALL, D. and BETTIGNIES, H.-C. DE (1968) The French Business Elite. *European Business* **3**:1–10.

HALL, D. BETTIGNIES, H.-C. DE and AMADO-FISCHGRUND, G. (1969) The European Business Elite. *European Business*, October: 45–55.

HALSEY, A. H. (1972) Higher Education. In A. H. Halsey (ed.) *Trends in British Society since 1900*. London: Macmillan.

——— (1974) Education and Social Mobility in Britain since World War II. Unpublished paper, Oxford University.

HANDY, C. B. (1977) Business Schools – Missionaries or Mercenaries? *International Management Development* **4**:3–5.

HANNAH, L. (1976) *The Rise of the Corporate Economy*. London: Macmillan.

HARBISON, F. and MYERS, C. A. (1959) *Management in the Industrial World*. New York: McGraw-Hill.

HARMON, F. (1977) European Top Managers' Struggle for Survival. *European Business* **28**(1):4–19.

HEKIMIAN, J. S. (1969) Closing the Gap between Business and the Schools. *Financial Executive* **37**:52–4.

HELLER, R. (1973) The State of British Boardrooms. *Management Today*, May.

HOFSTEDE, G. (1978) Businessmen and Business School Faculty: A Comparison of Value Systems *Journal of Management Studies* **15**(1).

HOLL, P. (1975) Effect of Control Type on the Performance of the Firm in the UK. *Journal of Industrial Economics* **23**:257–71.

HOOPER, SIR F. (1960) *Management Survey: The Significance of Management in the Modern Community*. Harmondsworth: Penguin.

d'HUGHES, P. and PESLIER, M. (1969) *Les Professions en France*. Paris: Presses Universitaires de France.

HUGHES, B. C. (1977) The Graduate. *The Financial Post Magazine*, September: 11–18.

HUMBLET, J. (1966) *Les Cadres d'Entreprise*. Paris: Editions Universitaires.

HUSSAIN, A. (1976) The Economy and the Educational System in Capitalistic Societies. *Economy and Society* 5(4): 413–34.

HUTTON, G. (1953) *We Too Can Prosper: The Promise of Productivity*. London.

ILLICH, I. (1970) *Deschooling Society*. Harmondsworth: Penguin.

Industrial Management (1971) A Lesson for Business Schools. July.

INSEE (Institut National de la Statistique et des Études Économiques) (1972) Un Million de Cadres Supérieurs Dénombrés au Recensement de 1968. 40:50–4.

International Management Development (1977) Management Education in France. 2:10–14.

JACQUEMIN, A. P. and DE JONG, H. W. (1977) *European Industrial Organisation*. London: Macmillan.

JACQUIN, F. (1955) *Les Cadres de l'Industrie et du Commerce*. Paris: A. Colin.

JALLAND, M. (1973) Concepts in Marketing Management. Unpublished paper, MBS.

JENNY, F. and WEBER, A-P (1974) L'Evolution de la Concentration Industrielle en France de 1961 à 1969.

JOHNSON, T. (1972) *Professions and Power*. London: Macmillan.

KELSALL, R. K., POOLE, A., and KUHN, A. (1974) *Graduates: the Sociology of an Elite*. London: Tavistock.

KENNEDY, W. P. (1976) Institutional Response to Economic Growth: Capital Markets in Britain to 1914. In L. Hannah (ed.) *Management Strategy and Business Development*. London: Macmillan.

KING, R. (1969) *Education*. London: Longman.

KITZINGER, U. (1976) Inaugural address, INSEAD, September.

KOSCIUSKO-MORIZET, J. (1973) *La 'Mafia' Polytechnicienne*. Paris: Le Seuil.

KUMAR, K. (1976) Industrialism and Post-Industrialism: Reflections on a Putative Transition. *Sociological Review* 24:439–78.

LAWRENCE, S. (1972) Professor Ball: Man of the Moment. *Personnel Management*, October: 18–19.

LEE, J. (1921) *Management: A Study of Industrial Organisation*. London: Pitman.

LEGGATT, T. W. (1972) *The Training of British Managers*. London: HMSO.

LEGGATT, T. W. (1978) Managers in Industry: Their Background and Education. *Sociological Review* 26:807–25.

LEGGE, K. (1978) *Power, Innovation and Problem-Solving in Personnel Management*. London and New York: McGraw-Hill.

LE MORE, H. (1976) *Classes Possédantes et Classes Dirigeantes*. Thèse de troisième cycle. Paris.

Le Point (1978) Les Salaires des Cadres 1978. *Le Point* 277:73–82.

LESLIE, N. (1978) How Barclays is Grappling with 'Universal' Banking. *Financial Times* 3 March: 10.

LIVINGSTON, J. S. (1971) The Myth of the Well-Educated Manager. *Harvard Business Review*, January–February.

LONDON BUSINESS SCHOOL (1970) *Annual Report.*

—— (1973) *Annual Report.*

—— (1975) *Annual Report.*

—— (1978) *Annual Report.*

LUPTON, T. (1972) Business Education, British Style. *Newsletter*, Centre for Business Research, Manchester Business School, Spring: 3–5.

LUPTON, T. and WILSON, S. (1959) The Social Background and Connections of Top Decision Makers. *Manchester School*: 27.

McCLELLAND, W. G. (1971) Myth Squared. *Management Education and Development* 2 : 58–63.

McEWAN, A. (1977) Britons Excel at Europe's School for Go-Getters. *Johannesburg Star.* January 13.

McGIVERING, I. C., MATTHEWS, D. G. J., and SCOTT, W. H. (1960) *Management in Britain: a General Characterisation.* Liverpool University Press.

MANCHESTER BUSINESS SCHOOL (1968) *Annual Report.*

—— (1971) *Annual Report.*

—— (1974) *Annual Report.*

MANN, R. (ed.) (1970) *The Arts of Top Management* London: McGraw-Hill.

MANSELL, C. (1972) Fontainebleau's Keen Cadets. *Management Today* July: 73–5 and 118–20.

MARCEAU, J. (1976) *The Social Origins, Educational Experience and Career Paths of a Young Business Elite.* Fontainebleau: INSEAD.

—— (1977) *Class and Status in France.* Oxford: Oxford University Press.

MARCEAU, J. THOMAS, A. B. and WHITLEY, R. D. (1978) Business and the State: Management Education and Business Elites in France and Great Britain. In G. Littlejohn *et al.* (eds) *Power and the State.* London: Croom Helm.

MARGERISON, C. (1978) Making Tomorrow's Managers. *Management Today* May 87–8 : 152.

MARRIS, R. (1964) *The Economic Theory of 'Managerial' Capitalism.* London: Macmillan.

—— (1971a) An Introduction to Theories of Corporate Growth. In R. Marris and A. Wood (eds) *The Corporate Economy.*

—— (1971b) The Modern Corporation and Economic Theory. In R. Marris and A. Wood (eds), *The Corporate Economy.*

—— (1972) Why Economics Needs a Theory of the Firm. *Economic Journal* 82 : 321–52.

MARRIS, R. and WOOD, A. (eds) (1971), *The Corporate Economy.* London: Macmillan.

MATHEWSON, W. (1976) The French Penchant for Having MBAs from American Schools Seems to Fade, *The Wall Street Journal* 24 August.

MAURICE, M. *et al.* (1967) *Les Cadres et l'Entreprise*, Université de Paris Institut des Sciences Sociales du Travail.

MELROSE-WOODMAN, J. (1978) *Profile of the British Manager*. London: BIM.

MELUCCI, A. (1974) *Idéologies et Pratiques Patronales pendant l'Industrialisation: le Cas de la France*. Doctorat de troisieme cycle, Paris.

MILLS, C. W. (1956) *The Power Elite*. New York: Oxford University Press.

MINISTRY OF EDUCATION (1947) *Education for Management, Management Subjects in Technical and Commerical Colleges*. London: HMSO.

MONJARDET, D. (1972) Carrière des Dirigeants et Contrôle de l'Entreprise. *Sociologie du Travail* 13(2): 131–44.

MORIN, F. (1974) *La Structure Financière du Capitalisme Francais*. Paris: Calmann-Levy.

MORVAN, Y. (1972) *La Concentration de l'Industrie en France*. Paris: A. Colin.

MOSSON, T. M. (1965) *Management Education in Five European Countries*. London: Business Publications.

――― (1972) And Now a Word from our Sponsors ... *Management Education and Development* 3: 74–8.

NATIONAL ECONOMIC DEVELOPMENT COUNCIL (1963) *Conditions Favourable to Faster Growth*. London: HMSO.

NELSON, LORD (1964) *Management Education and the British Business Schools: Report on the 1964 appeal and statement on future policy*. London: Foundation for Management Education.

NEWCOMER, M. (1955) *The Big Business Executive*. Columbia University Press.

NICHOLS, T. (1969) *Ownership, Control and Ideology*. London: Allen and Unwin.

NORMANBROOK, RT HON. LORD (1964) *British Business Schools: The Cost*. London: BIM.

NYMAN, S. and SILBERSTON, A. (1978) The Ownership and Control of Industry. *Oxford Economic Papers* 30: 74–103.

OFFE, C. (1976) *Industry and Inequality*. London: Arnold.

PAHL, R. E. and WINKLER, J. T. (1974) The Economic Elite: Theory and Practice. In P. Stanworth and A. Giddens (eds) *Elites and Power in British Society*. London: Cambridge University Press.

PARKER, H. (1970) Introduction to R. Mann (ed.) *The Arts of Top Management*. London: McGraw-Hill.

PARODI, M. (1971) *L'Economie et la Société Francaise de 1945 à 1970*. Paris: A. Colin.

PARTRIDGE, SIR J. (1970) What's Wrong with Business Education? *Economist*, 21 November.

Patronat Français (1968) La Commission 'Entreprise-École de Guerre' d'égage les Principes de Base d'un Système Efficace de Perfectionnement des Cadres-Supérieurs 287: 4–10.

PAYNE, P. L. (1967) The Emergence of the Large-Scale Company in Great Britain, 1870–1914. *Economic History Review* 20: 519–42.

PENROSE, E. T. (1959) *The Theory of the Growth of the Firm*. Oxford: Blackwell.

PERROW, C. (1972) *Complex Organisations*. Glenview, Ill.: Scott, Foresman.

POLITICAL AND ECONOMIC PLANNING (1965) *Attitudes in British Management*. Harmondsworth: Penguin.

────── (1965) *Thrusters and Sleepers: A Study of Attitudes in Industrial Management*. London: Allen and Unwin.

POLLARD, S. (1965) *The Genesis of Modern Management*. London: Arnold.

────── (1969) *The Development of the British Economy 1914–1967*. London: Arnold.

PRAIS, S. J. (1976) *The Evolution of Giant Firms in Britain*. London: Cambridge University Press.

PRIOURET, R. (1963) *Les Origines du Patronat Française*. Paris: Grasset.

────── (1968) *La France et la Management*. Paris: Denoël et Hommes et Techniques.

PUGH, D. S. and HICKSON, D. (1976) *Organisational Structure in its Context*. Farnborough: Saxon House.

RADICE, H. (1971) Control Type, Profitability and Growth in Large Firms. *Economic Journal* 81: 547–62.

RICHARDSON, G. B. (1972) The Organisation of Industry. *Economic Journal* 82:883–96.

ROBBINS REPORT (1963) *Higher Education*. Cmnd 2154, London: HMSO.

ROBERTSON, A. (1965) Management Education in Britain: The Recent History. In R. Malik (ed.) *Penguin Survey of Business and Industry 1965*. Harmondsworth: Penguin Books.

────── (1970) Business Schools – Is the Backlash Justified? *Management Decision* 4: 12–15.

ROSE, H. R. (1970) *Management Education in the 70s: Growth and Issues*. London: HMSO.

ROWLEY, A. (1974) *The Barons of European Industry*. London: Croom Helm.

SALAIS, R. (1970) Les Niveaux de Diplômes dans chaque Catégorie Professionelle. *Economie et Statistique* 9: 49–57.

SÉDILLOT, R. (1976) Les Affaires s'enseignnent à Fontainebleau. *La Vie Française* 49, 6 December.

SERVAN-SCHREIBER, J.-J. (1967) *Le Défi Américain*. Paris: Denoël. Translated 1969 as *The American Challenge*, Harmondsworth: Penguin.

SHANKS, M. (1963) Britain's 'Harvard' Begins to Take Shape. *Financial Times*, 17 June.

SIBBALD, A. (1978) A Case of Education. *Management Today*, July: 19–22.

SLOCUM, A. (1966) *Occupational Careers: A Sociological Perspective*. Chicago: Aldine.

SMITH, J. H. (1961) Management and the Universities. *Listener*, 20 July.

SORRELL, M. (1966) Finding Tomorrow's Managers. *Management Today* 112: 60–63.

SPIEGELBERG, R. (1973) *The City*. London: Quartet Books.

STANWORTH, P and GIDDENS, A. (1974) An Economic Elite: A Demographic Profile of Company Chairmen. In P. Stanworth and A. Giddens (eds) *Elites and Power in British Society*. London: Cambridge University Press.

────── (1975) The Modern Corporate Economy: Interlocking Directorships in Britain 1906–70. *Sociological Review* 23: 5–28.

STEELE, J. and WARD, L. (1974) MBAs: Mobile, Well-Situated, Well-Paid. *Harvard Business Review*, January–February: 99–100.

STINCHCOMBE, A. L. (1959) Bureaucratic and Craft Administration of Production: A Comparative Study. *Administrative Science Quarterly* 2:168–87.

STORY, J. and PARROTT, M. (1977) An Essay on Management in France – Does it Work? *International Herald Tribune*, 5 May.

TABLE RONDE (1978) Cadres: l'Avenir est aux 'Généralistes'. *Le Point* 277 (January) 74–5.

THOENIG, J.-.C. (1973) *L'Ere des Technocrates: le cas des Ponts-et-Chaussées*, Paris: Editions d'Organisation.

THOMAS, A. B. (1978) The British Business Elite: the Case of the Retail Sector. *Sociological Review* 26, 305–26.

———(1980) Management and Education: Rationalization and Reproduction in British Business. *International Studies of Management and Organization* 10 : 71–109.

THOMSON, D. (1965) *England in the Twentieth Century*. Harmondsworth: Penguin Books.

Times (1973) Business Graduates: Their Eyes are Bluer Now. 26 March.

Times (1976) Next Steps for Business Schools. 12 July.

TURNER, G. (1969) *Business in Britain*. London: Eyre and Spottiswoode.

TWIGGER, T. (1978) The Managerial Career. *Management Today*, December, 55–7, 114.

TYLER, W. (1977) *The Sociology of Educational Inequality*. London: Methuen.

UNION DES INDUSTRIES MÉTALLURGIQUES ET MINIÈRES (1970) *Ingénieurs et Cadres*. Paris.

UNIVERSITIES CENTRAL COUNCIL ON ADMISSIONS (1968) *Statistical Supplement to the Sixth Report, 1967–68*. London: HMSO.

———(1974) *Statistical Supplement to the Twelfth Report, 1973–74*. London: HMSO.

URWICK, L. (1950) A British Graduate School of Business. *Management Review* 9.

——— (1954) *Is Management a Profession?* London: Urwick, Orr and Partners.

——— (1957) *Leadership in the Twentieth Century*. London: Pitman.

UTTON, M. A. (1970) *Industrial Concentration*. Harmondsworth: Penguin.

VAN DEN BERG, J. (1969) Can Europe Close the 'Management Gap'? *McKinsey Quarterly*, Fall: 24–34.

VERNON, R. (ed.) (1974) *Big Business and the State*. London: Macmillan.

VEYRET, G. (1968) La France Cherche ses Business Schools. *L'Expansion*, Avril: 113–16.

WARD, L. and ATHOS, A. (1972) *Student Expectations of Corporate Life*, Boston Harvard Graduate School of Business Administration, Division of Research.

WATLING, T. (1970) *Plan for Promotion: Advancement and the Manager*. London: Business Books.

WESTERGAARD, J. and RESLER, H. (1975) *Class in a Capitalist Society*. London: Heinemann.

WESTON, R. (1972) Management Education and Research – A Survey of Comments and Issues. *Newsletter*, Centre for Business Research, Manchester Business School. Summer: 8–11.

WHEATCROFT, M. (1970) *The Revolution in British Management Education*. London: Pitman.

WHITEHEAD, T. N. (1947) *Leadership in a Free Society*. Cambridge, Mass.: Harvard University Press.

WHITLEY, R. D. (1973) Commonalities and Connections Among Directors of Large Financial Institutions. *Sociological Review* 21:613–32.

—— (1974) The City and Industry: The Directors of Large Companies, their Characteristics and Connections. In P. Stanworth and A. Giddens (eds) *Elites and Power in British Society*. London: Cambridge University Press.

WHITLEY, R. D. and THOMAS, A. B. (1980) A New Business Elite? The Background and Early Careers of Business School Graduates. *Manchester Business School Review* 5:6–17.

WHYTE, W. (1956) *The Organisation Man*. Harmondsworth: Penguin.

WILLIAMS, L. J. (1971) *Britain and the World Economy 1919–1970*. London: Fontana.

WILLIAMSON, O. E. (1964) *The Economics of Discretionary Behaviour: Managerial Objectives in a Theory of the Firm*. Englewood Cliffs, N.J.: Prentice-Hall.

—— (1970) *Corporate Control and Business Behaviour*. Englewood Cliffs, N.J.: Prentice-Hall.

—— (1971) Managerial Discretion, Organisation Form and the Multi Division Hypothesis. In Marris and Wood (eds) *The Corporate Economy*.

—— (1975) *Markets and Hierarchies*. New York: Free Press.

WILLIG, J. C. (1970) Organisation Man or Entrepreneur: Europe's Business School Managers. *European Business* 27:21–30.

WILLIG, J.-C. (1971) Send the Bosses Back to School! Complain Young MBAs. *European Business* 28:20–26.

XARDEL, D. (1978) *Les Managers*. Paris: Grasset.

ZEHNDER, E. (1975) *Survey of Business School Graduates in Europe*. London: Egon Zehnder International.

ZEITLIN, M. (1974) Corporate Ownership and Control: The Large Corporation and the Capitalist Class. *American Journal of Sociology* 79:1073–119.

ZEITLIN, M. and RATCLIFF, R. E. (1975) Research Methods for the Analysis of the Internal Structure of Dominant Classes: the Case of Landlords and Capitalists in Chile. *Latin American Research Review* 10(3):5–61.

Name index

Aldcroft, D. H. 161, 221
Alford, B. W. E. 19, 21, 221
Amado-Fischgrund, G. 93, 226
Allen, V. L. 40, 44, 221
Andreff, W. 13, 221
Anthony, P. D. 24, 221
Ashton, D. N. 3, 221

Bain, J. S. 13, 222
Baldwin, A. 58, 222
Ball, R. J. 45, 49–51, 53–4, 222
Barker, T. C. 20, 222
Baumol, W. 14, 222
Beaudeux, P. 26, 165, 171, 222
Berridge, T. 27, 174, 222
Bettignies, H.-C. de 204, 226
Bevin, E. 36
Birnbaum, P. 23, 204, 207–08, 222
Boltanski, L. 7, 20, 25–6, 153, 179, 183, 204, 208
Bottomore, T. 5, 222
Bouchet, J.-L. 15–16, 222
Boudon, R. 3, 222
Bourdieu, P. ix–x, 3, 7, 20, 25–6, 29, 153, 179, 183, 204, 208, 211

Bowie, J. A. 32, 223
Bowles, S. 3, 223
Boyd, D. 94, 223
Brabowski, H. G. 13, 223
Braverman, H. 219, 223
Burch, P. H. 19, 223
Burns, T. 14, 223

Carré, J.-J. 161, 223
Chandler, A. D. 10, 13, 15–21, 23, 26, 223
Channon, D. F. 15, 18–19, 21, 172, 223
Chester, T. E. 43, 218, 224
Child, J. 15, 19, 24, 31, 33, 36, 224
Clark, D. G. 178, 194, 204, 224
Clements, R. V. 19, 160, 174, 204, 206, 224
Coleman, D. C. 186, 224
Collins, R. 4, 224
Copeman, G. H. 205–06, 224
Cornwell, R. 87, 224

Daems, H. 21, 23, 223
Daniel, W. W. 58, 224

Subject index